World Development

Development

An essential text

Barry Baker

New Internationalist

World Development: an essential text
Published in 2011 by:
New Internationalist™ Publications Ltd
55 Rectory Road
Oxford
OX4 1BW, UK

Front cover photographs
Main image of 12-year-old Rasinatu from Burkina Faso: Chris Brazier/
New Internationalist.
Background images: Mark Henley/Panos (Mumbai cityscape); George Osodi/
Panos (construction workers in Lagos, Nigeria); Sven Torfinn/Panos (women
at an income-generating project in Patuakhali, Bangladesh).

Edited for New Internationalist by Chris Brazier
Designed for New Internationalist by Andrew Kokotka

Author's acknowledgements
This book is dedicated to Trevor Welham, a great friend and colleague.
We always planned to do this together. I would like to acknowledge the
contribution made by Matt Brown and Catherine Murphy with their help
and advice on content and also give my sincere thanks to Chris Brazier and
Andy Kokotka for their patience and creativity in editing and design.

Printed in Italy by Graphicom

British Library Cataloguing-in-Publication Data
A catalogue record for this book is available from the British Library.

Library of Congress Cataloguing-in-Publication Data.
A catalogue record for this book is available from the Library of Congress.

ISBN 978-1-906523-96-1

Contents

1 Development

What is development and how can it be measured?

* Definitions of development can be complex and often have a cultural basis. Development involves education, health, democracy, human rights, income, well-being and sustainability.
* Poverty is a key factor in development and measurements of poverty may vary from country to country and region to region.
* Useful measures of development may include a range of economic, social and political indicators and include GNP, GDP, GNI, HDI, HPI and GDI.
* Income distribution within a country or region can be measured and provides evidence about the level of inequality of wealth within the population.
* Explanations for the unequal distribution of wealth and resources in the population may vary from one country to another.
* Meeting basic human needs has an impact on the physical and human environment.

Key points

What do I think of Western civilization? I think it would be a very good idea.

Mohandas K Gandhi, (1869-1948), known as Mahatma, which means 'Great Soul'

Mahatma Gandhi was the spiritual and political leader of India during the Indian independence movement and inspired civil rights movements throughout the world with his philosophy of nonviolent opposition to oppression. He led the simplest of lives and opposed the social changes that rapid industrialization was causing in the Western world. At that time, most people in the West viewed India as a backward and uncivilized country and knew little of its rich culture and history. Gandhi's reply to the question posed to him indicated his doubts about the Western model of social organization. Western civilization is still often seen as synonymous with development, so Gandhi's perspective is still very relevant to modern arguments about the way forward.

What is meant by development?

There are some words in the English language that have acquired an aura of positive meaning. 'Community' is one such word and 'development' is another. If people talk about community we immediately conjure up the idea of people acting together for the greater good. In the same way, 'development' is associated with a general sense of things getting better over a period of time – improvement. Defining the word precisely is more difficult because it is a value-laden term. For some people it means increasing levels of wealth in order to combat poverty while for others the term relates much more to improved social conditions. Another group sees the idea of continuous development or growth as representing the unsustainable use of resources, environmental degradation and threats to social cohesion.

So what do we mean by development? One definition that is often quoted is that it represents an 'ideal state to be achieved by human effort'. This implies that development should be concerned with enhancing human rights and welfare and not just with improving people's income or wealth. Making progress towards development has no single recipe because of the social, cultural and economic diversity of the global population.

History of the development idea

The modern notion of development can be traced back to the inaugural speech of US President Harry S Truman in 1949. In his speech he stated that the benefits of scientific and industrial progress should be made available to 'underdeveloped' areas and he spoke of this development being based on 'the concepts of democratic fair dealing'. This was during the period at the start of the Cold War and there is no doubt that Truman's motives were political. He was aware that the Marshall Plan of 1947, whereby the US gave significant amounts of aid to western European countries, not only helped those countries to revive their industries but also secured their adherence to the US social and political model, thereby indirectly combating the communism then dominating the Soviet Union and eastern Europe. Truman envisaged 'development' as having a similar effect in global terms.

In the 1950s global tensions continued to rise between the West and the communist East. War broke out in Korea involving the Western

powers and Korea's neighbour, communist China. In the same period, African and Asian countries increasingly claimed independence from their former colonial powers – and both the West and the Soviet bloc competed to gain influence over these newly independent countries. The term 'Third World' – originally coined in French as *tiers monde* – arose in this period to describe developing countries as a group – those neither part of the capitalist West nor the communist East.

Some of these 'Third World' countries convened a conference in Bandung, Indonesia, in 1955 in an attempt to set out their own agenda, independent of the strategic competition between Washington and Moscow – this became known as the non-aligned group. The common characteristic of most of these newly independent countries – and they were joined by many more new African nations during the 1960s – was their low level of wealth and their lack of industry. Realizing that they needed access to financial and technical resources if they were to improve their national income and develop their own industries, increasing numbers of developing countries rejected non-alignment and accepted aid. But they paid a high price in having to accept along with the aid the economic, political and cultural philosophies of their sponsors.

Yes we can! School-children with a smile in Burkina Faso might be considered primary targets for development efforts.

The North-South divide

The Brandt Report was an important event in changing the views of many people about the nature of world development. It was written as a review of international issues in 1980 by the Independent Commission, first chaired by Willy Brandt, the former West German Chancellor. This landmark report drew attention to the stark difference in the characteristics of countries in the developed and the developing world, which increasingly became known as the Global North and South.

The North-South divide is the line that separates the rich North, or the developed world, from the poor South. This line of division splits the globe into two main parts. The 'North' embraces North America, Europe, Russia, South Korea, Japan – as well as Australia and New Zealand, despite their location in the Southern Hemisphere. The countries within this group are generally more economically developed because of their ability to trade manufactured goods of high value. The poor 'South' includes the remainder of the Southern Hemisphere. Countries in this group have to rely on export incomes derived from intermediate goods and primary commodities which are of lower value. This North/South terminology is still in common use and is considered by many to be less pejorative than other alternatives such as rich/poor or developed/developing.

Political convenience may have been the main reason for the growth of the idea of international development in the 1960s, but improvements in communications also made more people aware of the global discrepancies in wealth and the scale of mass hunger and malnutrition. Charities focusing on conditions in the South, such as Oxfam and CARE, emerged and aid became the accepted way for

Updated view of the North/South divide.

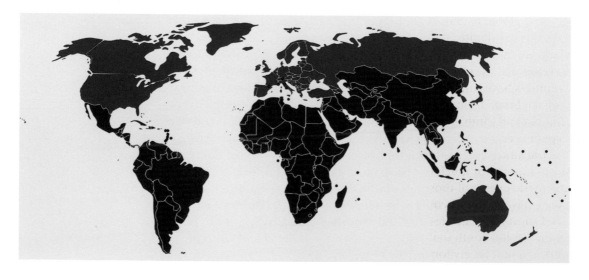

resources to be transferred to countries struggling to industrialize. People started to believe that social justice could be achieved by making the wealth of countries more equal.

Development progress in the last 50 years

Progress since the 1960s has been patchy at best and will be discussed more thoroughly later in the book. There is no doubt that one of the problems has been the simplistic notion of development that has been prevalent over the last 50 years. Development has been widely seen as a process aiming to make countries conform more closely to the model in the Global North, based on industrialization and the intensive exploitation and consumption of natural resources. Agriculture in poorer countries – much of which is conducted by farmers growing food for their own families' subsistence – has been seen as part of the problem because it is not organized in large, efficient, mechanized units. Subsistence farmers have been seen as people who must be helped out of poverty because their income is low – even those who are living comfortably on what they grow.

How successful has development been in the last 50 years? It is difficult to be positive. Over 25% of the 4.5 billion people living in developing countries do not reach the age of 40, whilst nearly 1.3 billion people have no access to clean water. Although the global GDP increased tenfold between 1950 and 2000 the increased incomes were so unfairly distributed that the average income of the world's five richest countries is over 70 times greater than that of the five poorest countries. Food security is a major problem for many millions of people and over 800 million people living in developing countries are classified as undernourished.

The global pattern is not simple. The majority of countries have experienced significant increases in wealth and standard of living but there are far too many important exceptions to be able to claim that development has been successful. A significant number of African countries have suffered economically because of wars (including Angola, Sierra Leone and Rwanda) and AIDS (including South Africa, Zambia and Zimbabwe). Some of the former Soviet bloc countries have experienced major economic problems as they have tried to cope with the transition to a market economy. Other countries which rely on only a few exports for much of their income are very vulnerable to changes in the market value of those commodities – when the value drops, it can create havoc, leaving countries with no way to pay off their debts. As this brief summary indicates, the list of problems experienced by countries of the Global South that have not been resolved by international development is very long indeed.

'How successful has development been in the last 50 years? It is difficult to be positive. Over

one quarter

of the 4.5 billion people living in developing countries do not reach the age of 40.'

Measures of economic well-being

Making comparisons between countries and regions in order to measure their progress is not straightforward. What do you want to compare?

GDP (Gross Domestic Product), GNP (Gross National Product) and GNI (Gross National Income) are the most common ways of comparing economic development between countries. They measure the value of the goods and services produced in a country but GNP and GNI also take into account any income generated abroad by industry based in the home country and so are usually seen as a more accurate measure of economic development than GDP. GNI has become the standard way of measuring the level of wealth within a country. Just measuring the total gross value of GNI can be very misleading, however, because it does not take account of the population of each country. For this reason, GNI figures are usually shown as 'per capita'– the total wealth of the country divided by its population.

All three of these measures provide, however, limited information about levels of development within a country. Rising levels of GDP, GNI and GNP do indicate increasing levels of wealth within a country but that does not necessarily result in improved social conditions, including education and healthcare, for the general population. In other cases the per capita level might give a misleading indication about the true levels of wealth of individuals – hiding the huge discrepancies that usually exist between rich and poor. Uneven distribution of wealth is a feature of almost all countries.

Another criticism of these economic measures is that they only take account of the official economy and do not consider the value of the informal economy that is much more a feature of developing countries,

Percentage of population living below the poverty line in selected countries

Country	% living on less than $1.25/day (2008)	% living on less than $2/day (2008)	% living below national poverty line
Bangladesh	49.6	81.3	49.8
China	15.9	36.3	2.8
DR Congo	59.2	79.5	71.3
Ethiopia	39	77.5	44.2
El Salvador	11	20.5	37.2
India	41.6	75.6	28.6
Indonesia	21.4	53.8	16
Kenya	19.7	39.9	52
Malawi	73.9	90.4	65.3
Turkey	2.7	9	27

UN Human Development Report 2008

including subsistence farming. Many consider that they also reflect a gender bias because the unpaid domestic work of many women is not counted. Wealth indicators can give us a general picture of the differences that may exist between countries but we should be wary of using them too literally.

The poor in Bangkok, Thailand, cluster along the *klongs* or canals, as here in Klong Toey.

If measuring wealth is difficult, what about measuring poverty? The ability to measure levels of poverty within a country or region is an important ingredient of any assessment of levels of development and GNP, GNI and GDP are not suited to that purpose. The most common measure of poverty within a country is the percentage of the population who live below the poverty line. The poverty line can be drawn by using a standardized measure – the UN Development Programme, for example, uses $1.25 or $2 a day – or a national poverty line which is decided by the country itself. The data for selected countries in the table opposite shows very wide variations and highlights the problems in comparing poverty levels in different countries if you use their own national poverty line.

This data is useful but it is also limited because it gives no indication of how far people are below the poverty line. For instance, it cannot detect any increase in the levels of income of the poorest groups that might still leave them below the poverty line. A more sophisticated version of this measure is the poverty gap ratio, which measures the average distance of the poor below the chosen poverty line and therefore gives an indication of the severity of income poverty. It is calculated as the mean shortfall of the total population from the poverty line (counting the non-poor as having zero shortfall), expressed as a percentage of the poverty line. Data is not available for all countries on an annual basis but in 2007 the poverty gap in India was 10.8% and in Indonesia 7.1%. The higher the number, the more severe is the poverty problem.

$$\text{Poverty gap ratio} = \frac{\text{Average shortfall of people whose earnings are below the poverty line}}{\text{Poverty line (e.g. \$1.25)}} \times 100$$

Social measures of development

Economic growth may not be sustainable when it results in negative impacts on the environment or has a destructive effect on society by encouraging increasing levels of inequality. Other measures have been developed that take account of a wider range of factors so as to assess the levels of development within countries and regions more accurately.

Social measures of development use a wide range of information and include health, education, gender equality and access to democracy. The most commonly used measure of social development is the

Human Development Index (HDI) rankings

Highest			Lowest		
Rank	Country	Score	Rank	Country	Score
1	Norway	0.938	160	Mali	0.309
2	Australia	0.937	161	Burkina Faso	0.305
3	New Zealand	0.907	162	Liberia	0.300
4	US	0.902	163	Chad	0.295
5	Ireland	0.895	164	Guinea Bissau	0.289
6	Liechtenstein	0.891	165	Mozambique	0.284
7	Netherlands	0.890	166	Burundi	0.282
8	Canada	0.888	167	Niger	0.261
9	Sweden	0.885	168	Dem. Rep. of Congo	0.239
10	Germany	0.885	169	Zimbabwe	0.140
26	UK	0.849			

UN Human Development Report 2010

Human Development Index (HDI) produced by the United Nations Development Programme. This considers the three most important measures of development to be:

- Levels of wealth within the country as measured by GDP per capita and adjusted in purchasing power parity (PPP)
- Health – measured by average life expectancy
- Education – measured by the percentage of the population in education at a particular age (primary, secondary and tertiary) and literacy levels (educational attainment).

The variables are combined in a composite index ranging from 0 (the lowest level of development) to 1 (the highest level of development). In the 2010 report the highest index score was 0.938 (Norway) and the lowest 0.140 (Zimbabwe). There were 25 UN member states not included in the 2010 HDI list because of the lack of data from those countries. The UN introduced a refinement of its HDI measurement in 2010 by also including in its report an HDI adjusted for inequality. This takes account of inequalities in the distribution of health, education and income in the country. The inequality-adjusted HDI is, on average, 25% less than the unadjusted HDI, much less in developed countries but more in developing countries.

There are some important criticisms of the use of HDI. Data from some developing countries may not be very reliable and may be difficult to confirm. The measures chosen, moreover, may seem very arbitrary to some because there are other ways of measuring relative qualities in health and education. The same criticism of GDP per capita, that it does not measure unequal distribution within the country, can be levelled at HDI. There is no indication in the education index about access to education for all groups in society, while the continuation of wealthy students through to tertiary education can hide the fact that it is difficult for children of poorer families to enter primary education. Nevertheless, there is a widespread use of HDI to compare development levels and it does reveal clear global patterns.

Some things that are important to development, such as levels of happiness within a country, are very difficult to measure quantitatively and therefore difficult to compare. The UN *Human Development Report* (first published in 1990) contains three other measures of development. The first recognizes the strong link between development and poverty and attempts to measure not just economic poverty but the wider implications of poverty. The Human Poverty Index used in the report is a composite measure, like the HDI, using the following data about a country:

- The percentage of the population living below the poverty line
- Adult literacy rate
- Percentage of the population who do not have access to clean water

- The probability at birth of not surviving to the age of 40
- The percentage of children under five who are underweight.

An index is calculated for each of these factors and the HPI value is calculated as a single index. The index calculated using the criteria above is referred to as HPI-1.

It is difficult to obtain the data from all developing countries to rank them using HPI. UNHDR calculated the Human Poverty Index for 2007 using only the data for the top 22 HDI-ranked countries and amended criteria to create HPI-2 (see table below).

Measuring gender inequality

In addition to its other measures, the *Human Development Report* includes tools to measure gender inequality. The Gender-Related Development Index (GDI) uses the HDI and adjusts it to take account of any inequalities between males and females. For example a large discrepancy in literacy rates between males and females caused by low female access to education will reduce the GDI. GDI is not a measure in and of itself but comparisons between HDI and GDI can help in identifying issues of

Human Poverty Index, 2007

Rank	Country	HPI-2	Probability at birth of not surviving to age 60 (%)	People lacking functional literacy skills (%)	Long-term unemployment (%)	Population below 50% of median income (%)
1	Sweden	6.3	6.7	7.5	1.1	6.5
2	Norway	6.8	7.9	7.9	0.5	6.4
3	Netherlands	8.1	8.3	10.5	1.8	7.3
4	Finland	8.1	9.4	10.4	1.8	5.4
5	Denmark	8.2	10.3	9.6	0.8	5.6
6	Germany	10.3	8.6	14.4	5.8	8.4
7	Switzerland	10.7	7.2	15.9	1.5	7.6
8	Canada	10.9	8.1	14.6	0.5	11.4
9	Luxembourg	11.1	9.2	-	1.2	6.0
10	Austria	11.1	8.8	-	1.3	7.7
13	Australia	12.1	7.3	17.0	0.9	12.2
16	UK	14.8	8.7	21.8	1.2	12.5
17	US	15.4	11.6	20.0	0.4	17.0
18	Ireland	16.0	8.7	22.6	1.5	16.2

UN Human Development Report 2007

gender inequality.

The Gender Empowerment Measure (GEM), meanwhile, attempts to quantify the equality of representation of men and women in the political and economic decision-making process. Using these measures the report identified 22 countries as having particularly low human development; all of them were in Africa.

Basic needs

The United Nations has stated what it believes to be our basic human material and social needs and these make a good starting place when evaluating whether there has been any progress in world development. The UN basic human needs are;

- Food, shelter, clothing and fuel.
- Clean water, sanitation, transport, healthcare and employment.
- A healthy and safe environment.
- An ability to take part in decision making.

There are almost seven billion people on the planet and meeting the needs of such a large population inevitably has an impact on the physical and human environment. Those impacts are not uniform and they vary according to a whole range of factors, including population density, whether the location is urban or rural and the nature of the predominant traditions or cultures.

Providing food for families and individuals is one of the most basic human needs. Growing food is an activity that may be small scale, and for subsistence purposes, or large scale and commercial. The way we grow our food is a contentious topic. Its impacts are not always obvious.

Much of the food consumed in Western countries is imported. In the UK, for example, 40% of the food comes from overseas. Such imported food bears a significant environmental footprint, not just due to its transportation but also because of the inputs necessary for its cultivation. Asparagus is a case in point. This vegetable has become much more common on supermarket shelves in the last few years. Although it is possible to grow it in Britain, its growing period there is limited to a couple of months in the spring. It is also a thirsty plant that thrives in moist conditions. Nevertheless, because consumers are prepared to pay quite a high price for what is perceived to be something of a luxury item, supermarkets are prepared to transport the vegetable over long distances. Much of the asparagus that appears in British supermarkets is air freighted from Peru. High up in the Andes the growing season is longer but the large quantities of water needed by the plant have to be taken from underground supplies (see box overleaf).

For subsistence farmers in many developing countries the biggest

Asparagus growing in the Ica Valley, Peru

Asparagus grown in Peru and sold in the UK is commonly held up as a symbol of unacceptable food miles, but a report has raised an even more urgent problem: its water footprint.

The study, by the development charity Progressio, has found that industrial production of asparagus in Peru's Ica Valley is depleting the area's water resources so fast that smaller farmers and local families are finding wells running dry. Water to the main city in the valley is also under threat, it says. It warns that the export of the luxury vegetable, much of it to British supermarkets, is unsustainable in its current form.

The Ica Valley is a desert area in the Andes and one of the driest places on earth. The asparagus beds developed in the last decade require constant irrigation, with the result that the local water table has plummeted since 2002 when extraction overtook replenishment. In some places it has fallen by eight metres each year, one of the fastest rates of aquifer depletion in the world.

The UK is the world's sixth-largest importer of 'virtual water', that is, water needed to produce the goods it buys from other countries, according to the Worldwide Fund for Nature. Much of this virtual water consumption is directly related to the boom in high-value food imports in recent years. The market in fresh asparagus is typical; it barely existed before the end of the 1990s. Now the UK is the third-largest importer of fresh Peruvian asparagus, consuming 6.5 million kilos a year.

The Guardian, 15 September 2010

A worker weighs asparagus at a processing plant in the Peruvian city of Ica.

Feature

Water in Rulindo, Rwanda

The installation of improved public water systems has changed the farming practices of many households. In order to purchase water, revenue has to be generated, so many households are now planting cash crops, in particular coffee, instead of cassava, beans, maize and other crops that have historically fed their family members. This has introduced much uncertainty and anxiety into the lives of subsistence farmers. If the price of coffee decreases on the world market, the trivial purchasing power of subsistence farmers also diminishes, further compromising not only their ability to purchase water but their ability to feed themselves, and their overall economic well-being. And as more farmers move into coffee production, the price of coffee will surely decrease, further jeopardizing subsistence farming in rural Rwanda.

Price of purity: Rwandans are going into debt to pay for drinking water.

Because it now costs money to irrigate, many households have stopped cultivating crops that require irrigation, like tomatoes, peppers, onions, passion fruit and *ibinyomoro* (tree tomatoes). These fruits and vegetables not only fed the family, but surpluses (usually 30% of the total yield) were taken to the local market to sell, generating revenue for desperately needed goods (clothing, tools, etc) that the household was unable to make.

Lastly, all the households I interviewed complained about the recent privatization of the improved public taps. Until three months ago, the taps were run by a local water collective, and the cost to fill each jerry can was five Rwandan francs. Then the district government entered into a contract with a local entrepreneur to manage all the improved water systems. The price doubled, with, according to the households I interviewed, no notable improvement in the quality or quantity of water. For the first time in these villages, some people are going into debt to pay for access to drinking water.

Michael J Mascarenhas, *New York Times* website, September 2010

Feature

problem they face in growing their crops is access to water. Providing access to clean water is a major objective of many development schemes and many farmers have benefited from the progress that has been made in improving water supplies to rural areas in the developing world. Sometimes the result of improved water supplies is not what had been predicted, however, and may exacerbate differences in wealth and opportunity amongst poor farmers.

More than 70% of Rwanda's farmers are subsistence farmers

producing very little surplus to sell to buy clothes and other goods for their families. Many of them lack access to water and this prevents the irrigation of their crops in the dry season. With no irrigation their crop yields are low and they have no money to invest in the things they need to increase yields. It is the classic cycle of poverty.

The box on page 17 focuses on a project to improve water supplies in Rulindo District, north of Kigali. It highlights the issues subsistence farmers have to confront when their only access to the 'improved' water supply is through taps owned by a private supplier.

Agribusiness

Farm systems in the developed world have completely different characteristics. They are mostly distinguished by their large-scale operations and high quantities of inputs. The intensity of agricultural practices on the farms requires the support of specialists in technology, chemicals, biotechnology and advice and information. The contrasts with subsistence farming could not be more marked.

The term agribusiness evolved in the 1970s and was used to describe the increasing number of inputs to farming in the developed world. It includes farming, seed supply, agricultural chemicals, wholesaling, processing, distribution and retail sales. The term has come to represent different things to different people. For people within the food supply industry it is a convenient way to describe the wide range of business and agriculture activities involved in modern food production. For many others the term has a negative connotation associated with corporate farming. It is all about large, vertically integrated food production businesses who, with profit as their only motive, cause damage to the environment, reduce food quality and cause social damage in rural areas in particular. There is plenty of evidence to consider.

Agribusiness grew rapidly with the coming of the Green Revolution in the 1960s. New seed varieties, the need for fertilizers and other biochemicals and a revolution in farm machinery meant the industry grew rapidly. Almost all farms in the developed world use the products and technology sold by agribusiness and increasingly farming in the developing world is becoming just as dependent.

United States CASE STUDY

Agriculture in North Dakota

North Dakota is the most westerly state of the Midwest region. The 12 states included in this region are often referred to as the 'Heartland of America'. The rural character of the state is evident in the farms and small towns that dot the landscape.

A grain elevator in Velva, North Dakota – wind turbines are visible in the distance.

North Dakota farming characteristics

Climate and soil

North Dakota has a sub-humid continental climate.

The annual precipitation is between 300mm and 450mm per year.

The average January temperature is -9°C and the average July temperature 21°C.

Extreme weather is a feature of the region. The highest recorded temperature is 48°C and the lowest -50°C – both recorded in 1936.

Soils range from fertile, black loam in the Red River Valley to more porous, sandy soils in the west.

Data

North Dakota Agricultural Census 2007

Total farmland (hectares)	16,055,749
% of total land area	89.8
Cropland (hectares)	11,139,864
% of total farmland	69.4
Woodland (hectares)	84,649
% of total farmland	0.6
Pastureland (hectares)	4,216,377
% of total farmland	26.3
Average farm size (hectares)	502

Farms by size (%)

1-40 hectares	15.0
40-200 hectares	33.3
200-400 hectares	14.7
400-800 hectares	16.8
Over 800 hectares	20.3

Farms by sales (%)

Less than $9,999/year	42.1
$10,000 to $49,999	12.9
$50,000 to $99,999	9.0
$100,000 to $499,999	24.6
More than $500,000	11.3

Characteristics of principal farm operators 1997-2007

	1997	2002	2007
Average operator age (years)	51.4	54.4	56.5
Percentage with farming as their primary occupation	72.3	70.7	57.9
Men	30,863	28,125	28,314
Women	1,485	2,494	3,656

Top 5 agriculture commodities, 2009

	Value of receipts thousand $	% of total state farm receipts	% of US value
1. Wheat	1,869,016	29.4	16.5
2. Soybeans	1,025,580	16.1	3.4
3. Corn	806,121	12.7	1.9
4. Cattle and calves	596,094	9.4	1.4
5. Barley	360,010	5.7	35.7

There are 1.7 million dairy cattle in North Dakota (2009) producing 219 million litres of milk a year.

Farm ownership in North Dakota is not typical of normal patterns of ownership in the US. Corporate ownership of farms in the state has been illegal since 1933 and the majority of the farms are owned by individuals and their families. The (Federal) Homesteads Act of 1862 gave ownership of 160 acres (65 hectares) of land to anyone over 21 who had registered, improved and worked their land for five years. The size of the land given to the new farmers was based on the size of the farms in the wetter eastern areas and was too small for the extensive farming necessary in the drier Midwest. In 1909 the Enlarged Homesteads Act allocated 320 acres (130 hectares) to farmers prepared to accept more marginal land that could not be irrigated. The overfarming of these marginal areas was one of the causes of the 'dustbowl disaster' of the 1930s in the Midwest states.

Farming on a huge scale

Although 'family farms' still predominate in North Dakota, the scale of agriculture is a long way from any idyllic notion of an intimate hands-on family operation. Typical wheat farms in North Dakota are highly capitalized and consist of several thousand hectares with every piece of farm machinery and modern farm technology used to its maximum effect. These wheat farms are made up of 20 or more of the original homesteaded sections of land, each of which at one time contained 'family farms'. The customers for the produce are not local but national and frequently international.

This movement to fewer and larger farms is typical of agricultural changes that have occurred in the US and in every other country of the Global North over the last 50 years. In 1930, 64% of the farms were less than 500 acres in size but by 1978, only 40% of the farms were that small. The largest farms in the United States, those with annual sales greater than $500,000 a year, make up 2.5% of all farms; yet they account for 40% of farm output and a similar pattern is found in North Dakota. The growth of large farms in the US has been assisted by the subsidies that farmers are given by the government as 'farm income stabilization'. The US government paid $15.4 billion in subsidies to American farmers in 2009. The average payment to farmers was $48,000 but over 60% of the total subsidy was paid to just 10% of the biggest farms and the subsidy has acted as an incentive to industrialize agriculture. The crops which have the highest subsidies are feed grain (in other words, grain that will be fed to animals, mostly corn), cotton, wheat, rice and soybeans. Most of these are extensively grown in North Dakota.

The growth of larger farm units has had a significant social and environmental impact. Mechanization has meant fewer jobs for farm workers and the tendency of large farms to procure their inputs from outside their local area has weakened the farm's links with the local community. Larger farms have often developed direct marketing relationships with large food processors and bypass local buyers. Although the law forbids the ownership of farms by corporations in North Dakota, many of the larger farms have contracts with large firms to buy and process their produce. These big companies often have control of most or all aspects of food production right through to the consumer – a process known as vertical integration. One example is Continental Grain, which processes and sells pork and poultry, operates feedlots, and sells nutritionally enhanced corn to be used as feed for poultry and livestock. Another is Koch Industries, which owns cattle ranches, feedlots, fertilizer and agricultural chemicals, as well as seed and feed processing plants.

Rural decline

Rural decline has been a problem in the Midwest states for many years. The increasing pace of the industrialization of agriculture has resulted in those communities which are close to major processing plants seeing increased farm production while other, more remote communities have suffered. Commodity agriculture (grain, beef, dairy, pork) remains, but it is in bigger hands. Industrialized agriculture has created a pattern of agricultural haves and have-nots and the overall impact has been to lessen the influence of agriculture in the state. The result has been severe rural depopulation, which is evidenced by thousands of abandoned farmsteads and 'ghost towns'.

Confined Animal Feeding Operations (CAFOs) are the ultimate outcome of this continuing industrialization of agriculture. These gather together into one small area all the elements of animal food production, including the animals themselves, both live and dead, feed, manure and urine. Feed is brought to the animals rather than their grazing or seeking feed in pastures and fields. Beef cattle, dairy cattle, pigs and poultry may all be produced in CAFOs. Their use in rural areas has become widespread across the US. One mega dairy in Indiana has 32,000 cows in giant sheds on a 17,000-acre site and produces over a million litres of milk every day. Many of the CAFO poultry farms contain over a million live chicks at any one time.

Pigs in a Missouri factory farm. Just one person operates this farm, covering 4,000 hogs in two 'barns'. The pigs spend their whole lives in this confined space before being slaughtered at the age of five-and-a-half months.

Problems with CAFOs

Animal welfare is a major concern in relation to CAFOs: animals are treated as elements of factory production. Another major issue is the disposal of the huge quantities of animal waste produced within CAFOs. The waste is often stored in large lagoons, and leakage and ruptures from these can discharge vast amounts of animal sewage into streams, aquifers and wetlands. The stench from the waste generated by CAFOs can extend for large areas around the farm site. The US Environmental Protection Agency warns: 'The environmental impacts resulting from mismanagement of CAFO wastes include, among others, excess nutrients in water (such as nitrogen and phosphorus), which can contribute to low levels of dissolved oxygen (fish kills), and decomposing organic matter that can contribute to toxic algal blooms. Contamination from runoff or lagoon leakage can degrade water resources, and can contribute to illness by exposing people to wastes and pathogens in their drinking water. Dust and odours can contribute to respiratory problems in workers and nearby residents.'

The advantages for the CAFO operators are clear. They enjoy economies of scale and are able to claim farm subsidies because their activities are classified as farming and not as industrial activity. There is a proposal for a 1,500-cow megadairy in Carrington, North Dakota, that has met some local opposition and is still under consideration. The arguments against it are clear, but it is less easy to see why any community would welcome a CAFO with open arms.

Communities accept CAFOs because of:
- The need for jobs – even in such a mechanized operation, some jobs are created by CAFOs
- The need for local authorities to increase their tax base so as to provide rural services
- The need to bolster a declining agricultural economy
- The knowledge that other communities will accept the CAFO if they do not
- The belief that big operations can afford modern pollution-prevention technologies
- The feeling that communities are powerless against large farmers and corporations.

North Dakota has seen the growth of CAFOs within its state boundaries. The state government is, however, so sensitive about the subject that it has made it illegal to photograph a CAFO without the permission of the owner.

Positive developments

Other developments in agriculture are more hopeful and sustainable. In recent years there has, for example, been a resurgence of interest in organic and free range foods. Some people have questioned the viability of industrial agriculture practices and have turned to organic produce from family farms in the interests of both food quality and animal welfare. This type of farming is possible where there are a significant number of affluent urban and suburban consumers willing to pay a premium for organic or free-range produce. The size of the farms varies from small units run as a hobby or part-time venture, to much larger farms backed by wealthy families, which use the latest technology and require large amounts of capital. The increasing number of smaller farms shown in recent surveys is in part a result of the growth of these smaller organic farms but also reflects the increasing number of part-time and 'hobby' farmers. This has, however, not altered the overall pattern of agricultural dominance by large farms and industrial agriculture. ■

Why are some countries more developed than others?

* *There are certain key historical events and processes that have contributed to the modern world economic order. These include the slave trade, colonialism, industrialization, the Cold War, international debt and the rise of newly industrialized countries (NICs).*
* *There are a range of theories that attempt to account for the variations in development between countries. These include modernist theory, dependency theory, Marxist theory and post-development theory.*
* *Each theory may have a different interpretation as to why a country has ended up with a particular level of development.*
* *Poverty is not just a problem in developing countries, though wealthier countries are more able to provide welfare support to protect the poorest.*
* *Indigenous cultures are important in the development process.*

Key points

Dependency theory

It is apparent that, however you measure them, there are huge variations in levels of development – the North-South line is merely the most graphic demonstration of this. Why are there such contrasts in wealth and all the associated factors such as healthcare and levels of nutrition? Many seek to explain this by looking back at global history over the last 500 years. Dependency theory is one such perspective that developed in the 1970s, most famously through the work of the Marxist economist Andre Gunder Frank. According to this theory, resources flow from a poor 'periphery' of countries to a rich 'core' of wealthy states. This flow of resources works to the advantage of the richer countries. Dependency theorists identify three stages that have led to this inequality in the distribution of wealth and human development.

Stage 1 Mercantile capitalism

During the 15th and 16th centuries, European merchants sailed around the globe looking for supplies of goods that would fetch a high price in European markets, such as spices, cloths and jewels. More European goods were produced to trade for the purchase of these goods and the merchants became very powerful.

As well as being able to bargain and barter they could also use threats and force to secure advantageous terms of trade. The negotiations did not take place on an equal basis and damage was done to many of the previously prosperous and stable societies they traded with. Europeans are often surprised to learn that well-developed societies and cultures existed in Africa for centuries before it was colonized by the European major powers. The ancient kingdom of Benin is only one example.

Stage 2 Colonialism

During the colonial period – between the 16th and 20th centuries – European countries took direct political control of land around the world. The land was exploited for cheap food, resources and labour. In some cases, such as Indian cotton cloth production, industries were closed down to prevent competition with European manufacturers. During this period, particularly in Africa in the 19th century, borders between countries were arbitrarily drawn for the convenience of the colonial power and little attention was paid to social groupings or previous history. Local food production was replaced on the best land by cash cropping for export and huge plantations and estates were established, owned by companies and individuals from the colonizing countries.

Stage 3 Neo-colonialism

Dependency theorists identify the period that followed the end of colonial rule (which mostly occurred in the mid-20th century) as the most powerful influence on current global development. Although the colonial powers gave up direct political rule, they continued to exert enormous influence through their continuing economic power. Former colonies were left with economies that had been constructed for the benefit of their foreign rulers, and with little opportunity to change the basis on which they interacted with the global marketplace. Much of this influence today is associated with the overwhelming size and power of the transnational companies that are such a dominant feature of world trade.

The continued influence of the colonial period during Stage 3 occurred because of a variety of factors:

- The colonial powers' ability to influence government decisions
- The high dependence on resources developed in the colonial period. This made ex-colonies economically vulnerable because of the fluctuation of commodity prices on the global market
- A lack of experience or participation in democracy that made it difficult for democratic models to develop. This often resulted in authoritarian government, frequently supported by the old colonial power
- A low skill base in management of business because the colonists rarely employed local people for those types of jobs. This meant a continued dependence on the old colonial power for expertise and investment.

Dependency theory is essentially an anti-capitalist perspective and as a result its interpretation of history places most of the blame for inequalities in development on the rich, mostly Western nations. Nation-states are seen as having little real power and their economic progress is determined by their relationship with that system.

This emphasis on countries having little control over their levels of development is key to the dependency theorists, who see the important decisions as still being made by a group of dominant countries at the

A container ship on the river Elbe in Hamburg, Germany – Europe's second-largest port.

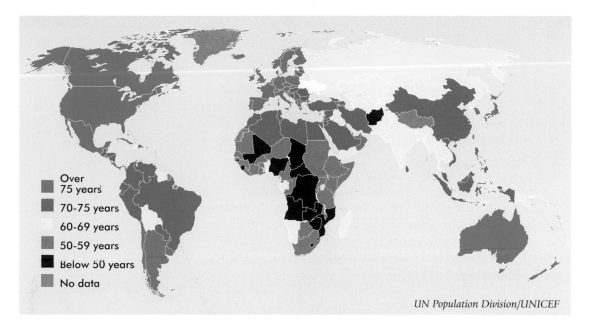

Legend:
- Over 75 years
- 70-75 years
- 60-69 years
- 50-59 years
- Below 50 years
- No data

UN Population Division/UNICEF

core of the system. The countries that own the capital and make the investment decisions have tended to be located in Europe, North America and Japan, although that dominance has been challenged in recent years. The core-periphery relationship that exists between countries has resulted in many developing countries being forced to become producers of raw materials for rich countries, which would then process them into goods that attracted a much higher price in the market. This relationship has often been referred to as 'the international division of labour'.

This explanation as to why some countries are more developed than others leads to the argument that, if poor countries are to improve their levels of wealth and development, they need to break out of the system and enter a self-sustaining development path. One way of doing this might be to have a government policy that protects its domestic producers of certain goods from foreign competition. South Korea is one country that followed this route, and some argue that this is what enabled it to join the ranks of industrialized, high-income nations.

World systems theory is similar to dependency theory and suggests there is a third group of countries, the *semi-periphery*, which is intermediate between the core and periphery. The semi-periphery is industrialized, but with less sophisticated technology than in the core and no control of finances. By this theory, the rise of one group of semi-peripheries tends to be at the cost of another group but the unequal structure of the world economy remains the same. It is interesting to look for evidence of this in the changing status of some developing countries.

Modernization theory
Modernization theory is the other dominant explanation for the differences that exist in development levels. According to modernization theory, underdeveloped countries can strengthen their

Life expectancy at birth, 2009. The gulf between rich and poor countries is clearly illustrated by differences in average life expectancy.

economies by being introduced to modern methods in technology, agriculture and industrial production. The view that countries pass through stages of economic development is most closely associated with the work of Walt Whitman Rostow (*The Stages of Economic Growth: A non-communist manifesto*, 1960). Rostow was a US economist and political theorist who worked for Presidents JF Kennedy and LB Johnson in the 1960s. He was a staunch anti-communist whose views on economic growth have become a cornerstone of modernization theory. In direct contrast to dependency theory, this sees the answers to uneven development as lying in the internal structures, governance and culture of a country. Through his work on the growth of industrialization in the UK and the US, Rostow identified five stages through which all developing societies must pass.

Stage 1 Traditional society
- Pre-Newtonian levels of technology and science
- Subsistence agriculture economy
- Hierarchical social structure largely based on birth rather than ability.

Stage 2 Pre-conditions for take-off
- Change occurs across a range of institutions often because of some external impulse, such as invasion
- Agricultural output increases because of improved technology
- Trade between regions starts to increase as communications start to improve
- Some industries start to develop, particularly extractive industries such as coal and iron ore
- An entrepreneurial élite emerges that is willing to reinvest its wealth
- Rational scientific ideas emerge and become more widely accepted.

Stage 3 Take-off
- A rise in investment to at least 10% of GDP
- One or two manufacturing industries emerge, possibly iron and steel or textiles
- Rapid improvements in infrastructure.

Stage 4 The drive to maturity
- A period of consolidation
- Use of science and technology is extended and mechanization develops
- Rate of investment remains high (10-20%)
- Political reforms continue and allow extension of voting rights
- International trade becomes more significant.

Stage 5 The age of high mass consumption
*   Growth of consumer industries
*   Rapid increase in levels of personal wealth and ownership of property
*   Stable political and social system
*   High levels of education
*   Significant increase in international trade.

Rostow recognized that his model was a simplified version of what really happened as countries developed. The complex political, economic and social processes that are happening in all countries take place in circumstances that vary from 'primitive' cultures to sophisticated societies. The important thing for Rostow was to describe the common stages that each country went through as it 'developed'. The model is descriptive and provides no explanation for the movement from one stage of the model to the next but the focus on internal change in the model is an important contrast to dependency theory.

Modernization theorists do not see the legacy of a country's history as an overwhelmingly important influence. For them, it is the decisions taken within the country that have the greatest impact on development. This theory fits in with the view of modern neoliberals that development is best served when there is little government intervention and markets are allowed to function without interference. They believe that huge bureaucracies and state regulations hinder private investment and distort prices, making development increasingly difficult. According to this theory, this is why countries that have embraced the free market, such

An illustration showing US President Harry Truman's face on the ancient Egyptian Sphinx. It was drawn by cartoonist Polyp for a special issue of *New Internationalist* magazine called 'Development: a guide to the ruins', written by Wolfgang Sachs (see overleaf).

as India, Brazil and China, have made such rapid economic progress in recent years. Countries that have attempted to adopt alternative socialist strategies such as Tanzania and Russia have eventually had to admit failure and adopt neoliberal principles in order to achieve economic growth and development.

Other theories of development

Although modernization and dependency theories are the most commonly discussed approaches to development, there are other views. 'Post-development theory' sees the whole concept and practice of development as a reflection of Western/Northern hegemony over the rest of the world. According to this view, modern development theory has been constructed by academics who are guided by the dominant underlying political ideology. Any development process guided by this academic and political coalition reflects Western ideas in its direction and outcomes. The result is a socially constructed view of development which suggests that the aim of development is to reflect the 'pattern of Western hegemony'.

"the idea of development stands like a ruin in the intellectual landscape"

Wolfgang Sachs

The theory is associated with Arturo Escobar and Wolfgang Sachs. Supporters of the theory argue that development was always unjust, never worked, and has now obviously failed. For them the idea of a middle-class, Western lifestyle imposed upon developing countries may neither be a realistic nor a desirable goal for the majority of the world's population. The actions that developing countries are encouraged to take to 'develop' require the loss, or even the deliberate extermination, of indigenous cultures.

'Post-structuralist theory', meanwhile, is a neo-Marxist theory that calls for a process of synthesis to explain different levels of development. It suggests that instead of focusing on the causes of current levels of development in a country or region, we should try to understand the unique effects of social and environmental processes at any given moment in time – 'everything matters'. Its recognition of the need to look outside the culture-bound explanations of the modernization and dependency theorists echoes post-development ideas.

Each of these competing explanations for uneven development can point to evidence from different parts of the globe to support their arguments and it is one of the great challenges for students of world development to be able to examine that evidence closely and reach their own conclusions. How would the theories interpret the development history of Mozambique (see case study opposite)?

CASE STUDY

The development history of Mozambique

MOZAMBIQUE

■, Maputo

Key statistics for Mozambique

Total population	22.9 million
Adult literacy rate	54%
Infant mortality rate	96 per 1,000 live births
GNI per capita	$440
Life expectancy	48 years
Number of adults living with HIV	1.5 million
Population below the poverty line	55%

The Portuguese first reached Mozambique in 1498 and set up trading posts and forts along the coast which they used to visit on their voyages to the Far East. Gradually they moved further inland looking for gold and slaves to sell. Portugal's influence in the region grew slowly, as it was more interested in developing trade with India and the Far East and in colonizing Brazil.

At the start of the 20th century the Portuguese used large private companies to administer Mozambique, many of them owned by the British. It was during this time that the British were largely responsible for building railway connections to neighbouring countries and supplying cheap labour to the mines and plantations of its nearby colonies and South Africa.

Although many European countries granted independence to their colonies after World War Two, Portugal still clung to its

colonies and many of its citizens emigrated to Mozambique. Pressure for independence intensified within Mozambique as other African countries won their liberation and FRELIMO (Front for the Liberation of

Mozambique) was formed in 1962. It started an armed campaign against Portuguese colonial rule and, after years of sporadic fighting and political change, Mozambique became independent in 1975.

After independence FRELIMO established a one-party state allied to the Soviet bloc and outlawed rival political activity. FRELIMO eliminated political pluralism, religious educational institutions and the role of traditional authorities.

The government gave support to the liberation movements in South Africa and Zimbabwe and the governments of those two countries responded by financing an armed rebel movement in central Mozambique called the Mozambican National Resistance (RENAMO). The situation within the country became murderously chaotic as a civil war and sabotage of its infrastructure by neighbouring states was followed by economic collapse.

During most of the civil war there was no effective government within the country and an estimated one million people were killed. A further 1.7 million refugees fled to neighbouring countries and several million more were internally displaced. The civil war ended in 1992 under a new constitution that guaranteed free elections and a multi-party political system.

By 1995 more than 1.7 million refugees had returned from Malawi, Zimbabwe, Swaziland, Zambia, Tanzania and South Africa and four million displaced people had returned to their areas of origin.

Progress in Mozambique

Mozambique is one of the world's 20 poorest countries and is 165th out of 169 in in the UN Human Development Index rankings. It is, however, recognized as one of Africa's most successful examples of post-conflict reconstruction and economic recovery. Since the end of the civil war its economic growth (averaging 9% annually) has been well above the average for Africa

---

The Throne of Weapons

This sculpture is made out of decommissioned weapons from the Mozambique civil war (1977-92), which claimed almost one million lives and left five million people displaced. It represents both the tragedy of that war and the human triumph of those who achieved a lasting peace. It was made by the Mozambican artist Cristóvão Canhavato (Kester) in 2001 for the Transforming Arms into Tools project, where some of the seven million guns left in the country were voluntarily exchanged for useful tools and hardware.

BBC History of the World in 100 Objects

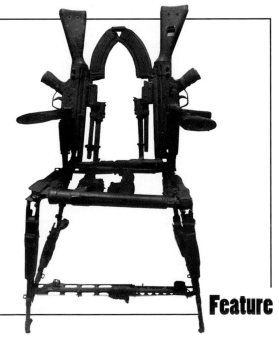

Feature

and it has succeeded in reducing the proportion of Mozambicans who live below the poverty line from 69% in 2003 to 54% in 2008. This is ahead of the targets set by the government in its first Poverty Reduction Strategy (PARPA).

The country has successfully held three elections since the end of the civil war, the most recent in 2009, and achieved a political stability that many thought was impossible. Its progress has been impressive. The 2008 Millennium Development Goals (MDG) national progress report estimated that Mozambique was likely or has the potential to achieve 12 of the 21 MDG targets – among them, those relating to poverty, under-five mortality, maternal mortality, malaria and the establishment of an open trading and financial system.

Largely as a result of its political stability and high rates of poverty, the country has also attracted strong donor support and high inflows of foreign direct investment. Foreign aid represents 15% of Mozambique's gross domestic product, compared with 6-8% for the rest of sub-Saharan Africa.

In spite of its progress, Mozambique faces many problems. Around 70% of its population live in rural areas where they struggle to make a living out of subsistence farming. Periodic drought affecting the interior of the country has forced many to move to the coast, with negative environmental consequences. Half of the country's 22 million population are children and over half of those live below the poverty line. One of Mozambique's biggest

challenges is to translate its economic gains into improved child and maternal health and well-being.

According to UNICEF, another major problem is the disparity that exists in income, education, health and nutritional status – as well as access to safe water and sanitation – between rural and urban areas; between men and women, boys and girls; and between those that are educated and those that are not.

AIDS is the greatest threat to Mozambique's development. There are about 1.6 million people living with HIV and about 350,000 children have lost their parents to AIDS-related illnesses. The government has invested money in measures to reduce the spread of the disease but orphaned children are particularly affected by food insecurity and malnutrition. Natural disasters increase the problems of those living in poverty, who are most vulnerable to the periodic droughts and floods.

But does any of this shed any light on the question that heads this chapter? Why is Mozambique less developed than other countries? The extreme poverty that is at the root of Mozambique's low levels of development can be explained from a number of different perspectives. Developed countries have the opportunity to shield the less well off in their populations from the levels of poverty experienced in the poorest countries by using their national wealth to provide welfare support. That does not mean that poverty is not also a big problem in developed countries, as is demonstrated by the next case study, on poverty in the UK. ■

United Kingdom

CASE STUDY

Poverty in the UK

UK poverty facts

- Nearly 13 million people live in poverty in the UK
- 3.8 million children in the UK are living in poverty
- 2.2 million pensioners in the UK are living in poverty
- 7.2 million adults of working age are living in poverty in the UK
- 70% of Bangladeshi children in the UK are poor
- Women form the majority in the UK's poorest groups
- London has a higher proportion of people living in poverty than any other region in the UK
- The UK has a higher proportion of its population living in relative poverty than most other European countries: of the 27 EU countries, only 6 have a higher rate than the UK.

Data

'Individuals, families and groups in the population can be said to be in poverty when they lack the resources to obtain the types of diet, participate in the activities, and have the living conditions and amenities which are customary, or are at least widely encouraged and approved, in the societies in which they belong.'

P Townsend, *Poverty in the United Kingdom* 1979

Witness

The main cause of poverty is low income, arising from unemployment, low wages or the low level of welfare benefits.

Income poverty

The most commonly used definition of low income is a household income that is 60% or less of the average (median) British household income. In 2009, the 60% threshold was worth:

- £119 (around $190) per week for a single adult with no dependent children

- £206 per week for a couple with no dependent children
- £202 per week for a single adult with two dependent children under 14
- £288 per week for a couple with two dependent children under 14.

This is measured after income tax, council tax and housing costs (including rent, mortgage repayments, buildings insurance and water charges) have been deducted. It represents what the household has available to spend on everything else it

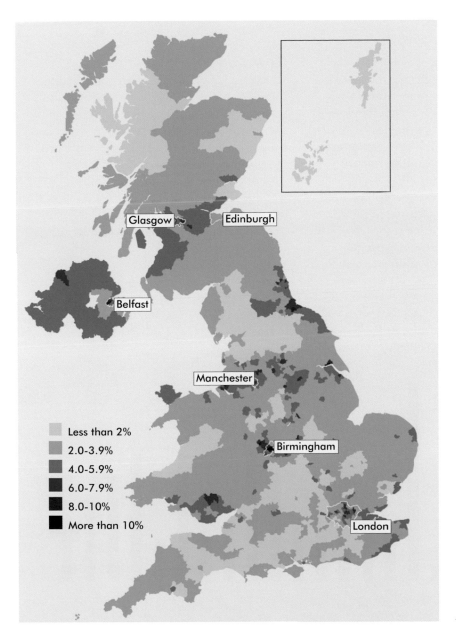

Glasgow

Edinburgh

Belfast

Manchester

Birmingham

London

Less than 2%
2.0-3.9%
4.0-5.9%
6.0-7.9%
8.0-10%
More than 10%

Regional unemployment rates in the UK, June 2010.

needs, from food and heating to travel and entertainment. Using this measure, nearly 13 million people in the UK are living below the poverty line. Measures of poverty in developed countries are normally more generous than those in developing countries.

Unemployment

Levels of unemployment in the UK are subject to considerable variation. The national level of unemployment in June 2010 was 7.7%, but this was expected to rise steeply because of the economic recession and decisions taken by the government to cut public spending so as to reduce the budget deficit. The risk of unemployment is higher for those with low skills, those from certain minority ethnic groups, and for those living in low employment areas such as the northeast of England and South Wales. The map on page 35 shows the wide variations in rates of unemployment across the UK.

Other people may be unemployed because they experience barriers to finding work, such as having caring responsibilities or through discrimination because of gender, age, ethnicity, disability or sexual orientation.

Low wages

Having a job is not necessarily a guarantee of freedom from poverty. In 2009, 61% of income-poor children came from households where one or more parent was in work. Low wages, part-time work and not having two adults in work in a household all increase the risk of poverty. The national minimum wage (NMW) is a legal right which covers almost all workers in the UK. It became law in 1999 to make some employers pay a more realistic living wage. When it was introduced, the minimum wage caused a lot of controversy and was criticized by businesses in general

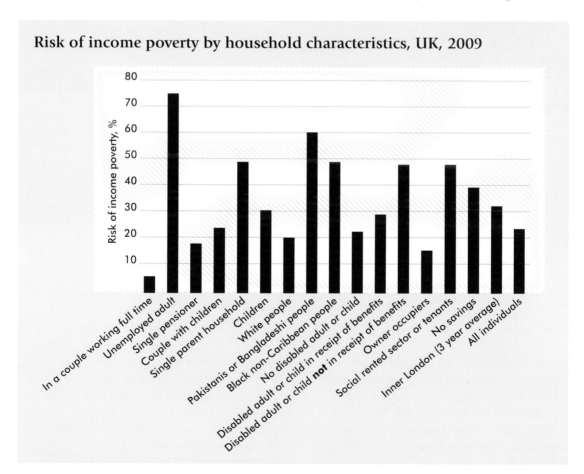

Risk of income poverty by household characteristics, UK, 2009

because they believed that it would add to their costs and make it harder for them to compete. It has since, however, been generally accepted. In October 2010 the NMW for different groups of workers was set as below:

- £5.93 (around $9.50) an hour for workers aged 21 and over
- £4.92 an hour for workers aged 18 to 20
- £3.64 an hour for workers aged 16 to 17.

The London Living Wage was introduced by Mayor of London Ken Livingstone and set at well above the national minimum wage level. It is an advisory rather than legal minimum and in 2010 it was £7.85 an hour.

Benefits, or welfare payments, are often thought of as the protection needed to keep people above the poverty level in a welfare state such as the UK, but benefit levels are frequently set too low to prevent claimants living below the poverty line.

The impact of poverty

The impacts of poverty are wide ranging and complex. When you are poor in the UK you are likely to suffer more illness and have a shorter life expectancy, your access to educational opportunities will be limited

> *We know what makes us ill.*
> *When we are ill we are told*
> *That it's you who will heal us.*
> *When we come to you*
> *Our rags are torn off us and you listen all*
> *over our naked body.*
> *As to the cause of our illness one glance at*
> *our rags would tell you more.*
> *It is the same cause that wears out our*
> *bodies and our clothes.*
>
> Bertolt Brecht (1898-1956):
> 'Worker's Speech to a Doctor'

compared to more affluent people, you are less likely to find work and more likely to be homeless. All of these ill-effects of poverty are reflected in statistical data but there are other less obvious impacts that can be just as damaging, such as the difficulty of retaining self-respect and self-esteem when your control over your own life appears to be so limited.

Child poverty in the UK

Almost 20% (3.9 million) of children in the UK live in severe poverty, in households where, in 2009, the total income was less

Children from poor families are at 10 times the risk of sudden infant death as children from better-off homes. Babies from disadvantaged families are more likely to be born underweight – an average of 200 grams less than children from the richest families. Poorer children are two-and-a-half times more likely to suffer chronic illness when toddlers and twice as likely to have cerebral palsy, according to the report 'Health Consequences of Poverty for Children'.

Children living in disadvantaged families are more than three times as likely to suffer from mental-health disorders as those in well-off families and infants under three years old in families with an annual income of less than £10,400 are twice as likely to suffer from asthma as those from families earning over £52,000.

End Child Poverty Report 2010

Data

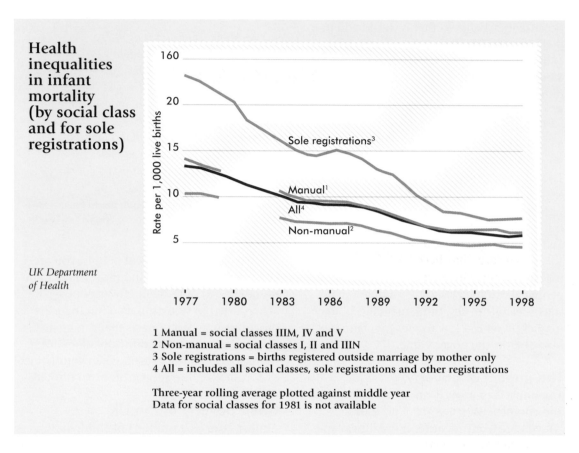

Health inequalities in infant mortality (by social class and for sole registrations)

UK Department of Health

Rate per 1,000 live births

Sole registrations[3]

Manual[1]

All[4]

Non-manual[2]

160

20

15

10

5

1977 1980 1983 1986 1989 1992 1995 1998

1 Manual = social classes IIIM, IV and V
2 Non-manual = social classes I, II and IIIN
3 Sole registrations = births registered outside marriage by mother only
4 All = includes all social classes, sole registrations and other registrations

Three-year rolling average plotted against middle year
Data for social classes for 1981 is not available

than £254 a week. There are wide regional variations – for example, 40% of children in the northeast of England live in low-income households compared with 22% in the southeast. London also has a high number of children living in poor households (36%), despite also having the country's biggest proportion of high earners.

The links between child poverty and multiple deprivation have been investigated by social scientists for many years and its negative impacts have been made clear.

The graph above shows the direct impact of social class on child mortality since 1977. Although the gap has narrowed over the ensuing three decades, there is still a significant difference between the mortality rates of children born in single parent or 'lower' class families (5.9 infant deaths per thousand births) and children born in middle and upper class families (4.9 infant deaths per thousand births). Poorer children on average experience worse health during their childhoods and the effects of this may last far beyond childhood. Three-year-olds in households with incomes below about £10,000 are 2.5 times more likely to suffer chronic illness than children in households with incomes above £52,000.

Child poverty also has a negative impact on educational achievement. On average, poorer children score less well on a range of

Pupils in England who score at or above level 2 for reading at Key Stage 1:
Poorest tenth of areas – 73% of pupils
Richest tenth – 93% of pupils.
Children who get 5 GCSEs at A*-C grade:
Children eligible for free school meals – 35.5%
Children not eligible for free school meals – 62.9%

Department for Children, Schools and Families, National Curriculum Assessment, GCSE and
Equivalent Attainment and Post-16 Attainment by Pupil Characteristics, in England 2006/07

Data

educational measures such as reading tests and GCSE results (the public exam at age 16).

Improving educational opportunities for poorer children has become an important political topic. Universities are encouraged to increase the number of students they enrol from low-income households and to take account of the disadvantaged education they may have received compared to children from wealthier families. Politicians from different political perspectives regularly propose changes in the school system with the aim of raising student achievement and opportunity but none have so far succeeded in challenging the class divide in educational attainment.

In 1999 the Labour government made a pledge to eradicate child poverty completely by 2020 and introduced changes to benefit legislation, the tax system and social security changes so as to achieve its aim. Although the Institute of Fiscal Studies estimates that, over the next 13 years, over 600,000 people were lifted out of poverty, this has hardly reduced the overall poverty rate at all. The measures have included:

- Tax credits for low-income earners
- Tax credit support for parents and universal child benefit
- National minimum wage
- Increased support for people with disabilities
- Increased spending on education, health and housing
- Measures to help the unemployed return to work.

There is a large degree of self-interest for all governments in their attempts to reduce child poverty. After all, it is not only children from poorer families themselves who are affected if they are unable to fulfil their potential. Research by the Joseph Rowntree Foundation suggests that by limiting a child's educational attainment and reducing the skills available to employers, child poverty impedes national economic growth and costs the UK at least £25 billion a year.

What individuals think about poverty is directly linked to their notions of fairness. Is it fair that society should attempt to help people who are poorer? Does a fair society necessarily involve making people more equal in wealth and opportunity? ■

Education and language in South Africa

Key statistics for South Africa	
Total population	50.1 million
Adult literacy rate	89%
Infant mortality rate	43 per 1,000 live births
Life expectancy	52 years
Number of adults living with HIV	5.7 million
Population below poverty line	50%

Background: apartheid in South Africa

Apartheid was a system of legal racial segregation enforced by the National Party government in South Africa between 1948 and 1994. Residential areas, schools, transport, and even doors and benches were all separated. Residential areas were segregated by means of forcible removals. 'Blacks', 'coloureds' and 'Indians' all had to live in different areas and their homes were subject to being bulldozed, especially if the local authorities thought they were too close to a 'white settlement'.

Apartheid was confronted by internal resistance, both violent and nonviolent, as well as by international action. There was an international trade embargo on South Africa throughout the apartheid era. The 'white' racial group retained all power and wealth, forcing 'blacks' deeper into poverty.

The education system during apartheid was designed to keep 'blacks' down. Only the two official languages of English and Afrikaans were used in the classroom. Funding for the medical care and education facilities in townships was kept to a minimum. Jobs for those living in townships were menial and very low paid.

In the Soweto uprising (1976) thousands of black students walked from their schools to Orlando stadium. The march was triggered by a police massacre of 23 students protesting at the mandatory use of Afrikaans as an official language of instruction in black schools. By the time the students reached the stadium, up to 10,000 were marching, carrying placards. According to eyewitnesses, a very small minority of students saw a police patrol and threw stones. One police officer fired a shot, causing chaos and panic, and around 600 people died. The Soweto uprising became a focal point for opposition.

Apartheid eventually ended in 1994

when Nelson Mandela, the long-imprisoned leader of the African National Congress, was elected as the first black president of South Africa. After the ending of apartheid, cultural diversity was included as a key objective of the new national constitution. A law was passed that required all national languages to be used in schools.

Education and language

Since the end of apartheid there has been a fierce argument in South Africa about the languages in which students should be taught. Research has shown that children are more likely to learn and retain information if they are taught in their mother tongue. UNESCO defines 'mother-tongue education' as: 'education which uses as its medium of instruction a person's mother tongue, that is, the language which a person has acquired in early years and which normally has become his/her natural instrument of thought and communication'.

However, there are now 11 official languages in South Africa: English, Afrikaans, Xhosa, Zulu, Ndebele, Sepedi, Sesotho, Setswana, Siswati, Tshivenda and Xitsonga.

Since 1994, there has been little progress made in teaching subjects such as science, geography and history in African languages – most South Africans live in poor rural or semi-rural areas and the reality is that the African languages used in these areas are limited to the vernacular subjects. The problem is that the local African languages do not have the vocabulary to support core subjects like science and so these are taught in English. It is argued that South Africa is already

spending a high percentage of its resources on education and cannot afford to spend more on developing the curriculum and materials, training and retraining teachers, or producing and distributing materials.

The other major factor is that Matriculation Examinations are done in English. These have to be passed by students if they are to be admitted to university and this entrenches English as the language of power and success. Some feel that the education system is still creating apartheid-like division amongst South African schoolchildren.

South Africa's colonial past and the social, economic and environmental damage caused by apartheid are vital influences upon the country's development. But the cultural issues that inhibit educational progress also have an impact on levels of development within the country. ∎

Pupils at a newly integrated school in Cape Town.

Percentage speakers of the top five languages are:

Zulu 23.8%   Xhosa 17.6%   Afrikaans 13.3%
Sepedi 9.4%   English 8.2%

Data

③ **Inequality** Ineq...

Why do levels of development vary within countries and regions?

* *There are variations in development between urban and rural areas within developing countries.*
* *There are theoretical models that try to explain these variations.*
* *Industrialization has been identified as a way of accelerating development in many developing countries.*
* *Newly industrialized countries (NICs) have transformed their economies using strategies such as export-led growth and import substitution.*
* *Physical and social factors can contribute to the disparity between regions.*

Key points

All countries develop unevenly, with some areas ending up poorer than others. England is one of the starkest examples of uneven development in the rich world, not least because there is such a clear north/south divide. Indicators show that the north has higher unemployment, lower wage levels and lower house prices than the south of England,

66% The average house price on the south coast of England is this much larger than the average house price in the north.
54.9 years Average healthy life expectancy in Middlehaven, Middlesbrough, against 86 years in Didcot, Oxfordshire.
10 years Boys born in Manchester are likely to die this much younger than those in the London borough of Kensington and Chelsea
90% of areas with highest rates of emergency hospital admissions due to alcohol are in the north.

Source: *The Observer* 28 October 2007

Data

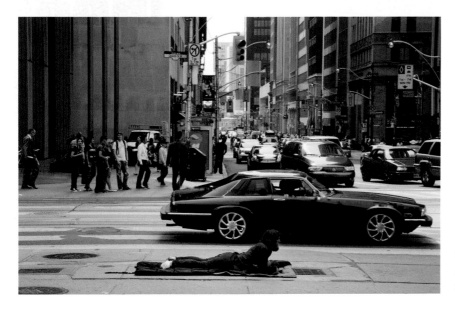

Left behind: a homeless man lies beside a busy street in Toronto, Canada.

particularly the southeast. There are also marked differences in social indicators such as the incidence of some diseases and even life expectancy, as these statistics suggest.

Explanations for regional differences within countries

Developing countries suffer similar disparities in levels of wealth and rates of economic growth between different areas.

According to dependency theorists (see Chapter 2), the concept of core and periphery may provide a partial explanation for this uneven development within some countries of the Global South. By their explanation, a wealthy élite exists even in the poorest of societies, and those in the élite will use their wealth and power to influence investment decisions in favour of their own area, helping to facilitate faster economic growth there than elsewhere.

In free market or neoliberal theory, by contrast, regional differences should not exist. According to this view, if one region attracts more investment than others, then supply and demand should cause labour costs to increase. Those areas or regions where labour costs have not risen will then become more attractive as labour costs there will be cheaper. If this does not happen, they say, it is because of some interference in the market mechanism that prevents the correction taking place.

The reality is, however, that there are regional differences in most countries and arguably the most convincing explanation for this was provided by Gunnar Myrdal with his model of cumulative causation.

Cumulative causation

In this model an initial investment, such as a decision to build a large new factory, sets off a series of positive feedbacks that reinforce the attractiveness of the area to further investment. Other companies may

> **'In terms of life chances, the only line within another European country that is comparable to the [UK] North-South divide is that which used to separate East and West Germany.'**
>
> Danny Dorling, Professor of Human Geography at Sheffield University, quoted in *The Observer*, 28 October 2007.

be encouraged to follow because they may provide component materials for the factory. Companies who provide a similar service or type of goods may take advantage of the skilled workforce created by the initial investment. As employment opportunity increases in the area, higher sums of money raised through local taxation can be spent on improving infrastructure and schools or on providing more leisure facilities. All of these things make the area more attractive to further investment.

Myrdal's model went further and offered an explanation for why regions with lower levels of development may find it difficult to break out of an unequal relationship with wealthier and more powerful neighbours. The economically powerful core area will have access to a larger market and companies operating in that core area can benefit from economies of scale that are not available to producers in the peripheral areas. With their higher incomes, companies in the core region can invest

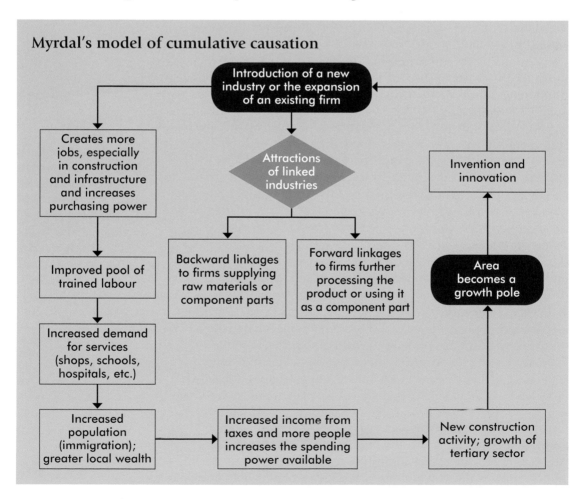

Myrdal's model of cumulative causation

Introduction of a new industry or the expansion of an existing firm

Creates more jobs, especially in construction and infrastructure and increases purchasing power

Attractions of linked industries

Invention and innovation

Improved pool of trained labour

Backward linkages to firms supplying raw materials or component parts

Forward linkages to firms further processing the product or using it as a component part

Area becomes a growth pole

Increased demand for services (shops, schools, hospitals, etc.)

Increased population (immigration); greater local wealth

Increased income from taxes and more people increases the spending power available

New construction activity; growth of tertiary sector

in more efficient methods of production and more advanced products. All of these things reinforce the advantage of companies in the core area and make it very difficult for companies in the peripheral region to survive without some sort of trade protection.

Peripheral areas may actually be helped by development in the core area. If there are resources in the peripheral area that are required by the core area, the improved communications required to export the materials may also benefit the general economy of the peripheral region and assist its growth. Increasing levels of wealth in the core region may result in higher demand for products or resources from the peripheral region and this trickle-down effect may help to stimulate development. This drifting downwards of high levels of wealth to the poor is one of the key elements in neo-conservative economics.

A growth pole is formed by the jobs created within the core area. The wages paid to the people employed result in demand for extra services, which in turn create more jobs. This process is called the 'positive multiplier effect'. It explains why many governments offer rich rewards to transnational corporations prepared to invest in a region or country. The larger the investment, the greater the multiplier effect will be. The model also forecasts that the opposite will happen when a major industry or factory closes. Workers will lose their jobs, have less money to spend, require fewer services and so more jobs will be lost. This is the negative multiplier effect.

Myrdal's model has a relevance that goes beyond an explanation for the differences in development of regions within nation states. It can also be applied to patterns of global development. The traditional core areas are western Europe, the US and Japan. They have enjoyed a competitive advantage compared to the industries in the peripheral areas of the world, such as most of Asia and all of Africa. The peripheral regions cannot compete with the core region without some form of protection such as trade barriers and tariffs.

All recent global trade talks have focused on the removal of trade barriers and the movement towards global free trade because 'free marketers' have claimed that it would stimulate world trade and lead to increased prosperity. Others see the frailty of industry in peripheral zones as much more of a problem. There are countries and regions that have bucked the trend and rejected the conventional Western economic model for development and emphasized social equality. The Indian state of Kerala is one of these (see the case study on page 55).

Export-led growth and industrialization
The developing countries that have been most successful in achieving high rates of economic growth and in raising their overall level of

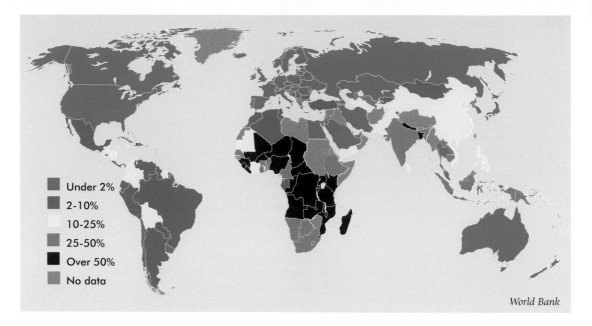

World Bank

national income are those that have managed to industrialize. In the middle of the 20th century a group of countries decided that only higher levels of industrialization would lead to increasing levels of wealth and development. That group of countries included Brazil, India, Mexico and South Korea, among others. The methods used varied from country to country but there are some common features in the strategies they chose.

The first route was export-led growth, sometimes referred to as 'export valorization'. In adopting an export-led growth policy, a country will encourage industries that have a potentially large export market by giving them loans and other incentives to expand. Little attention is given to the domestic economy as the low levels of wealth mean there is little demand. The domestic market only becomes a factor once the export industries have grown to a level where the increasing wage levels they pay the workers have created a larger demand. This approach has been a feature of some rapid-growth economies, possibly because it is the preferred route of the International Monetary Fund and the World Bank, which have funded some of the developments.

Import substitution

A second possible route to rapid industrial growth is import substitution. Countries using this route have chosen products that they have previously imported and manufactured them within their own country instead. The newly formed industry is initially unable to compete with the inevitably cheaper goods produced by more established manufacturers and so, in the early stages of import substitution, some protection is needed for domestic producers. This usually takes the form of high taxes and duties or quotas on imported goods. The rapid growth of motor-cycle manufacture in Japan, for example, is substantially attributable to the early protection of its own industry. The risk for countries opting for this route is that other countries will respond to high

Percentage of population below the international poverty line of $1.25 per day, 2009.

levels of tax on their goods by imposing new taxes or duties of their own. This could lead to the spread of 'protectionism'.

The importance of external factors in industrial growth

Although economists sometimes refer to 'autarkic development' as a type of development that has taken place without any outside help, the reality is that, in a globalized world, this is almost impossible and all industrial growth has been influenced by external factors.

The early growth of some Asian economies such as Japan, South Korea and Taiwan took place at a time when the US was investing huge amounts of money in these Pacific Rim countries to try to stem the growth of communism in the region. There are also examples of the importance of geopolitics in other regions.

Foreign direct investment (FDI) has been important where companies have established production centres in other countries. They may have done this because of cost advantages in production or to avoid trade restrictions on imported goods. Transnational corporations have become so large and powerful that they can negotiate with governments to maximize their manufacturing advantages.

The growth of NICs

The first wave of countries that achieved rapid growth in the 1960s are often collectively referred to as Newly Industrialized Countries (NICs). There is no agreed list but among them are the Asian Tiger economies of South Korea, Taiwan, Singapore and Hong Kong. Countries like Thailand and the Philippines that have industrialized since the 1980s are referred to as second-generation NICs. All of these countries have experienced very rapid growth in GNI (at least 10% per annum) caused by a huge growth in manufacturing output.

The growth of NICs has been very important in world development. Before these countries became successful, industrial output was centred on Europe and North America. The rest of the world was mainly a peripheral region supplying raw materials to this core area (the 'Old International Division of Labour'). NICs broke this pattern of development and manufacturing industry has become much more diversified, with massive implications for future development.

The rapid growth of industry in NICs has had profound social, economic, political and environmental consequences in those countries. While there are many common features in the emergence of the NICs they each have an individual story to tell about the circumstances that led to their growth and the impact of that growth on the country, as indicated by the case studies of Brazil and China that follow.

Brazil CASE STUDY Poverty in northeast Brazil

Key statistics for Brazil	
Total population	193.7 million
GNI per capita	$8,070
Infant mortality rate	17 per 1,000 live births
Life expectancy	73 years
Adult literacy rate	90%

Regional disparity and development

Brazil has been one of the global success stories in the last decade because of the high rates of economic growth and the progress it has made in achieving many of the Millennium Development Goals. The northeast is the poorest part of Brazil and it has not been able to match the economic progress of the southeast. This brief case study looks at the key features of the region and outlines some of the attempts that have been made to reduce poverty levels.

The northeast of Brazil is made up of nine states covering 18% of the country's land area and is home to 53 million people. A large area of the northeast is divided into large ranches owned by a few families. Poverty has led to large-scale migration from the northeast to the large cities in the south of the country, such as Rio de Janeiro and São Paulo.

The northeast is diverse but is generally much drier than the rest of Brazil. It has, on average, less than 750 mm of rainfall every year and is locally known as the 'Caatinga'

or drought zone. Drought is periodic and often linked to El Niño (the regional climatic variation that depends on Pacific Ocean currents) but in June 2010 prolonged heavy rainfall brought disastrous flooding.

It is one of the poorest areas in North and South America but has made a lot of recent progress. GNI per capita for Brazil was $8,070 in 2009 but wealth levels in the northeast are much lower.

Reasons for poverty in NE Brazil

- The remoteness of rural areas and the difficult environment have contributed to the poverty of a predominantly rural population
- It is a peripheral region, away from the economic core of Brazil in the southeast and has received little investment
- There has been an over-reliance on agriculture which has been made worse by a large drop in the world price of coffee
- There is massive inequality in the region – the poorest 20% own 2% of the wealth.

Impact of poverty

- 50% of the population live on less than $2 a day
- There is a generally high illiteracy rate (25%) but this is as high as 50% in some areas
- Significant numbers of young people have migrated out of the region over recent decades and this has made poverty worse
- Around 20% of deaths in the region are linked to poor water quality.

Brazil has made remarkable progress in reducing infant mortality rates across the country (18 per thousand births in 2008 compared with 46 in 1990) through both better healthcare and rising incomes. The rate remains much higher in the northeast, however, again because of the combined effect of income poverty and poorer access to healthcare, especially hospitals.

The Brazilian president up to 2010, Luiz Inácio (Lula) da Silva, was born in the northeast and the area has received a lot of government help and internal investment in the last 10 years. Some of the schemes detailed below are the result of top-down government action and some have arisen from bottom-up local action to try to alleviate the impacts of poverty in the region.

Solutions

Government grant

A family grant has been introduced by the government – it means that families receive $36 a month.

To get the family grant, parents must

Jadson Mendes Costa, 18, was released from labour conditions on a farm akin to slavery.

ensure that their children stay in education and receive a number of vaccinations. The scheme is thus particularly targeted at reducing infant mortality and illiteracy.

Oxfam million cistern project
Oxfam, working with local NGOs, has funded one million cisterns in the northeast of Brazil.
- Oxfam has trained local people in how to install the cisterns
- Each cistern holds 15,000 litres of water – enough to supply a family for the year
- The cistern has a built-in filter that reduces the risk of waterborne disease
- Water can also be used for irrigation and many families have been able to grow green vegetables for the first time – significantly improving their diet
- Oxfam also helped the families with seeds and training to help them grow new crops such as coffee and vegetables.

Coffee Growers' Association
The Piata Coffee Growers' Association (ASCAMP) was formed in the early 1990s and is run by local farmers. In 1997 ASCAMP received money from the World Bank to build a small coffee factory because many farmers used to sell unprocessed coffee at a very low price. The only coffee-processing factories in the area were 100 kilometres away and very expensive.
- By selling coffee as a collective growers get a better price. Tools and knowledge are also shared
- The new factory charged one third of the price of the other factories
- Since 1997 there has been a big increase in coffee production in the area, creating over 3,000 jobs
- Waste from the processing of coffee is used by the farmers as organic fertilizer.

Sobradinho Dam
The Sobradinho Dam is a hydroelectric dam built on the São Francisco River in the state of Bahia. Completed in 1982, the dam generates 1,050 megawatts of electricity.
- The lake formed by the dam is 320 kilometres long and is the 12th-largest artificial lake in the world
- Around 50,000 people were forced to move because of the dam construction. Most were given only minimal compensation and many received none
- The dam has allowed irrigation of crops in an arid area and increased food production in the region and also the number of jobs in agriculture. However, large landowners have benefited most from its construction
- Many small landowners have been unable to use the water from the reservoir because they cannot afford the pumps required to channel it to their land
- The dam generates 60% of the region's hydroelectric power and has led to a significant increase in industry in the region
- The dam is a good example of a top-down solution that depends on the 'trickle down' of benefits to the poor. ■

China CASE STUDY

Rapid industrial growth in China

China has been ruled by the Communist Party since 1949, when the People's Liberation Army led by Mao Zedong drove the nationalists from the mainland to seek refuge in Taiwan (then Formosa). For 30 years after that the country was subjected to extraordinarily strict political and social control. Millions were executed and Chinese society experienced brutal upheaval and repression, particularly during the Mao-inspired Great Leap Forward (1958-61) and Cultural Revolution (1966-76). During this time all major industry in China was state owned, as was all agricultural land.

After Mao's death reforms were introduced and in 1978, after years of state control of all productive assets, the government of China embarked on a major programme of economic reform. In the first stage the reforms focused on:

- The 'decollectivization' of agricultural land, with the land divided into private plots for each household. Each farmer was given use of the land but not ownership. This increased agricultural productivity and rural incomes
- Opening up the country to foreign investment

Special Economic Zones (SEZ)
1. Pudong District, Shanghai Municipality
2. Xiamen, Fujian Province
3. Shantou, Guangdong Province
4. Shenzhen, Guangdong Province
5. Zhuhai, Guangdong Province
6. Hainan Province

- Giving permission for private businesses to start up.

The second stage of the reform process, in the late 1980s, involved the privatization and contracting out of much of the state-owned industries. The state's assets were sold to private investors, although the state retained control of some key sectors such as banking and energy supplies. At the same time price controls and protectionist policies were lifted as the country moved towards a free-market economy.

Other important measures were the setting up of Special Economic Zones (SEZs) in predominantly coastal locations to encourage foreign direct investment, and joining the World Trade Organization in 2001.

SEZs in particular have become an important element in China's rapid growth with their reduced taxes and tariffs.

Government policy favoured the coastal regions in its aim to attract foreign investment and new technology. Labour costs are relatively low throughout China but in the coastal regions they were better educated and more skilled. The lack of trade unions was also a factor in attracting inward investment.

All aspects of infrastructure (road, rail, air, communications) are more developed on the coast than in the interior.

As 90% of China's international trade passes through its seaports it was logical to locate manufacturing facilities near to the ports.

Between 1978 and 2010 the Chinese economy grew by an average of 9.5% a year, making it the fastest-growing economy in the world. In 2009 it became the second largest economy in the world after the US and private-sector growth accounted for more than 70% of GDP. There are now over

A labourer takes a rest beside a billboard at a construction site in Chengdu.

10 million small businesses in China. In 1979 primary goods and primary processed goods accounted for 75% of all Chinese exports and by 2009 95% of its exports were manufactured goods.

The state gave its early support to this rapid industrialization process by investing heavily in energy production, in some industries such as iron and steel, and in transport infrastructure. At this stage of the reforms some industries received subsidies but most of those were withdrawn as a condition of joining the WTO and China embarked on an export-led strategy of growth. The state has assisted the export of Chinese goods by keeping the value of its currency (the renmimbi) artificially low. The policy has

> *iPhone4 is sold in the US, Europe and elsewhere, but it was assembled in China. As the world's centre for the processing of IT products, China's environment is paying the price. Printed Circuit Board (PCB) and battery power production especially create heavy metal pollution and have particularly serious consequences.*
>
> *The Guardian,* June 2010

Witness

been criticized by other countries, notably the US, because they believe that it gives China an unfair advantage in world trade and is causing problems in the financial markets. It looks set to become a very important topic in trade negotiations over the next few years.

In the 1980s and 1990s exports were dependent on cheap toys, textiles and other goods but in the last decade China has switched to the production of high-value sophisticated information and communication technology. Over 700 million people in China own mobile phones and it is now the largest global market for car producers, with 13 million cars and vans sold in 2009.

China is still a communist state and it seems strange that it should make such rapid growth with a strategy that includes so many free-market features. However, the stability provided by the state has been an important factor in encouraging the foreign investment that China needed.

The social and environmental impacts of such profound change in China have been huge. Some 500 million Chinese people have been lifted out of poverty in the last 30 years by the extra wealth generated by industrial growth. Wages have increased and living standards have improved for millions of people. At the same time everybody has benefited from the improvements to the infrastructure and the increase in the range of consumer products.

Growth has, however, had a very negative impact on the environment. China has become the world's largest producer of renewable energy but it has also become the largest emitter of CO_2 and other greenhouse gases. Manufacturing industry has created water, land and air pollution and environmental controls in factories have been inadequate.

The result is that two-thirds of Chinese cities are either moderately or severely polluted and 7 of the 10 most polluted cities in the world are in China. Respiratory and heart disease, made worse by the pollution, are the leading causes of death in China. In addition, 90% of urban water bodies in China are severely polluted and 300 million Chinese people have to drink contaminated water. The situation might improve as the Chinese government has become more aware of the need to make manufacturers more accountable – it now keeps detailed corporate violation records of pollution incidents, allowing manufacturers to check the efficacy of component suppliers.

The largest social impact of growth has certainly been the migration of millions of people to the industrial cities. Agricultural output has risen but the increase has been achieved through the increased use of machinery and modern farming techniques and agricultural wages have fallen a long way

The Chinese authorities are about to begin the country's first national census in 10 years. More than six million workers have been hired for the huge task in the world's most populous country. The authorities hope the census will clarify the number of migrant workers, which by some estimates is said to be more than 200 million.

BBC news, November 2010

Witness

behind the wages migrants can find in the city. This is the biggest migration of people on earth and movement on such a scale has clear consequences both for rural areas, where the migrants leave a distorted population profile, and for the cities, where the rates of population increase are unsustainable.

There is a more detailed discussion of the issues raised by such vast internal migration in China in Chapter 11. ∎

Kerala, India CASE STUDY
Education for all – a strategy for growth?

Key statistics for India

Total population	1,198 million
GNI per capita	$1,170
Infant mortality rate	50 per 1,000 live births
Life expectancy	64 years
Adult literacy rate	63%
Primary school enrolment/attendance	83%

Overcoming regional disparities within a country can be a problem in a developed or developing country. Some regions within larger countries develop unique characteristics that make their development quite different from the rest of the country. India is the seventh largest country in the world in area and the second largest in population size (1.2 billion). It is made up of 28 states and seven territories and one of the most serious problems faced by the Indian government is the regional differences in socio-economic development, poverty and availability of infrastructure in a country which has one of the fastest economic growth rates in the world.

The pattern of uneven development is complex. Some states, such as Maharashtra, have achieved very high growth rates (9% average per year) but in others, such as Madhya Pradesh, growth rates are much lower (4%). Rural areas, such as Bihar, tend to have high poverty rates but rural Punjab has one of

the lowest poverty rates in the country.

India has implemented five-year plans that have attempted to reduce regional disparities, encouraging industrial development in the interior regions by offering things such as tax relief and cheap land, but industries still tend to concentrate around urban areas and port cities. The OECD produced an Economic Survey of India 2007 which suggested that improving economic growth rates in Indian states depended on their introducing market-oriented reforms and liberalizing their economies – the standard neoliberal prescription for development. By contrast, one state has achieved higher levels of development than the majority of other Indian states by taking a completely different route and become a *cause célèbre* for supporters of non-Western based models of development. Kerala's high levels of development have been achieved through an emphasis on greater social equality rather

> *'The Kerala evidence suggests that literate men have literate sons, but literate women have literate families... Female literacy and education are crucial determinants of child survival, general health and hygiene.'*
>
> India.gov.in

Witness

than on increased wealth.

Kerala is a small state with a population of 32 million in the southern tip of India. It makes up roughly 1% of the land area of the country. India has a rapidly developing economy but per-capita income is still very low – the World Bank ranks it 161st out of 213 countries for GNI per person.

Only 30 years ago Kerala was one of India's poorest states but that situation has changed. Average wealth levels in Kerala have increased markedly in recent years and in 2009 it was ranked 6th richest of the 22 Indian states. Although in global terms incomes there are still very low, Kerala has a much higher life expectancy (75 years) than the rest of India (64 years) and an infant mortality rate (14 deaths per thousand births) which is much lower than the rest of India (52 deaths per thousand births). The diversity of its population – 60% Hindu, 20% Muslim, 20% Christian – would be a recipe for unrest in other parts of India but multiculturalism, gender equality and more liberal interpretations of caste status are embedded in the culture of Kerala.

If Kerala were a country and not a state its HDI ranking would be 75th (out of 175 countries) compared to India's national ranking of 134th. The strength of its social indicators compared to its economic poverty has made it an essential case study for people who are interested in world development issues.

The achievements of the education system in Kerala have been recognized as key to understanding how this has happened.

At the Janaranjini preschool in the state of Kerala in rural southern India, children aren't building castles in the sand. Instead, as they sit cross-legged in front of a thin layer of sand, they are learning the fundamentals of reading and mathematics.

Three-year-old VS Madhav twirls letters of his native Malayalam – the language of Kerala – into the sand with his left forefinger while his classmate, four-year-old Neethu Saji, writes Arabic numerals more quickly than her teacher can call them out.

'I also learned like this. My father also like this,' says N Revindhran, who is a volunteer at the public library that runs this preschool, locally referred to as a *kalari*. 'This is the ancient model [of schooling],' Revindhran explains.

Education in Kerala represents a success story that many nations might wish to emulate.

Christian Science Monitor May 2005

Feature

Schoolchildren ride home by autorickshaw in Kochi, Kerala.

Kerala's adult literacy rate of 91% puts it closer to the US than to the rest of India (65%) and India's National Literacy Mission declared total literacy in the state in 1991. How has this impressive record of educational achievement happened?

The first part of the answer is historical. The roots of Kerala's literacy culture can be traced back at least to the Hindu rulers of the 19th century, in the early days of the British Empire. The Queen of Trivandrum issued a royal decree in 1817 that said: 'The state should defray the entire cost of the education of its people in order that there might be no backwardness in the spread of enlightenment.' Succeeding rulers built schools for the general population and promoted elementary education, while Christian missionaries helped by setting up schools for the poor and oppressed.

In the early 20th century, social reformers in the region continued the drive for education for the lower castes and for girls. All of this helped progress and by 1961 the state had double the literacy rate of the rest of India: 55% compared with the Indian average of 28%.

Politics is also part of the explanation. The Communist Party of India (CPI) has ruled the state for much of the past 50 years. The CPI attempted to introduce major social reforms in the 1960s and 1970s and the first and most important of these was land reform. Their land-reform legislation set a limit on private ownership and created a more even distribution of wealth by taking wealth from the previous landowners. Today a larger percentage of people own the land on which they work than in any other state in India. The national government blocked land reform for 10 years but the legislation was eventually passed in 1970 and was an important factor in reinforcing the importance of education to the people of Kerala.

In 2009 37% of Kerala's annual budget was spent on education and the state supported 12,271 schools. There is a primary school within three kilometres of every settlement. One of the most impressive elements in the education success story in Kerala is the equal opportunity it offers to women – 88% of women in the state are literate (compared with the national Indian rate of 54%) and there are more women than men in higher education.

In some ways Kerala has been a victim of

'When every family owns a piece of land, no matter how small, they have a sense of belonging. Then they can plan for the future, and education of their children becomes a part of that planning.'

PK Ravindran

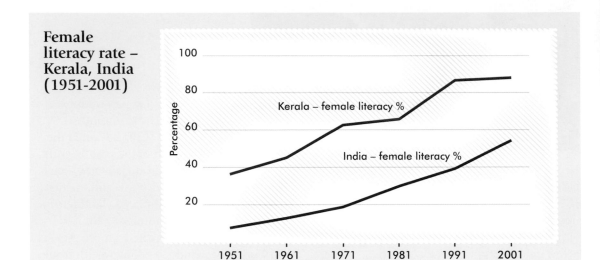

Female literacy rate – Kerala, India (1951-2001)

Kerala – female literacy %

India – female literacy %

Percentage

100
80
60
40
20

1951   1961   1971   1981   1991   2001

its own education success. The state has not been able to provide its literate population with enough work and rural unemployment is high. There is little industry, and although the state government has taken steps to liberalize the economy there are few major corporations and manufacturing companies operating in Kerala. The answer for many Keralans has been to migrate to find work. Their high standards of educational achievement have made finding work, in construction, IT and the service industries much easier than for other groups of workers. As a result, other Indian states, the US and particularly the Middle East are home to large numbers of workers from Kerala. In the Middle East alone there are an estimated 2.1 million workers from Kerala and the money they send home is very important to the economy of the state.

In 2008 non-resident Indians sent home $32 billion, making India a major beneficiary of migrant remittances. The money sent home represents only a little less than the total annual amount of foreign direct investment

that India receives ($36.6 billion as of 2009). Kerala is particularly dependent on these foreign remittances and they are estimated to make up 20% of the state's annual income. In 2009 the official net state domestic product per capita for Kerala was equivalent to $1,168 (Indian state average $1,009) but if the value of remittances is added it becomes $1,436 – making it the richest Indian state.

Kerala is not the only part of the world where the indicators for education and healthcare far exceed what would normally be expected based on relatively low levels of income. Cuba has been the subject of a debilitating US-led trade embargo for many years but has still managed to deliver education and healthcare that are the envy of many other much 'richer' countries. Case studies like these emphasize the need to maintain an open mind about what might be the potential routes for development in countries and regions and lead some critics to question what we are actually trying to achieve by the process of development. ■

4 Globalization

Is globalization a positive influence on development?

* *Globalization is a complex process with economic, political and cultural dimensions. There is evidence of the impact of globalization in virtually all countries of the world.*
* *Transnational corporations (TNCs) have played a major role in the globalization process. Their role in the global economy needs careful analysis.*
* *National governments increasingly face problems that are too big for them to deal with independently and require global decision-making, such as climate change and combating terrorism.*
* *Cultural globalization has occurred through increasingly sophisticated information and communication systems as well as the growth in tourism and cosmopolitan lifestyles.*
* *There are major institutions that play a significant role in the globalization of trade and finance. Prime among these are the World Bank, the International Monetary Fund and the World Trade Organization.*

Key points

The process of globalization

Globalization is a word that has entered the modern lexicon and its use is so common that we rarely think about the complex process the term describes. The world becoming global is the simplest of definitions. Many academics who study the process start with this simple definition and then add further elements. A lot of definitions focus just on trade and business. A more comprehensive commonly used definition is the following by Guy Brainbant: 'Globalization not only includes opening up of world trade, development of advanced means of communication, internationalization of financial markets, growing importance of multinational corporations, population migrations and more generally increased mobility of persons, goods, capital, data and ideas but also infections, diseases and pollution.'

Listing some of the things that happen as a result of globalization makes it easier to recognize. There is the interaction and integration among people, companies, and governments of different nations, for example, which is mostly driven by international trade and investment and is made much easier by information technology. The process of globalization has impacts on the environment, on culture, on political systems, on economic development, and on human well-being in societies all over the world.

The rise of free-market capitalism

Although some features of globalization have a very long history, it is more recently associated with a process that has seen the spread of a type of free-market capitalism to almost every country. The end of the Cold War, following the collapse of the Soviet bloc in 1989-91, is generally recognized as the start of globalization as we understand it today.

The release from the strictures of Soviet-style control led many countries to adopt more market-orientated economic systems and to try negotiating reductions in barriers to trade. International bodies such as the World Trade Organization were active in these negotiations and agreements were established to promote trade in goods, services and investment. Large corporations greatly increased their global influence by building foreign factories and establishing production and marketing arrangements with foreign partners. The most important agent of change in the globalization process has been the growth of these large transnational corporations (TNCs). They are almost entirely based in the Global North and operate by making the same product, often with local variations, in different countries and selling it all over the world.

> 'Globalization not only includes opening up of world trade... but also infections, diseases and pollution.'
>
> Guy Brainbant

Globalization and social change

Just as important as the products they sell, these companies have brought operating and production methods to the countries where they operate that have led to important social changes. George Ritzer called this process 'McDonaldization' in his 1990 book *The McDonaldization of Society*. The importance of TNCs to the globalization process cannot be overestimated. As capitalism has spread around the world, even countries whose economies have previously been state-controlled have allowed such businesses to operate with the aim of increasing national wealth levels. China is the most obvious example of this change in economic orientation. Governments in the Global South are urged to remove any restrictions on the operation of transnational corporations as they seek to

Key symbols of
Western consumer
culture in the
Ukrainian capital,
Kiev, which was part
of the communist
Soviet Union until
1991.

encourage foreign direct investment.

The reduction of government intervention in the economy and the
consequent privatization of many services is one of the key neoliberal
principles that has underpinned the spread of globalization. As far as
neoliberals are concerned, to participate effectively in the global market,
national governments must not interfere too much. Whereas in the 1970s
most developing countries were expected to have a 'Five Year Plan' for
development, that degree of government direction and involvement is
frowned upon by proponents of free-market globalization and even the
centrally controlled economy of China has been opened up to the forces
of free enterprise.

Governments all over the developing world have been forced to
privatize the provision of basic services because they have come under
pressure to reduce government spending. This is a neoliberal prescription
for economic health and is usually included as a loan condition
when a developing country which is experiencing financial difficulties
borrows money from the International Monetary Fund (IMF). The
implementation of this economic and social 'medicine' generally came in
the form of Structural Adjustment Programmes (SAPs) and these became
notorious among those who worked in international development
because of their disproportionate impact upon the poor – UNICEF, for
example, felt obliged to campaign during the 1980s for what it called
'adjustment with a human face'.

The privatization of Dar es Salaam's water supply

The story of water in most cities in the developing world is that the group paying the most is the poor, because they have to resort to the water vendors who peddle this precious commodity around the streets. But in Dar es Salaam it is not only the poor. Decades of neglect and underinvestment in the city's water infrastructure mean that fewer than 100,000 households – in a city of 3.5 million people – have running water.

Privatization of water-supply systems has always been controversial in the developing world, and in sub-Saharan Africa in particular. The conflicting motives of foreign companies, which want to maximize profit, and governments, which seek – in theory at least – to improve access to water for people with limited means to pay, means that so far there have been precious few success stories.

Still, the World Bank and International Monetary Fund had little doubt that it was the best way forward for the Dar es Salaam Water and Sewage Authority (Dawasa). They made the privatization of Dawasa's assets a condition for Tanzania receiving massive debt relief. When no buyer emerged, the Bank removed its demand that the assets be sold. But it made clear that a $143.5-million loan package for upgrading the city's water infrastructure would be forthcoming only if a private company operated the water system.

1 August 2003 was the day City Water took charge of Dar es Salaam's water, and the day it started haemorrhaging money. Not only was the company unable to meet revenue collection targets agreed in the contract – and which were crucial to attain if it was to make a profit – City Water was collecting less money than its state-run predecessor. At the same time, though, the people of the capital saw their water bills rising.

The Guardian 16 August 2007

Feature

SAPs have gained such a bad name that the World Bank and the IMF have replaced them with Poverty Reduction Strategy Papers (PRSP), though these contain some similar economic prescriptions. The forced privatization of the public water supply in Tanzania in 1996 is an example of the actions that developing countries have been forced to take at the insistance of the IMF and the World Bank (see box).

In 2005, Tanzania cancelled its contract with City Water, a wholly owned subsidiary of the British company Biwater, after it failed to meet its obligations under the original contract to supply water to the city. The contract had been backed by the British government and the World

Bank. Biwater went to an international tribunal to claim damages against the Tanzanian government but its claim was rejected because the panel 'found that water and sewerage services had deteriorated' since City Water had taken control in 2003. The tribunal ordered Biwater to pay $8 million in damages and fees to Dawasa, the state water utility in Dar es Salaam.

Contrasting views on globalization

Not everybody believes that globalization is a new phenomenon and sceptics argue that it is not historically unprecedented. They contend that if you look at the statistical evidence of world flows of trade, investments and labour since the start of the 19th century the pattern is very similar. As far as they are concerned, globalization is a 'myth' which is no more than a continuation of the integration of national economies that has been happening for the last 200 years. They point out that most of the capital and the companies benefiting from global trade and foreign direct investment are still largely concentrated in North America, Europe and East Asia. These sceptics believe that neoliberals have underestimated the continuing power of national governments, which continue to be key to maintaining world order. They prefer to talk in terms of an internationalized world with the state still playing a vital part in regulating economic activities.

Transformationalists, on the other hand, have a longer-term perspective on the process of globalization. They argue that it is neither a good nor a bad thing but rather an ongoing process that may continue or gradually disappear. From this perspective, globalization is transforming the ways in which states and businesses influence each other and the traditional law-making authority of states is gradually being weakened. However they do not think that states will disappear or necessarily become more powerful, they just see globalization as an ongoing process which will continue to interact with other economic and political movements. According to transformationalists such as Colin Hay, 'It is a tendency to which there are countertendencies'.

Global process and global consequences

The huge increase in manufacturing and trade in the last 30 years has magnified the international consequences of all its associated activities: from extraction through production and transportation to retail. The consequence of this is that the environmental and social impacts of globalization extend far beyond the boundaries of individual countries. Using dirty coal to make steel in eastern Europe or China has implications for acid rain and climate change for all countries, not just for the countries where the production takes place. This

'The evidence clearly shows that water privatization has been a disastrous policy for poor people around the world, but the World Bank insisted on imposing water privatization in Tanzania in return for much-needed debt relief.'

World Development Movement

atmospheric 'pollution of the commons' becomes an international issue that requires international co-operation and decision-making. Even terrorist activity has been globalized because of the way in which communication has changed – information and finance can be moved around the globe very quickly and the response to terrorism therefore has to be international. Unfortunately, attempts at international co-operation to deal with such large-scale threats is not always successful, as with the Doha (WTO) trade talks in 2008 and the climate change talks in Copenhagen in 2009.

The world's money markets are at the heart of the globalization process. Improvements in communications technology have facilitated an increasingly free flow of capital and as a result financial markets around the world have become ever more integrated. The bankers and stockbrokers operating the markets belong to transnational corporations capable of moving huge sums of money around the globe almost instantaneously. The Bank of International Settlements estimates that the daily average turnover in global foreign exchange markets is $3.98 trillion. Economic events in one part of the world can have an immediate impact on other global markets. The financial markets have grown more quickly than the regulatory bodies needed to control them and the clearest evidence for this was the 'credit crunch' of 2007/8 that started in the US property market but spread rapidly all over the world. One cause of the problem was the complexity of financial packages called derivatives, which hid the 'toxic' debt of mortgages that could never be repaid. This was compounded by the lightning speed of worldwide trading. Together they brought the global finance system very close to collapse and the impacts of the crisis are still being felt worldwide today.

Social and environmental impacts of globalization

The globalization process clearly causes profound economic change but its social and environmental impacts are just as powerful. Supporters of the positive outcomes of globalization argue that there are fewer dictatorships and more democratic governments than there were 30 years ago. They claim that this is because the spread of capitalism encourages a political system of liberal democracy – though in China and Vietnam there is no sign as yet of authoritarian one-party states being threatened by the rampant capitalism now being pursued. It is true that decisions about aid and investment often depend upon the nature of democracy within a country. This encourages democratic government and although in many countries democracy is neither well established nor stable, elections are increasingly monitored by observers from other countries who assess the fairness of the process

A cartoon by Kate Charlesworth representing popular feeling against bankers during the Western financial crisis of 2008-09.

and the legitimacy of the result.

Another political impact of globalization has been the perceived need to develop supra-national groups to deal with issues more effectively than is possible for an individual nation-state. The European Union is an example of this. It is not just a trading bloc but an attempt to increase the global political influence of its member states. It is a logical response to issues that are transnational in nature such as climate change, cross-boundary water and air pollution, over-fishing of the oceans, the spread of invasive species, the threat of terrorism and international drug smuggling.

Since many corporations seek to cut costs by building factories in developing countries with less environmental regulation, globalization and free trade may increase pollution. There is a long list of examples of the damage caused by industrial activity in developing countries – oil production in the Niger Delta and chemical production in India are among the most well-known examples. Imposing environmental controls on production would increase costs and potentially have an impact on the manufacturer's ability to compete. There are those who argue that it is wrong to impose such regulation on developing countries because, by deterring potential investors, it may prevent them from raising their living standards.

The spread of Western values

Globalization has had a profound impact on culture, largely through the existence of very powerful world information and communications systems. It is difficult to quantify the impact of the digital age on the human population but nobody will deny its significance or the power it has in transmitting messages that affect culture and behaviour on a global scale. Most of the references to globalization's impact on society refer to an 'Americanization' of consumer culture exemplified by the prevalence of US fast food companies such as McDonald's and Coca-Cola, the domination of American television and film companies in the popular media and the powerful impact of the Western music industry on young people.

The rapid growth in the global tourist industry – prompted both by the reduced cost of travel and an increase in leisure time for many people – has also led to the spread of Western values to previously traditional societies. There are some people who think this influence has had a negative impact on those societies. That is a simplified summary of a process that has also assisted the growth of major religions and helped the English language to become the dominant global language. You can retrieve evidence of its many other diverse impacts on society and culture, and weighing the positive and negative elements of this evidence will help determine your view of the overall value of the globalization process.

Supra-national organizations

Supra-national organizations have had an enormous influence on the way in which globalization and world development have interacted. The World Bank, the International Monetary Fund and the World Trade Organization are the most important of these. They came into being at the United Nations Monetary and Financial Conference in New Hampshire, US, in 1944, which became better known as the Bretton Woods conference. At the conference the Allied nations from World War Two agreed to the setting up of the International Bank for Reconstruction and Development (IBRD), the General Agreement on Tariffs and Trade (GATT) and the International Monetary Fund (IMF). The role of these organizations was to regulate the international monetary and financial systems after the end of the War.

The World Bank

The IBRD is now part of the World Bank. The Bank was originally established to support reconstruction in Europe but today its function is to reduce global poverty. It has over 184 member countries and an annual budget of $24 billion (2009). It is involved in a wide range

of activities from major construction projects to policy making that it believes will encourage economic growth. Loans to member countries are given at preferential rates although grants can be given to the poorest countries.

Technically the World Bank is part of the United Nations but it has its own governance structure. It gets its money from three sources: subscriptions paid by member countries, bond flotations on the global finance markets and earnings from its assets. Members are shareholders in the bank but they do not have equal voting power. The number of votes allocated to each country is proportional to its contribution to the Bank. The United States holds 16.4% of the total vote, Japan 7.9%, Germany 4.5%, France 4.3% and the United Kingdom 4.3%. Changes in the Bank's Charter require an 85% majority and so the US can block any changes. In addition the President of the World Bank is nominated by the President of the United States and elected by the Board of Governors – which is dominated by the big contributors.

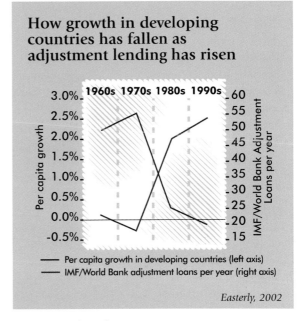

How growth in developing countries has fallen as adjustment lending has risen

— Per capita growth in developing countries (left axis)
— IMF/World Bank adjustment loans per year (right axis)

Easterly, 2002

The World Bank focuses its activities on developing countries. Between 2003 and 2009 it has, for example, provided $2 billion on grants, loans and credits to combat HIV and AIDS, $300 million of which went to Niger. Loans and grants given by the World Bank are, however, always conditional and opponents claim that its advocacy of free-market economic measures has been harmful to development in some countries – particularly where its 'shock' treatment has reduced government spending in weak and uncompetitive economies. The World Bank has also been involved in controversial projects such as the privatization of state enterprises.

With its Western-dominated governance structure, it is no surprise that some people in developing countries have argued that the actions of the World Bank foster the interests of Western countries and companies, show insufficient understanding of local needs in the Global South, and are sometimes based on an intellectual argument that blames the poor for their own condition. In addition, it is often criticized for the environmental impact of the projects it supports, including large dams and support for fossil-fuel extraction rather than renewable energy alternatives.

Defenders of the World Bank argue that it has substantially changed its philosophy and practices a lot in the last decade and that it is now

The IMF: the power and the folly

The closest thing we have had to a world government over the last two-and-a-half decades is not the United States, despite its own tendency to behave as if that were the case. Nor is it the United Nations, still flailing around trying to assert itself as it stumbles into the 21st century with a structure born of the power politics of 1945.

It is rather a secretive, unelected organization which has been hijacked by fundamentalists who have thereby gained the opportunity to dictate economic and social policy to almost every country in the world.

Sounds unlikely, doesn't it? Like the stuff of science fiction or the maddest conspiracy theory. If only that were so.

The organization is the International Monetary Fund (IMF), which is based in the American capital, Washington DC, and both the power it wields in the world and its appalling record in the misuse of that power should be one of the greatest scandals of our age...

When Lula [Brazil's president 2003-10] and the other political leaders of the Majority World have to swallow their principles at the behest of the IMF, is it not just a case of profligate, debt-ridden countries being shepherded back to the straight and narrow by an impartial international body of experts?

This is certainly what the IMF would like you to think – and it seems very successfully to have persuaded Western governments and media to that effect. The reality is shockingly different. The IMF has been taken over by fundamentalists as extreme and narrow-minded as an al-Qaeda lieutenant or a US Bible-Belt preacher.

The fundamentalism of the IMF lies in its religious adherence to the idea that the untrammelled free market is the solution to every economic problem. Its own equivalent of a holy commandment is the idea of 18th-century economist Adam Smith that the profit motive acts as an 'invisible hand' driving an economy towards efficiency. Even were we to accept that in a perfect model of a free market this would be so, the lesson of much recent economic theory has been that no such perfect market exists – least of all in the troubled economies of the Majority World over which the IMF primarily holds sway.

This picture of the IMF as an institution blinded by its own obsession has been most powerfully painted by no less an authority than Nobel Prizewinner and former World Bank chief economist Joseph Stiglitz, who notes: 'They are an institution that seems to believe in market fundamentalism but yet exists because of market failures – an internal contradiction that they've never come to terms with. An intellectually incoherent institution that says "we believe in markets" but what are they doing? Intervening in exchange-rate markets all the time. Bailing out Western creditors.'

Stiglitz makes it clear that he believes the IMF to be working in the interests of the Western financial community – an extraordinary indictment of an international institution, and one that in any sane world would prompt a formal public inquiry.

Chris Brazier, *New Internationalist*, 365, March 2004

 Witness

An office worker in Seoul protesting against the International Monetary Fund during the Korean economic crisis of 1997.

more responsive and flexible in its assessment of the requirements of developing countries.

The International Monetary Fund

Member countries of the World Bank are also required to join the International Monetary Fund. It has a similar governance structure to the World Bank but its function is to provide a systematic mechanism for foreign exchange transactions as well as to foster investment and promote global economic trade and growth. When it was formed after World War Two, the aim was to prevent global financial crises such as those of the 1920s and 1930s. To that end, member countries that get into financial trouble have access to funds to help their economies recover. Greece used that arrangement in 2009 when its economy was in danger of collapsing.

Criticisms of the organization are similar to those levelled at the World Bank. Money is loaned with conditions attached, generally a one-size-fits-all prescription involving privatization and reductions in government spending. The difference is that the IMF is much less concerned about its public image than the World Bank and sees itself as a purely financial institution rather than one concerned with development. This makes it less conducive to change and has led some to accuse it of 'free-market fundamentalism' (see box opposite).

Whatever people's attitude to them, there is no escaping the fact that the IMF and the World Bank are easily the largest public lenders of funds in the world and are therefore very important in global development terms.

The World Trade Organization

The World Trade Organization (WTO) is an international body that attempts to promote free trade by persuading countries to abolish tariffs, taxes and other barriers. As a consequence, it has been closely identified with the globalization process. Its job is to settle trade disputes and organize trade negotiations such as the unsuccessful Doha talks in 2008. It is a very powerful group whose decisions in trade disputes are absolute and it can enforce its decisions by imposing trade sanctions against countries that have breached the rules.

The WTO was set up in 1995, replacing the General Agreement on Tariffs and Trade (GATT) with a body that has a much wider remit and much more power. There are 153 member countries in the WTO. China was allowed to join at the end of 2001 but the US only lifted its objection to the entry of Russia to the organization in October 2010 and it is still not a full member. Supporters of the WTO claim that, by working to increase world trade, the organization is raising living standards around the world.

Critics of the WTO argue that it is too powerful because it can compel sovereign states to change laws and regulations by declaring them to be in violation of free trade rules. They contend that it is a 'club', run by the rich for the rich, and does not take enough account of the problems of poor countries or the impact of free trade on things such as workers' rights, child labour, the environment and health.

Globalization case studies

The case studies that follow highlight some of the impacts of globalization. The first examines the oil industry's foreign direct investment in Nigeria, while the second shows how a transnational corporation can become very influential and powerful through taking control of parts of the food supply chain. The third examines the impact of globalization on one country – Uganda – from a number of different angles.

Nigeria CASE STUDY

Dominated by oil

Key statistics for Nigeria	
Total population	154.7 million
GNI per capita	$1,140
Infant mortality rate	86 per 1,000 live births
Children under 5 who are underweight	29%
People not using an improved water source	42%
Human Development Index	0.423 (142nd of 169)

It was inevitable that the oil boom of the 1970s would have a profound impact on the development of Nigeria. Its proven oil reserves are estimated to be 36 billion barrels and natural gas reserves are well over 100 trillion cubic feet. Nigeria is a member of the Organization of Petroleum Exporting Countries (OPEC), and its crude oil production averages around 1.6 million barrels per day as of 2010 (US State Department figures).

The country's dependence on oil since the 1970s has been stark. In 2009 oil and gas exports accounted for more than 90% of export earnings and 80% of federal government revenue. The concentration on oil wealth has led to a devastating decline in traditional agriculture and a failure to develop manufacturing industry. Associated with this has been a massive migration to the cities and increasing poverty, particularly in rural areas. In spite of its oil revenues, basic infrastructure and social services collapsed and by 2002

Nigeria's per capita income had fallen to a quarter of its 1970 level.

Developing oil reserves demands expensive technology and expertise to which countries such as Nigeria do not have access. The world's major oil companies are all very heavily involved in exploiting Nigeria's oil reserves. At a time when oil prices are so high it would seem to be a foolproof way of making money but there have been a lot of problems. The Niger Delta has been the focus for most of the oil exploration and extraction and the issues caused by the industry have been reported by journalists, environmental groups and local campaigners. Severe ecological damage caused by oil spills, poor corporate relations with indigenous communities, sabotage of the oil infrastructure and personal security problems for staff working for the oil companies: all of these have adversely affected levels of foreign investment.

The high income from oil allows

the Nigerian currency (the naira) to be chronically overvalued and makes imported consumer goods cheap. This, together with the lack of dependable electricity and other industrial production factors, has undermined manufacturing and its ability to compete internationally. In addition, the distribution of the national income from oil and gas has been chronically uneven. Some people within government circles have become very rich but that wealth has not filtered down to the majority of the population. Corruption is endemic and the administrative difficulties encountered in any trading with Nigeria add to the problems of companies investing in the country.

These negative impacts associated with the exploitation of a natural resource have been seen in many other countries and the phenomenon is often referred to as the 'resource curse' or 'Dutch disease'. The classic case sees a flow of money into the country leading to currency appreciation, which increases the cost of the country's other exports. The result is de-industrialization as manufacturing industries are made less competitive by exports of oil and natural gas.

In the absence of coherent government

Oil spills in the Niger Delta

We reached the edge of the oil spill near the Nigerian village of Otuegwe after a long hike through cassava plantations. Ahead of us lay swamp. We waded into the warm tropical water and began swimming, cameras and notebooks held above our heads. We could smell the oil long before we saw it – the stench of garage forecourts and rotting vegetation hanging thickly in the air.

The farther we travelled, the more nauseous it became. Soon we were swimming in pools of light Nigerian crude, the best-quality oil in the world. One of the many hundreds of 40-year-old pipelines that crisscross the Niger Delta had corroded and spewed oil for several months.

Forest and farmland were now covered in a sheen of greasy oil. Drinking wells were polluted and people were distraught. No one knew how much oil had leaked. 'We lost our nets, huts and fishing pots,' said Chief Promise, village leader of Otuegwe and our guide. 'This is where we fished and farmed. We have lost our forest. We told Shell of the spill within days, but they did nothing for six months.'

That was the Niger Delta a few years ago, where, according to Nigerian academics, writers and environment groups, oil companies have acted with such impunity and recklessness that much of the region has been devastated by leaks.

In fact, more oil is spilled from the Delta's network of terminals, pipes, pumping stations and oil platforms every year than has been lost in the Gulf of Mexico, the site of a major ecological catastrophe caused by oil that has poured from a leak triggered by the explosion that wrecked BP's Deepwater Horizon rig last month.

John Vidal, *The Observer*, 30 May 2010

Witness

programmes, the major transnational oil corporations have launched their own community development programmes. The Niger Delta Development Commission (NDDC) was, for example, created to help catalyze economic and social development in the region, but it is widely perceived to be ineffective and opaque

There is a good business – as well as moral – case for companies such as Shell to contribute to poverty alleviation in the Niger Delta but this can realistically only happen if national planning and management and clear environmental planning and controls are in place. Beyond this the transnationals could make a contribution through the introduction of 'cleaner' technologies and more socially responsible corporate policies. ■

A child plays beside burning oil pools in Kigbara-Dere, in the Niger Delta.

The power and influence of corporations – Monsanto

MONSANTO

Monsanto is a US transnational agricultural biotechnology corporation based in Creve Coeur, Missouri. Previously an industrial chemical company, it diversified into agrochemicals and biotechnology in the mid-1990s. Today it is the leading producer of genetically modified (GM) seed and the world's leading producer of the herbicide glyphosate, which it markets as 'Roundup'. Monsanto, like many large companies, has a complicated business structure. Its company profile lists profits of $2.024 billion (2008) and the employment of 21,000 in the US. It is bigger than it seems, however. It has bought up and/or entered into licensing agreements with many other seed suppliers and research companies around the world and has enormous power in global agriculture and food supply. It now provides the technology for 90% of the world's GM seeds.

Its genetic modification of food crops often involves making them resistant to high levels of its own herbicide so that the crop can be sprayed to eliminate weeds. Agracetus, a company owned by Monsanto, produces 'Roundup Ready' soybean seed for the commercial market. Other Roundup Ready crops include corn and cotton, and Monsanto is trying to bring more to market, including wheat and rice.

Monsanto has caused global controversy through its aggressive marketing of its products and its willingness to use litigation against opponents of its practices. It has become a target of the anti-globalization movement and environmentalists. It is not hard to find evidence of why it is so controversial. The box gives details of a case that Monsanto brought against a small farmer in Canada.

Percy Schmeiser's battle with Monsanto has been showcased in a film and he has also gone back to court to sue Monsanto for polluting his land with GM crops. Other actions taken by Monsanto have caused widespread concern. Taking out a patent on something gives a company exclusive rights to sell and develop a new invention. We normally associate patents with products developed by the company but in the case of Monsanto and other biotech companies the patents are on naturally occurring plants and genes. The patent grants the company a temporary monopoly and bans farmers from saving seeds. It forces them to buy new seeds from the company each year or pay for a licence to use patented seeds they have saved. Monsanto has a large degree of control of this market in the developed and developing world and it has led to an increase in seed prices and a decrease in seed choice for farmers. Greenpeace and other environmental groups have called for an end to patents on seeds because they promote monoculture and hinder the development of new seeds. They warn that it could eventually lead to a situation where companies like Monsanto are in control of the whole food chain.

Finding evidence of the influence of TNCs is easy, and Monsanto is just one example. Controlling that influence to make sure that it works in the interests of the global community is much more difficult. TNCs are the fuel that drives the globalization process and governments are reluctant to interfere with their activities. Their influence can have global benefits but ultimately it is probably sensible to recognize that their primary purpose is to generate profits. ∎

Imagine yourself as a farmer. I know it's not easy, since few do it any more, but give it a shot. Picture yourself as a seasoned farmer on the Canadian prairies. You've been working your farm for 50 years, with your wife working at your side. Despite the vicissitudes of life, and heavy pressure from ever-enlarging mechanized farms around you, you're still there. Then, one day, you find a large seed and chemical company has filed suit against you – because they've found their genetically engineered plants on your land. First, you're wondering how representatives of this company came to be sniffing around on your land without your knowledge or permission, and second, you're perplexed because you've never bought the seed they accuse you of using. In fact, you've deliberately avoided using such seed, and have survived competition by saving your own, developing improved strains through the age-old process of natural plant breeding. Furthermore, despite their genetically modified seed having contaminated your own natural crop – an irreversible action with major long-term biological and financial implications for you and any farms around you – you find the courts are only interested in protecting the rights of the 'copyright holder' of the seed, even while acknowledging that the seed may have blown in from neighbouring fields or passing trucks. It turns out that it doesn't matter how the seed got onto your property, or whether or not you knew it was there. It's on your land, so you have to pay.

'Whether Mr Schmeiser (the farmer) knew of the matter or not matters not at all,' Roger Hughes, Monsanto attorney.

celsias.com

A German poster advertising a special showing of the film about Percy Schmeiser's battle, titled 'David versus Monsanto'.

Witness

Uganda CASE STUDY

Poverty reduction and the impact of globalization

UGANDA

Kampala

rara

Lake Victoria

Key statistics for Uganda	
Total population	32.7 million
GNI per capita	$460
Probability of not surviving to age 40	31.4%
Adult literacy rate	75%
Infant mortality rate	79 per 1,000 live births
Children under 5 who are underweight	20%
People not using an improved water source	33%
Human Development Index	0.514 (157th of 182)

Rural poverty in Uganda

Uganda is a poor country with a population of approximately 32 million people. Some 31% live below the national poverty line (2007). The majority of Ugandans (85%) live in rural areas and 10 million of those live in poverty. The poorest regions of the country are the north and northeast, where outbreaks of civil violence in the last 20 years have disrupted many lives. In 1999 the internally displaced population of Uganda was estimated at 622,000. The conflict was caused by The Lord's Resistance Army (LRA), which led a rebellion against the Ugandan government with appalling consequences for the local population over two decades.

The security situation has recently improved in northern Uganda but the understandable insecurity of the population is still a factor in any attempts to eradicate poverty. Improved governance has been dependent on the successful resolution of the conflict in the north. Although this has not been fully achieved, the situation is calmer and the LRA have moved to the eastern part of the Democratic Republic of Congo.

There are many other reasons for the high incidence of poverty in rural areas. The majority of the population are smallholder subsistence farmers who are unable to transport produce to markets because of a lack of vehicles and roads. The climate is erratic and the extreme variability of rainfall and soil fertility makes farming difficult. In addition there is no access to the advice and technology they need to increase production and reduce losses caused by pests and disease. Food shortages are a regular problem.

Health and social issues are another factor. The population is growing by 3.2% a year, doubling every 20 years, and AIDS has caused the deaths of a large number of young adults, leaving an estimated one million children without parents. Life for women in rural areas is particularly hard because of the lack of healthcare and social services. In addition, the division of land between sons has led to land fragmentation and a lack of ownership security.

Poverty Eradication and Action Plan

Uganda was one of the first countries in the developing world to produce its own poverty reduction strategy, the Poverty Eradication and Action Plan (PEAP), in 1997. The existence of a poverty reduction strategy in the country helped to make it the first HIPC (Heavily Indebted Poor Country) to be eligible for debt relief in 1998.

PEAP was established on five 'pillars'.

1. Improved economic management – including economic management, tax policy and trade policy.
2. Enhanced production, competitiveness and incomes assisted by private sector investment.
3. Improved security, conflict resolution and disaster management.
4. Good governance; with a focus on democracy, human rights, political governance, justice, law and order.
5. Human development; focused on education and skills development, health, water and sanitation.

Economic growth and employment-generation were thought to be necessary conditions for poverty eradication and growth was to be driven by agricultural modernization. The action plan identified the expansion of the private sector as an essential requirement for economic growth. It also specified the need for economic openness with no tariff protection from imports, which was the preferred approach of the IMF, and a move towards producing goods for export.

To deal directly with poverty, a Poverty Action Fund was set up to distribute the funds needed for the implementation of universal primary education, the expansion of primary healthcare, agricultural improvement programmes and other projects directly related to poverty relief. The Human Rights Commission has been working with the Ugandan government and a Ministry of Ethics and Integrity has been established to ensure that public funds are used properly. A Land Act has been introduced to strengthen the rights of the poor and the need to improve the infrastructure, particularly road transport, has been recognized. The UN and other international organizations have acknowledged the progress that Uganda has made and see its poverty reduction strategy as a vital part of the process.

The impact of globalization in Uganda – selected examples

At the same time as Uganda attempts to implement measures to reduce poverty within the country it is constantly being influenced by the forces of global change. A brief look at three separate stories reveals how globalization is having a major impact on the day-to-day life of all Ugandans.

Fishing in Lake Uganda

Lake Victoria/Uganda covers a total area of 68,800 square kilometres and ownership is split between Tanzania (49%), Uganda (45%) and Kenya (6%). The lake is the largest inland fishery in the world and in 2006 contributed more than 12% of Uganda's GDP. Uganda had over 20 fish factories and exported more than 30,000 tonnes of fish a year – worth over $150 million a year to its economy. Fish exports overtook cash crops such as coffee and cotton in terms of export earnings. Over 30 million people in East Africa depend on fishing for their livelihood and it provides a valuable source of food for millions of consumers in the region.

Fish have always been an important source of food to people living around the lake. The Nile Perch was introduced into the lake in the 1950s by British colonial officers and became a very important export product and source of food. Unfortunately it is a predatory fish and it has reduced the indigenous species in the lake to extinction levels and had a major impact on the lake ecosystem. Fish numbers in the lake have declined rapidly in the last few years because of overfishing, poor fishing methods such as seine nets which destroy fish breeding grounds, and illegal trade in small, young fish. Some fish factories have closed because there is no fish to process. Some of the illegally traded unprocessed fish, especially Nile Perch and Tilapia, has ended up in European markets. The overfishing of Lake Uganda is the result of the demand for its fish from the developed world – it has become part of the global food industry.

Tanzania has tried to protect its fishing industry by banning foreign fishing boats from its waters and Uganda is using patrol boats to try and prevent boats from Kenya fishing in Ugandan waters. Research estimates suggest that Uganda's total fish production is surpassing the sustainable target level by 27%, a yearly surfeit of 90,000 tonnes. The reduction in fish availability is driving up local prices and threatening the livelihood of millions of people. The only long-term solution is the adoption of sustainable fishing practices. These would include:

- Long-line fishing, a more sustainable alternative to using gill nets
- A reduction in the number of fish-processing plants to match the stocks of Nile perch
- Investment in aquaculture to raise other species for domestic and regional markets.

Second-hand clothes

The clothes that are frequently given to charities or other organizations in developed countries have increasingly found their way to the markets of developing countries. How can such innocuous acts of charity cause so much critical debate about their impact on traditional industries and cultures?

A flood of second-hand clothing from the West is undermining textiles produced in Africa. The Ugandan government has imposed a tax on the import of second-hand clothes

Human development outcomes in Uganda have been transformed by the introduction of free primary education for four children in each family, which has led to a massive increase in enrolment. Primary education is a central element of the PEAP. Now that quantity has increased so much, quality is critical.

Healthcare is being co-ordinated by the new health strategic plan. At the heart of this is the minimum health package. Service delivery is being improved by a number of mechanisms including better remuneration and training, better infrastructure, and better accountability to consumers through village health committees.

Uganda PEAP 2004

Feature

Ugandan manufacturers want their government to put controls on the importation of all second-hand clothing (commonly known as *mivumba*). They argue that the imported clothing – much of it donated to leading charities in the US and Europe before finding its way to Africa – is hampering the growth of the local textile industry. Joyce Rwakasisi, the Textile Development Agency co-ordinator, says the sector cannot develop when mivumba take up 85% of the market.

But while the Uganda National Bureau of Standards is to ban the importation of second-hand nightwear, stockings, bras and undergarments – primarily on health grounds – it will allow the continued importation of other second-hand clothes.

Western charity undermines African textiles

A photo and headline from *New Internationalist* magazine in 2004. This Bambara girl from central Mali is carrying strips of cotton woven by village craftspeople.

Uganda's textile sector used to employ 500,000 people and earn $100 million in annual exports, but has virtually been brought to its knees by the imports.

The country isn't alone. Neil Kearney, General Secretary of the International Textile Garment and Leather Workers Federation points out that in Zimbabwe some 20,000 textile and clothing jobs have disappeared directly or indirectly due to imported used clothing from the West. South Africa has lost 20,000 and Senegal 7,000 jobs, while Kenya, Mozambique, Tanzania, Togo, Côte d'Ivoire and Ghana have been hard hit too. 'In fact, hardly a nation in Africa has escaped the attention of the importers. In some cases, European charities specializing in the second-hand clothing trade, export and retail the goods themselves,' Kearney said.

But in finding a solution to this problem, not all support a ban on mivumba imports. Member of Parliament Jacob Oulanyah says: 'For Government to phase out second-hand clothes, it must have a deliberate policy for a substitute, which is not there at the moment.'

New Internationalist November 2004

Feature

Mobile phones reach Uganda's villages

Not far from the equator, a ribbon of red dirt track leads off the main road.

The track is lined with coffee bushes draped with vines of vanilla and miles of banana, yam and cassava plants.

These are *shambas*, smallholdings owned by subsistence farmers in the heart of Uganda, East Africa. Many live below the poverty line and there is no electricity.

In a village called Kkonkoma, on the roof of a small house there is an aerial. It is a mobile phone antenna for a home-based village telephone service run by 24-year-old entrepreneur Joseph Ssesanga and his family.

Neighbours make telephone calls from his house rather than walk down the dirt track to the nearest public telephone some five kilometres away.

Business in a box

The business began when Mr Ssesanga's mother, Nakakande Teopista, who was supporting the family by selling fish, learnt of small loans available to people wanting to start mobile phone businesses.

This is the Village Phone model, which provides a business in a box. With loans, budding entrepreneurs can buy a mobile phone, a car battery to charge it, and a booster antenna that can pick up signals from base stations situated up to 25 kilometres away. The handset is loaded with software that tracks revenues from every call. The loan providers, so-called microfinance institutions, take on the task of ordering the equipment and transporting it to those who cannot afford to travel long distances.

Paying for school

By making money on every call she sells, Ms Teopista managed to repay the loan in four months. She then began to invest.

The family now operates in six villages, employs phone operators and even provides a phone-charging service for those with their own handsets.

Mr Ssesanga now manages the operators, and he also cycles around the village offering services to passing neighbours.

The fortunes of his family have been transformed, he says.

'We were farmers, but seasons are a major problem. We grow vegetables, but sometimes they can be damaged and you lose everything.'

In contrast to such dire predicaments, the family can now afford school fees – secondary school is not free in Uganda – and has even opened a stationery shop in the nearest town.

Pioneered in Bangladesh

The Village Phone model was pioneered by Grameen Bank in Bangladesh. By providing small-scale loans it allowed rural women to lift themselves out of poverty. There are now 295,000 village phone operators countrywide in Bangladesh.

BBC News 2007

Feature

'My goat is sick. Its neck is swollen. It can't eat,' an old woman in a remote village in Uganda said. She spoke to a man passing by with a mobile phone.

'Let me see if I can help,' said Laban Rutagumirwa.

He sent off a text message that read 'goat bloat'. The message went to an agriculture information service devised by the Grameen Foundation and the Bill and Melinda Gates Foundation. A response came back shortly with instructions to mix a half kilo of rock salt with a litre of water and have the goat drink it. Two weeks later, Rutagumirwa was passing through the village and came across the old woman. She happily reported that her goat had recovered.

allAfrica.com, September 2010

Feature

to try to reduce their impact on domestic industries but traders have started to source their clothes from neighbouring countries like Congo where there is no import tax. It is a complex issue which causes arguments – even amongst charities.

Mobile phones

Only 15 years ago mobile phones were the size of a house brick and only used by a few people in industrialized countries. Today the industry has expanded to the extent that since 1994 10 billion mobile phones have been manufactured and in 2010 there were 5 billion mobile phones connected to networks worldwide. The biggest increase in use in recent years has been in India and Asia but the technology has also changed the lives of people in Uganda and every other African country. While the installation of cables for landlines was always seen as an impossibly expensive undertaking in most parts of sub-Saharan Africa, particularly in the rural areas, wireless technology has allowed Africans to jump a stage and make telephony accessible even to villagers in subsistence-farming communities.

Mobile phones are also helping farmers in Uganda gain information about the price they may receive for their crops before they go to market and also obtain advice about the care of their crops or animals.

The evidence portraying the impact of globalization is inevitably selective and the case studies only provide a limited insight into its impact in one small African country. Globalization benefits some and disadvantages others. It is too simple to say that there are usually economic gains but social and environmental costs – but it may not be far from the truth. ∎

⑤ **Population**

How does population growth affect development?

✱ *The relationship between population and development is complex and there are competing explanations.*

✱ *Population growth can be a factor in creating increased demand for basic services and also food insecurity.*

✱ *The relationship between the size of the human population, food supply and environmental sustainability is vital but subject to debate.*

✱ *The population structures of countries at different levels of development have their own characteristics and they pose different challenges.*

Key points

The world's population will pass the seven billion mark late in 2011. The relationship between population growth and development is the subject of a lot of debate. There are many who feel that the rapid growth rate of the human population is the biggest threat to an environmentally sustainable world. Others believe that a growing population is required to have a positive impact on economic growth. The graph opposite shows global population growth since 1750 and projected through to 2050.

Characteristics of population growth

The rapid growth of the global population has happened relatively recently in human terms and is often referred to as the 'population explosion'. The phrase is inevitably associated with high birth rates but the true characteristics of rapid population growth are more complicated. Fluctuations in birth and death rates are equally important in trying to explain changes in population levels. Nick Eberstadt, an American demographer, said that the reason for the population explosion is 'not

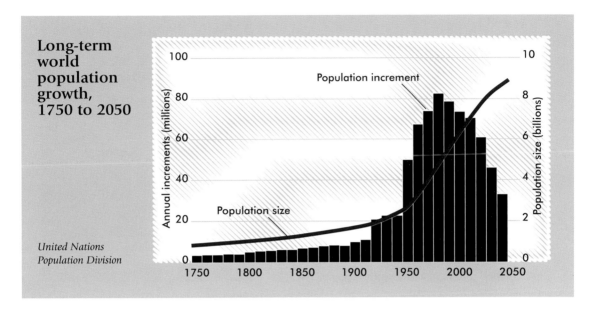

Long-term world population growth, 1750 to 2050

United Nations Population Division

because human beings started breeding like rabbits but because they stopped dying like flies'. How did the global population reach seven billion?

Demographic transition model

The demographic transition model was based on observations by Warren Thompson, an American demographer, of population changes in industrialized countries from 1750 onwards. His original model suggested that countries will pass through four stages of population growth, although modern versions of the model have extended this to five or even six stages.

Stage One or pre-modern stage

Death rates are high in this stage for a number of reasons, including a lack of knowledge of disease prevention and food shortages. The death rate is further increased by outbreaks of infectious diseases such as the plague or smallpox and other diseases such as cholera that are caused by a lack of clean drinking water or efficient sewage disposal. Only a minority of children survive childhood and there is little reason to control fertility so birth rates are also very high.

Stage Two or early industrial stage

The population starts to rise because of a drop in the death rate. The declining death rate is largely due to better food supply as a result of agricultural innovations and significant improvements in public health because of better drinking water supplies and sewage disposal as well as

The world at seven billion: highlights

1. World population reached 6 billion in October 1999 and it is estimated that it will reach 7 billion by the end of 2011.

2. World population is projected to reach 8 billion mark in 2028 and 9 billion in 2050. It is projected to stabilize at just above 10 billion after 2200.

3. It will have taken just 12 years for the world to add this most recent billion people. This is the same amount of time it took for the population to increase from five billion to six billion.

4. World population did not reach one billion until 1804. It took 123 years to reach 2 billion in 1927, 33 years to reach 3 billion in 1960, 14 years to reach 4 billion in 1974 and 13 years to reach 5 billion in 1987.

5. The highest rate of world population growth (2.04 per cent) occurred in the late 1960s. The current rate (1995-2000) is 1.2 per cent.

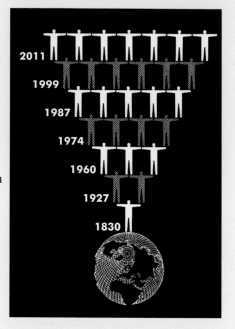

6. The largest annual increase to world population (86 million) took place in the late 1980s; the current annual increase is approximately 75 million.

7. Of the 75 million people currently added to the world each year, 95% live in the less developed regions.

8. Around 80% of the world population currently reside in the less developed regions. At the beginning of the century, 70% did so. By 2050, the share of the world population living in the currently less developed regions will have risen to 90%.

9. The population of the world is ageing. The median age increased from 23.5 years in 1950 to 26.4 years in 1999. By 2050, the median age is projected to reach 37.8 years. The number of people in the world aged 60 or older will also rise from the current 1 in 10 persons to be 2 in 9 by 2050; in developed countries, nearly 1 in 3 will then be aged 60 or older.

10. World life expectancy at birth is now at 65 years, having increased by a remarkable 20 years since 1950; by 2050 life expectancy is expected to exceed 76 years. However, in spite of these impressive gains, recent years have shown a devastating toll from AIDS in a number of countries.

11. Couples in developing countries today have on average 3 children each; 30 years ago they had 6. More than half of all couples in developing countries now use contraception.

12. The number of persons who have moved to another country has risen to over 125 million migrants today from 75 million in 1965.

13. The world has become increasingly urban. The majority of the world's population was urban for the first time in 2006.

United Nations Population Division

Feature

The demographic transition model

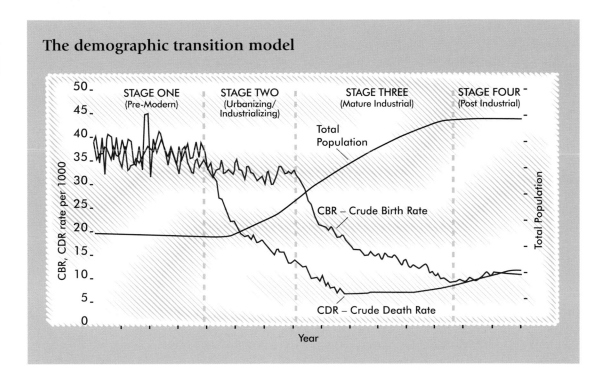

an increased awareness of the importance of personal hygiene. Just as important, though, is the beginning of a reduction in poverty levels and an improvement in female literacy.

The decline in the death rate is particularly evident in the reduction in infant mortality and the increased survival rates for young children mean that the population is increasingly youthful in profile.

Stage Three – the post-industrial stage

The birth rate starts to decline and the rate of population increase falls as the gap between birth and death rate is reduced. The fall in birth rate is due to a number of factors. The decline in childhood deaths means that parents can be more confident about the survival of children and feel less need for a large family. Increasing urbanization also reduces the value of child labour while at the same time raising the cost of the education and care of dependent children, making it more likely that people will have fewer children. A continuing decline in poverty levels has the same impact.

Just as important is the increasing literacy and employment of women and the social valuation of women beyond the traditional role of childbearing and motherhood. The entry of women into the workforce extends their life beyond the family and makes them increasingly influential in decisions concerning family planning. Improvements in contraception technology in the second half of the 20th century reinforced the decline in fertility but it is the change in values that is most important.

Stage Four – the late industrial or stable stage

The birth and death rates stabilize at a low level and the population level is high but stable. The population profile is less youthful and some demographers identify a fifth stage where the death rate is consistently above the birth rate and the population starts to decline. A few have claimed there is evidence of a sixth stage in some countries with a high Human Development Index (above 0.95) where there is an increase in birth rates.

The demographic transition model is not a predictor of population levels and does not attempt to provide accurate information about individual countries. It was based on observations of the early industrializing countries and, while some countries have passed through the stages of growth very quickly, such as China and Brazil, other poorer countries have stalled in Stage Two. The model does, however, highlight the importance of increased levels of wealth in reducing birth rates and population growth.

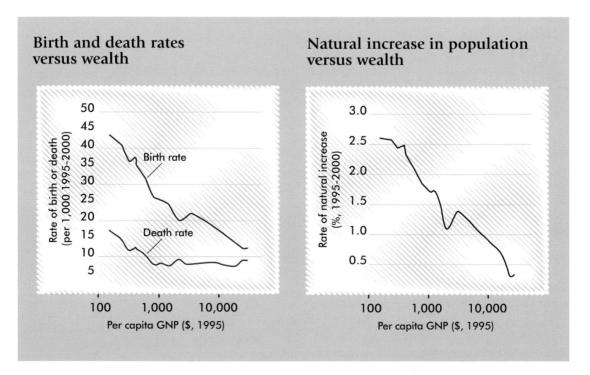

Birth and death rates versus wealth

Natural increase in population versus wealth

Why female empowerment is key

Population worriers make much of the projection of nine billion by 2050. But were it not for three decades of successful family planning that figure would be closer to 16 billion, points out Australian demographer Peter McDonald.

Here in Morocco, for example, only 5% of women used contraception in the late 1970s – today 63% do. But another crucial factor is the progress made in getting girls into school. This, more than anything, delays childbearing, encourages greater spacing between children or even opens out the option of not having children at all.

It's the perfect chicken and egg. Education means lower fertility – and lower fertility can mean more education. One of the immediate benefits of the so-called 'demographic dividend' that comes with fewer children being born is that school rolls fall, educational resources are not so over-stretched, and there is, in theory at any rate, more money available per child for education. In practice, the money may be wasted or misdirected. But in South Korea, for example, where the demographic dividend was invested in education, the results in terms of economic and social development over the past few decades have been astounding.

The same felicitous connection exists between health provision and fertility rates. Statistically, a child's chance of survival improves hugely in a smaller family where resources – both physical and emotional – tend to be more concentrated. And if children have a better chance of surviving, their parents will not feel they need to have so many. This is one of the reasons why in countries where there is the greatest poverty – those of sub-Saharan Africa, for example – women both have the most children and lose the most children as infants.

Vanessa Baird, *New Internationalist* 429, Jan/Feb 2010

Witness

Age structure matters

Population totals in themselves tell us very little about what impact that population may have on resource allocation within the country. The age structure of the population is one important factor and this varies enormously from one country to another. In some developing countries, such as Ethiopia and Indonesia, more than 50% of the population are under the age of 15. With a population profile like that, education and health services will demand a large proportion of the national budget. On the other hand, in the UK there are currently more people over the age of 60 than young people under the age of 16. The ageing population that is typical of most of the countries of the Global North is a result of falling fertility rates and a gradual rise in life expectancy. It raises some important issues that are difficult to resolve.

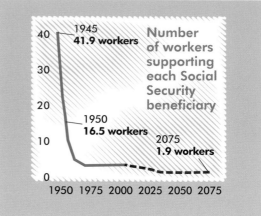

- The increased demand for pensions in a welfare state places a huge strain on the national budget. EU countries spend an average of 12% of their GDP on providing pensions for the elderly. The funding has to be provided by the income from taxes and other sources from a shrinking economically active portion of the population.

- Families are becoming less nuclear and caring for elderly relatives has increasingly become the responsibility of the state. This is very expensive. How to pay for elderly healthcare has become a big political issue in many countries. Should elderly people have to pay for their own care by using the money they wanted to pass on to their children or by selling their houses? Why should the state pay for the care of older people who frequently have more money than many taxpayers? This is an important debate that is likely to continue for some years.

- Politicians need to take account of the large number of older people as a proportion of the total electorate when they are making decisions about the allocation of resources. The demands made by

Examples of age structure graphs

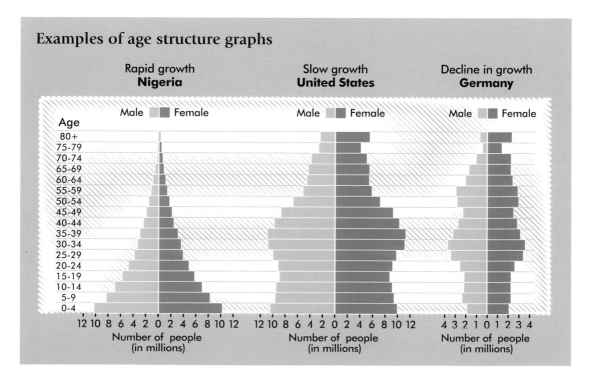

an elderly population are difficult to resist. They form a coherent, powerful group because their interests are so focused on factors caused by old age: the level of state pensions, access to healthcare, payment for care homes and the need for subsidized transport. There are no other groups of voters who have such a distinctive and cohesive profile and potential political influence.

The age structure of a population has implications for development because of the particular characteristics of each age group. The high proportion of the global population who are either of childbearing age now or who will be of childbearing age in the future means that even if the replacement population level of 2.1 children per woman was somehow achieved now, the global population would continue to rise for another 50 years. Some 44% of the population of Nigeria are under the age of 15. The fertility rate in the country is 5.8 children per woman and, even allowing for a future reduction in the fertility rate, the total population of Nigeria is predicted to increase from 130 million today to over 300 million in 2050. Statistics like these have for years stirred up debate about population growth and its impact on the earth's resources.

Waiting outside a maternity clinic in rural Burkina Faso.

The population debate in development revolves around the views of some people that the earth's resources cannot provide for an ever-increasing population (Malthusian) and those people who argue that the earth could support a much larger population if those resources were used more efficiently and distributed more fairly.

The Malthusian viewpoint

Thomas Malthus's essay on population and food supply, written at the end of the 18th century, has been very important in crystallizing opinion about the impacts of population growth. He suggested that population growth was a geometric progression (1, 2, 4, 8, 16 etc) and food supply only increased arithmetically (1,2,3,4,5 etc). As a consequence population would quickly outstrip food supply and only catastrophic events could resolve this imbalance (famine, disease, war etc). He was opposed to any social welfare provision (which meant the Poor Law in 18th-century Britain) because he considered that would only increase

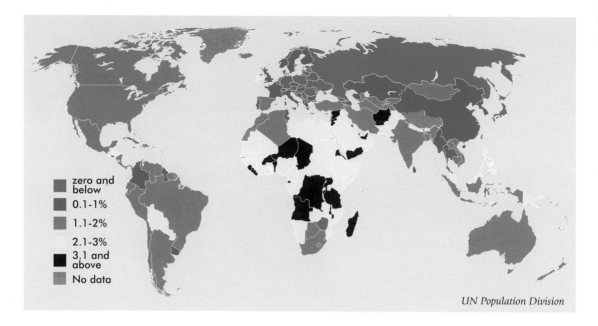

zero and below

0.1-1%

1.1-2%

2.1-3%

3.1 and above

No data

UN Population Division

the life expectancy of the least useful (the poor), whose numbers would multiply. Malthus believed that the middle classes were more able to show the restraint needed to control population growth.

Population annual growth rate 2000-2009.

For strict Malthusians, poverty today is the result of too many people in the world and they link current food shortages to the same issue. The obvious problem with Malthusian views has been the fact that although population has increased rapidly, food supply has not lagged behind in the way he predicted. This was a result of the agricultural revolution that increased food yields in the 19th and 20th centuries. The major improvements in transport and communication that also occurred meant that populations could be fed not only by domestic food supplies but by food grown in other parts of the world.

Neo-Malthusians have amended these views to argue that the increased industrial and agricultural activity needed to feed this much larger population is not sustainable and will lead to environmental disaster. These disasters may manifest themselves in different ways but include climate change, deforestation and desertification. They might agree that the earth is technically able to support a larger population in the short term but they will argue that it is only at the expense of its resource base. A major change from Malthus's original account of the link between population and food supply is that the blame for this situation has shifted from the poor to rich consumers in the developed world. The richest 20% of the earth's population currently consume 80% of the earth's resources.

The Malthusian question

John Beddington, the government's chief scientific adviser, warned this week of a 'perfect storm', with food, water and energy all dangerously depleted by 2030, thanks to population growth and rising prosperity. Next week the Optimum Population Trust will hold a conference at the Royal Statistical Society, arguing that the planet has room for 5 billion people at the most, and that the United Kingdom should be home to no more than about 18 million.

Such figures are unhelpful: they describe an alternative planet with an entirely notional history. Thomas Malthus, who warned that population growth would outstrip food supply, has been dismissed because food production has more or less kept up with population growth. That is one reason why we are all here, and why some are clinically obese.

But the Malthusian question has stimulated argument about the Earth's carrying capacity, which depends as much on human optimism as on ingenuity. 'If the world's population had the productivity of the Swiss, the consumption habits of the Chinese, the egalitarian instincts of the Swedes, and the social discipline of the Japanese, then the planet could support many times its current population without privation for anyone,' wrote Lester C Thurow in the very different world of 1986.

Yet human numbers continue to swell, at more than 9,000 an hour, 80 million a year – a rate that threatens a doubling in less than 50 years. Land for cultivation is dwindling. Wind and rain erode fertile soils. Water supplies are increasingly precarious. Once-fertile regions are threatened with sterility. The yield from the oceans has begun to fall. To make matters potentially worse, human numbers threaten the survival of other species of plant and animal. Humans depend not just on what they can extract from the soil, but what they can grow in it, and this yield is driven by an intricate ecological network of organisms. Even at the most conservative estimate, other species are being extinguished at 100 to 1,000 times the background rate observable in the fossil record.

Malthus's arguments were part of the inspiration for Charles Darwin's theory of evolution, and they have validity in the natural world. On the savannah, in the rainforests, and across the tundra, animal populations explode when times are good, and crash when food reserves are exhausted. Is homo sapiens an exception? Perhaps. Humans can consider each other's needs, and co-operate; there is also plenty of evidence that they choose not to. The Optimum Population Trust does not have the answers, but the questions remain, quite literally, vital.

The Guardian, 21 March 2009 **Feature**

However, they would also argue that rapid population growth in the poorer countries leads to economic stagnation, uncontrollable urbanization and environmental damage. For neo-Malthusians, population control should be the main objective of aid programmes. One such thinker, the US writer Robert D Kaplan, has even argued that population growth and the major problems that flow from it have caused some poor countries that were already weak to become unstable in a

way that could threaten the developed world, a view that some have summarized as a 'New Barbarism'. He would cite Somalia, commonly described as a failed state and home for potential terrorists, as a good example of what can happen in these circumstances.

The owner of the first ever condom shop in Tehran, Iran, shows off his wares.

Population growth as a positive factor in development

There are others, notably the influential Danish economist Ester Boserup, who see population growth as a process that can have a positive impact. In Boserup's theory, rising population density often induces agricultural innovation because land is used more intensively. Fertilizing, field preparation, irrigation and weed control become significant parts of farming practices. They demand longer hours from the farmer and higher inputs, a process she describes as agricultural intensification. This is an anti-Malthusian view of the world in which human ingenuity can resolve the problems caused when we reach a resource boundary and the Green Revolution of the late 20th century is an example of what can be achieved. Her cornucopian views have been welcomed by some but condemned by others who see her ideas as far too complacent given the clear evidence of environmental decline. Boserup was a feminist and there is no doubt that her ideas and research in the 1980s made a major contribution to the recognition of the important role of women in development.

Those people who support the arguments of Malthus or Boserup

Too many people?

Today there are around 6.8 billion people occupying this planet. That's up from 5.9 a decade ago. By 2050 it is projected to top 9 billion.

Talk of 'overpopulation' has been with us for some time. Already, in 1798, when there were a mere 978 million people in the world, mathematician Thomas Malthus was warning of an impending catastrophe as human numbers exceeded the capacity to grow food.

Often the cause of concern is the speed at which others – be they people of other races or social classes or religions or political allegiances – are reproducing themselves, threatening, presumably, to disturb the wellbeing of whatever dominant group the commentator belongs to.

This was epitomized recently by Michael Laws, Mayor of Wanganui District in New Zealand, who proposed that in order to tackle the problems of child abuse and murder, members of the 'appalling underclass' should be paid not to have children. 'If we gave $10,000 to certain people and said "we'll voluntarily sterilize you" then all of society would be better off,' he told the Dominion Post *newspaper.*

Most contemporary worries about population are less offensively expressed. For many, the issue is primarily an environmental one. The logic is simple. The more people there are, the more greenhouse gas is emitted, the more damage is done. Any attempts to reduce carbon emissions will be negated by runaway population growth.

This was echoed recently by the Financial Times *when it called for an international debate on population. A leader column argued: 'World population growth is making it harder to achieve cuts in carbon emissions' and went on to quote a disputed London School of Economics study maintaining that spending on family planning is 'five times more cost effective at cutting carbon dioxide emissions than the conventional low carbon technologies'.*

The UK-based Optimum Population Trust goes further, suggesting that to achieve sustainability we should be aiming to reduce global population by at least 1.7 billion people. How reasonable is all this? Is population really the big taboo that liberals won't touch?

Since the 1970s fertility has declined considerably, not just in countries like Morocco but worldwide. This makes for a global average of around 2.5 children per woman. In 76 countries the fertility rate has actually sunk below replacement level – which is set at around 2.1. This means that the current population is not reproducing itself. It's most noticeable in Europe but there are examples from every continent, including Africa.

In developing countries the average fertility rate fell by half, from six to three children, between 1950 and 2000. But in many countries of sub-Saharan Africa, women are still having five or more children on average.

In terms of the big global numbers, what happens in India and China, the two most populous countries, has the greatest impact. India today has a fertility rate of 2.7 (down from 3.5 in 1997) and is expected to hit replacement level in 2027. China's drop from 5 or 6 per woman before 1970 to around 1.5 today looks likely to persist. 'The accumulated evidence suggests that lifting the one child policy would not lead to a resurgence of uncontrollable population growth,' say researchers from the region. China, they say, 'would benefit from learning from its neighbours, Korea and Japan, how difficult it is to induce people to increase childbearing once fertility has fallen to a very low level.' As a consequence, China's population should start shrinking by 2023. According to the United Nations, 21 countries already had a declining population in the period 2000-2005.

Vanessa Baird, *New Internationalist 429,* **Jan/Feb 2010**

Witness

Other explanations of the impact of an increasing human population on the environment

IPAT
IPAT is an acronym that originated in the 1970s from a discussion between American economists and environmentalists. It is written as an equation –
$I = P \times A \times T$
– where I represents the human impact on the environment, P the size of the human population, A the affluence of the population and T the level of technology available to the population at that time.
The equation predicts an increasing impact on the environment because of rising global populations and affluence but also offers the possibility that the impact may be ameliorated by improved technology – by reducing waste in manufacturing processes, for example.

POET
P (Population) O (Organization) E (Environment) T (Technology) describes a model of social change developed by Otis Dudley Duncan in the 1960s. It is similar in that it sees the human impact on the environment as a product of the interaction between the level of population and technology available. But it places more emphasis on the organizational structure of society; including the type of government, business organization and the influence of cultures and traditions.

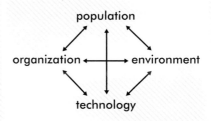

Club of Rome
The *Limits to Growth* was an influential report published in 1972 by The Club of Rome, a global thinktank now based in Switzerland. The group deals with a variety of international political issues but this report was about the impossibility of continuous economic growth due to the pressure of rising global populations on finite resources such as fossil fuels. Later reports from the group were less pessimistic and more hopeful about the ability of humankind to deal with potential environmental and economic catastrophes.

Feature

accept the inevitability of rapid population growth in the medium term at least. But that basic premise has been questioned in recent years as global evidence suggests that populations are not rising as fast as predicted in many parts of the world and raise the possibility that the huge numbers that statisticians predict for future global populations are not inevitable.

Is the global population increasing as fast as we think?

United Nations figures show that family size is decreasing in all countries, regardless of their stage of economic development. The most populous countries with below-replacement fertility are China, Brazil, Vietnam, Iran, Thailand and Korea, in order of population size. Although predicted to keep growing until 2050, world population should level out in the latter half of the century due to the effects of declining fertility.

Religion, immigration, female employment, contraception and economic growth may all have an influence on population growth. It is complex ingredients like this that prevent human population growth ever becoming an exact science and make it such fertile ground for debate.

The impact of population growth on food supply and environmental sustainability

Ultimately, the argument over global population growth boils down to questions of food supply and environmental sustainability, which have occupied the thoughts of eminent scientists from different disciplines for the past 50 years. The box opposite summarizes some of the key explanations and theories.

The Food and Agriculture Organization of the UN (FAO) has been relatively optimistic about food supplies in the future. It predicts rising food production, particularly in developing countries, associated with the use of improved agricultural technology. Many other individuals and organizations are more pessimistic about our ability to produce more food and deeply worried about the impact on the environment that further intensification of agriculture may bring.

A radical alternative opinion is that it is the way that we grow food that is causing the problem and not population numbers. According to this view, corporate food production is both environmentally destructive and unsustainable and is driving more efficient small farmers out of business.

The evidence of the impact of population growth on development arrives in our newspapers and on our televisions almost every day and it is often contradictory. It is a topic of fundamental importance to all students of world development.

Population and resources in Kenya

Key statistics on Kenya	
Total population	39.8 million
Population growth rate	2.9%
Fertility rate	4.9 children per woman
Annual number of births	1.5 million
GNI per capita	$770
Life expectancy	55 years
Infant mortality rate	55 per 1,000 live births
Adult literacy rate	87%

As shown by the graph below, Kenya's population has increased rapidly over the last 50 years and is projected to reach 85 million by 2050.

To what extent does Kenya support Malthus's view?

Kenya's circumstances make it ideal for evaluating Malthus's ideas and seeing if

Population and food production in Kenya, 1961-2006

Statistics from the UN Food and Agriculture Organization Database – they include cereals, meat, fruit and dairy production but exclude coffee, tea and tobacco

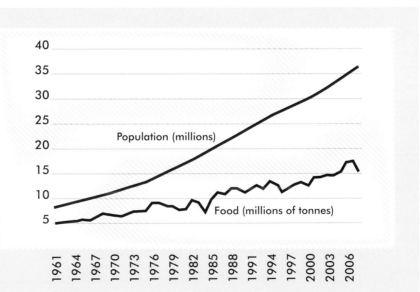

Population (millions)

Food (millions of tonnes)

Food per capita in Kenya, 1961-2006

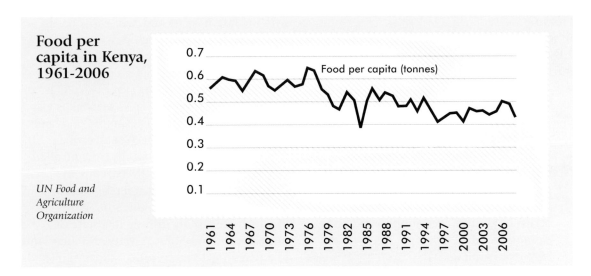

UN Food and Agriculture Organization

there is evidence of the positive and negative checks that his model predicts. In the graph above, the data supports the Malthusian model in which the geometric growth of the population outstrips the arithmetic growth of food production. Despite food production having increased by more than 300%, food production per person has actually fallen, leading to food insecurity which has been exacerbated by significant agricultural exports and by periodic droughts.

Negative checks

Famine
In September 2009, after three years of poor rains, Kenya declared a state of emergency as drought affected 10 million people. Food prices increased by up to 80% according to the World Food Programme, while Save the Children estimated that 1 in 3 children in parts of northeast Kenya were suffering from the effects of undernutrition. Widespread famine was only avoided by international and governmental aid which helped support around 6 million people.

Conflict
In addition to increasing food prices there is increasing concern about conflict over land. In the Mount Elgon region of northern Kenya, for example, the Sabaot Land Defence Force (SLDF) have emerged as an armed group. They claim they have taken up arms as members of the Sabaot ethnic group to defend land seized during the controversial 'Chebyuk 1 & 2' settlement schemes and now face eviction by the government under the 'Chebyuk 3' scheme. All three government plans were designed to resettle landless people and all have been marred by corruption and arbitrary land-grabbing, which has exacerbated ethnic tensions between the Sabaot, Iteso and Bukusu communities.

In total, Human Rights Watch reports over 600 SLDF killings and thousands of attacks, including rape and mutilation. Widespread human rights abuses have also been attributed to the Kenyan military, whose 2008 'Operation Save Lives' actually led to dozens of deaths and thousands of people being illegally detained.

Disease

In total the WHO estimates that around 70% of deaths in Kenya are attributable to infectious diseases, for example:

- HIV is prevalent in approximately 6.3% of Kenya's population (having fallen from a peak of 10% in 1990) and AIDS kills up to 130,000 people each year
- In 2008, 3,091 cases of cholera were reported by the World Health Organization – linked to poor drinking water (only 57% of Kenyan's have access to an improved supply) and poor sanitation (only 42% have access to improved sanitation)
- Malaria was responsible for around 40,000 deaths (many of them children under 5) in 2006. Reported cases of malaria have, however, fallen significantly in the last few years from over 9 million to 840,000 due in part to successful government and international projects.
- The high prevalence rates of these diseases have meant that life expectancy has fallen from 60 in 1990 to 54 in 2008.

Contraception and family planning

Contraception and family planning have become more widespread throughout Kenya, in large part due to better education about the risks of HIV, but also reflecting a growing middle class and changes in culture. According to the UN Population Fund, approximately 32% of women are using modern contraception and this has led to female fertility rates falling from a peak of 9 in 1963 to 4.8 in 2008, which will in turn slow the population growth rate in the future.

To what extent does Kenya support Boserup's view?

Food production has increased significantly over the last 50 years and, while this has in part been due to the development of new agricultural areas, technology and farming innovation have also played a significant role. The Machakos region, for example, is southeast of Nairobi. In 1937 Machakos was described as 'an appalling example of a large area of land which has been subjected to unco-ordinated and practically uncontrolled development by natives. Every phase of misuse of land is vividly and poignantly displayed in this reserve, the inhabitants of which are rapidly drifting to a state of hopeless and miserable poverty and their land to a parching desert of rocks, stones and sand' (Colin Maher, senior soil conservation officer for the British colonial authorities, 1937).

Despite this depressing description and a population that increased by over 600% during the last century, food production was able to outstrip population growth with an estimated 1,000% increase in crop production since 1930. This 'Machakos miracle' was initiated by a reduction in government constraints on agriculture and has been further developed by the work of local groups and, more recently, by NGOs such as Excellent Development. Changes have included:

- Terracing which reduced soil erosion and helped retain moisture, as well as increasing the area of land that could be successfully farmed
- Tree planting that reduced soil erosion, retained moisture, provided fuelwood (significantly reducing the time spent collecting fuel) while the fruit provided a valuable cash crop
- Changes in farming practice such as mixed planting, including pulses that help to fix the nitrogen in the soil, have reduced the need for expensive

agrochemicals

- Widespread use of composting, which has increased yields and reduced the need for agrochemicals
- A range of water conservation methods such as sand dams and cut-off drains have been extensively used, reducing the risk from drought.

In total, 76 new technologies were introduced, including 35 new crop varieties and 11 tilling and soil fertility practices, many of which were invented by the local Akamba community.

Conclusion

Kenya is a complex and diverse country that has many regional variations, reflecting different ethnic groups, climate zones and levels of globalization and development. As such, no single model could realistically be expected to fit the whole of the country. However, Kenya is facing declining food supplies per capita, which is exacerbated by the export of cash crops and by ethnic unrest over land ownership. With increasing concerns regarding land degradation and the impacts of climate change, it may well be that Kenya is near to exceeding its carrying capacity. There is nonetheless hope – as demonstrated in the model of food production in Machakos and the work to prevent HIV and malaria – that when communities work together and adopt new technologies and ideas the consequences of an expanding population may not be as dire as Malthus predicted. ■

Taking control: women at the largest Marie Stopes family planning clinic in Nairobi.

6 Aid & Debt Relief

Debt Aid & Aid & Relief Relief Re

What is the difference between aid and debt relief?

✴ Aid comes in two main forms: voluntary aid from charities and non-governmental organizations (NGOs); and Official Development Assistance (ODA) from national governments.

✴ Aid projects come in all shapes and sizes. They can be local or national in scale and may be characterized by top-down or bottom-up management.

✴ There are different opinions about the value of aid including those of Bauer, Sachs, Easterly and Escobar.

✴ Developing countries have been paying more money as repayment of their debts to governments and banks in developed countries than they have been receiving in aid.

✴ Some developing countries have been granted debt relief as part of the Heavily Indebted Poor Countries (HIPC) initiative.

Key points

What is aid?

There is much more controversy about the nature and value of aid than most people would imagine. As in other aspects of development studies, there are philosophical and practical differences in the views expressed by different groups, but even before that discussion can begin there are some basic points to be clarified.

Aid has been defined as the financial, technical, economic or military assistance given to developing countries that often results in a flow of money to the developing country at a concessionary rate. One source of aid are International Non-Governmental Organizations (INGOs) such as Oxfam, Save the Children and CARE. The aid they provide may be delivered in a variety of ways from emergency aid in times of crisis to assistance with local development projects.

A comparison of two aid providers: an NGO (Oxfam) and an international financial institution (the International Monetary Fund, or IMF).

	Oxfam	IMF
Started	1943	1945
Reason	To respond to famine in Nazi-occupied Greece	To create financial stability in world financial markets
Who set it up	A mixture of academics and religious groups in Oxford, UK	The four allied powers at the end of World War Two: France, Russia, Britain and the US
Aims	Oxfam's mission statement highlights the five key rights that Oxfam aims to provide: • The right to life and security • The right to a sustainable livelihood • The right to basic social services • The right to be heard • The right to equity This is based on three core values: empowerment, inclusiveness and accountability	The IMF states that its aim is 'to foster global monetary co-operation, secure financial stability, facilitate international trade, promote high employment and sustainable economic growth, and reduce poverty around the world'
How is it funded?	Through donations – Oxfam claim that 88% of donations are used to fund projects	The IMF is funded by payments from its member organizations. Contributions are proportional to a country's GDP
Who controls it?	Oxfam is a registered charity, overseen by a number of trustees. In recent years it has undergone a restructuring to support collaboration between the Oxfam affiliates in a range of different countries, including India, and to increase its international impact	The IMF is controlled by its member states. The number of votes is proportionate to the amount of money states pay each year. The US has control and an effective veto. The IMF has commonly been run by economists appointed by the EU with a neoliberal philosophy
Philosophy	Oxfam's work is founded on a rights-based approach and a belief in bottom-up development	The IMF traditionally has had a neoliberal philosophy. This means a belief in small government, free trade and in services being provided by private companies wherever possible. It inevitably has a top-down approach to development
Justification	Set up as a humanitarian agency to provide for people's basic needs in emergencies but evolved over the years to be just as concerned with human development over the long term. It accepts some government money but is mainly funded by individual donors who expect their money to be used to relieve poverty.	Set up by governments to prevent financial crises. Most key positions are held by economists with neoliberal beliefs. Its funds are largely provided by wealthy countries such as the US and the UK, which often hold similar neoliberal economic principles.

There is a tendency for rich countries to give more money to multilateral development banks such as the World Bank (WB) and the Asian Development Bank (ADB), where voting is weighted and they can have more influence over where the aid money goes, and less to the United Nations agencies where voting is equal and less of the money is returned to the donor countries. For example, in 2006-07, Australia gave more than $203.2 million to the World Bank and the Asian Development Bank, as compared to $60.6 million to UN agencies.

AID/WATCH

Witness

Aid may also come from Official Development Assistance (ODA). Put simply, this is official financing or other forms of assistance, given by governments to other countries so as to promote and implement development. Money from ODA may be given directly to the country concerned (bilateral aid) or to another organization to distribute such as the United Nations or the World Bank (multilateral aid).

The amount of money available as ODA depends entirely upon the decisions made by individual national governments. In the 1980s the UN set a target for OECD countries of 0.7% of GNP to be contributed to ODA – but this target has only been met by five countries: Denmark, Norway, Sweden, Luxembourg and the Netherlands.

How is aid given?

Aid may be in the form of grants, or of loans that have to be repaid at less than the market rate. Alternatively it can involve writing off debt. Debt levels in some developing countries have been unsustainable for many years – in many cases the repayments on debt incurred by previous generations have exceeded the amount received in new aid or loans. The issue of debt is discussed later in this chapter.

In attempting to make aid more effective, money has increasingly been given in the form of core funding, known as general budget support (GBS), or with funding earmarked for a particular sector, such as agriculture or health (known as sector-wide approaches, or SWAPs). In 2004 only $2 billion of the $79 billion global aid budget was in GBS form but the proportion has increased markedly in recent years. GBS or SWAPs funding enables governments to spend aid on recurring costs such as teachers' and health workers' salaries and makes it less likely that it will be spent on prestigious projects of little long-term value. It is likely that more aid programmes will be delivered through GBS in future but if this is to be successful there will have to be a long-term commitment from donor countries.

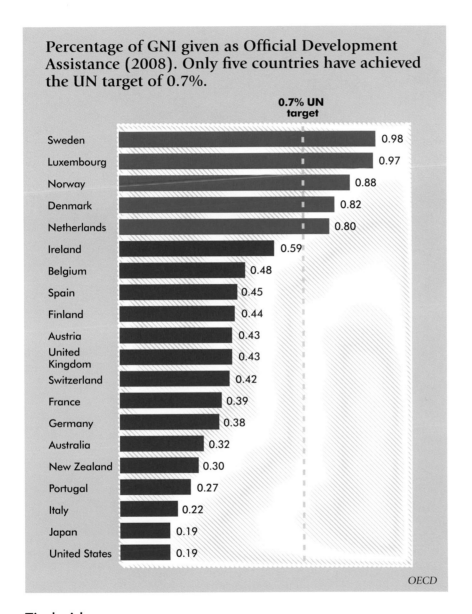

Percentage of GNI given as Official Development Assistance (2008). Only five countries have achieved the UN target of 0.7%.

0.7% UN target

Sweden	0.98
Luxembourg	0.97
Norway	0.88
Denmark	0.82
Netherlands	0.80
Ireland	0.59
Belgium	0.48
Spain	0.45
Finland	0.44
Austria	0.43
United Kingdom	0.43
Switzerland	0.42
France	0.39
Germany	0.38
Australia	0.32
New Zealand	0.30
Portugal	0.27
Italy	0.22
Japan	0.19
United States	0.19

OECD

Tied aid

Some aid packages are described as 'tied' aid because they are conditional and will only be given if the recipient country abides by certain conditions – such as purchasing certain goods from the donor country or building a road or dam with the aid money. Building projects often require the participation of contractors from the donor country. On other occasions money may be withheld if a country fails to hold elections or undertake structural changes to its economy. In

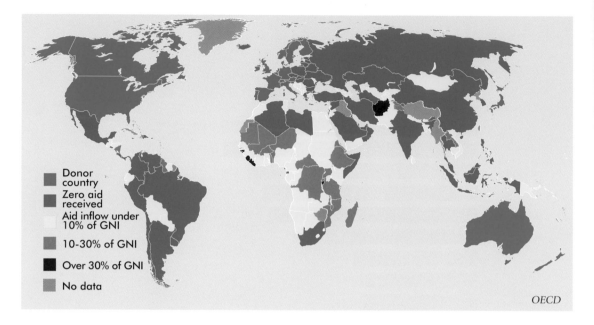

Donor
country

Zero aid
received

Aid inflow under
10% of GNI

10-30% of GNI

Over 30% of GNI

No data

OECD

these ways, donor countries seek to impose their own political doctrine on the receiving country.

Emergency food aid can save lives and there are times when it is desperately needed. However, most food aid channelled through the World Food Programme (WFP) and NGOs is sourced in the donor country. This is a form of tied aid. Aid organizations would prefer to receive cash, which would allow them to buy food locally or in neighbouring countries – this not only provides more appropriate and cheaper food but is also less likely to damage local markets. Over 90% of the food aid given by the US is in the form of tied aid so as to support its own farmers and food processors.

Aid as % of recipient GNI, 2008.

What is the value of aid?

There are arguments about the value of aid and its use in developing countries. Critics point out that the US contributes a relatively low percentage of its GNI but remains a major aid contributor, as you would expect from a country with the biggest economy in the world. However, most of its aid is given to countries to promote its own political and strategic interests or US exports. In 2008, for example, the largest recipients of US aid were Israel and Egypt (accounting between them for 25% of all US aid) – and many other key recipients were geopolitical allies in the 'war on terror' or the 'war on drugs'. Many donors undermine the quality of the aid they are providing by imposing their own preferred economic policy reforms. This 'conditionality' often obliges poor countries to implement policies based on dogma and ideology – for example, privatization and economic liberalization, which have a debatable impact on reducing poverty.

Of course, not all aid programmes have these characteristics. Aid from many countries and organizations is at the heart of programmes that attempt to improve the health of the poorest people in the developing world or make agriculture more productive to alleviate food supply problems. It is true, however, that the value of aid to countries in the developing world is the subject of intense debate.

Different perspectives on the nature and value of aid

Bauer – A neoliberal perspective

Neoliberals are least supportive of the principle of giving aid to developing countries and their views were expressed most clearly by the Austrian-British economist Peter Bauer (1915-2002). He took the view that aid is a form of protectionism that can destroy the entrepreneurial spirit in a country and slow down the development process. He stated that without foreign aid there would be no concept of 'Third World' countries – he believed that the aid programme politicized economies and directed money into the hands of governments rather than potentially profitable businesses. The result was, he argued, that interest groups competed for control of the aid money rather than engaging in more productive activities. He summed up his views by stating that aid has become 'an excellent method for transferring money from poor people in rich

Porters wait to deliver sacks of food aid in drought-hit Niger in 2010.

countries (through taxation) to rich people in poor countries'.

As a neoliberal, Bauer did not see the colonial period as the destructive event that dependency theorists describe. He believed that developed countries are investing in misguided aid projects as a consequence of the guilt they feel about their colonial past. He claimed that former colonies have actually done better than other developing countries, having benefited from close relationships with rich countries that have helped them with trade and technology transfers. He identified the rise of NICs as evidence for this claim. As far as Bauer is concerned, aid makes countries dependent on external help and has developed a momentum of its own that does not serve the interests of the majority in developing countries.

A social studies lesson in a school funded by voluntary aid in Nsanje district, Malawi.

Criticism from the left – a neo-Marxist view of aid.

It is not only the political right that believes that aid can be damaging to the interests of developing countries. Neo-Marxist interpretations of aid focus on the way that aid is often tied and gives the rich countries continued power over the poorer developing countries. Aid is seen as a form of imperialism because aid is almost invariably given, not to the poorest who need it most, but to countries where it can serve the strategic interest of the donor. They contend that it is often given to countries in support of a system that works against the interests of the poor. They would point to US aid to countries of strategic importance in the Middle East, such as Israel and Egypt, as examples of this process. Dependency theorists tend to view official aid programmes as an extension of the neo-colonial relationship in which rich countries continue to dictate the terms.

Polman – radical opposition to aid.

A more radical opposition to aid is expressed by Linda Polman. She argues that humanitarian aid has become a massive industry that often unwittingly supports war-mongering factions and allows them to continue fighting long after they would normally have to give up. She cites the way in which Hutu 'killers', who fled from Rwanda in 1994 after their part in the attempted genocide of the Tutsis, received food, shelter and support from international aid agencies while their surviving victims were left destitute. 'Without humanitarian aid,' she claims, 'the Hutus' war would almost certainly have ground to a halt.'

In the same way, Polman believes that the massive global aid programme spearheaded by Band Aid in 1984 was actually responsible for prolonging the civil war in Ethiopia. Her perspective on the current war in Afghanistan is similar.

The problems with aid programmes

Even those who support the use of aid to improve levels of development concede that aid is not always used in the right way, by the donor or the recipient. There are many examples of aid programmes where there have been one or more of the following problems:

- Aid given to corrupt or undemocratic governments
- Aid used to strengthen armed forces

Failed aid projects

The World Bank's private arm, the International Finance Corporation, has admitted that only half of its projects in Africa succeed. A key example is the oil pipeline it financed in Chad.

Project: Chad-Cameroon oil pipeline to the Atlantic Ocean

Donor: World Bank

Cost: $4.2 billion

Where it went wrong: The pipeline was the biggest development project in Africa when it was completed in 2003. It was funded on condition that the money be spent with international supervision to develop Chad. However, President Idris Deby's government announced in 2005 that oil money would go toward the general budget and the purchase of weapons, or else oil companies would be expelled. Oil money has since been consistently spent on regime survival and rigged elections.

Feature

> **Band Aid – Ethiopia 1984: Did it really make a difference?**
> Michael Buerk's first BBC report from the famine zone opened with the words, 'Dawn, and as the sun breaks through the piercing chill of night on the plains outside Korem, it lights up a biblical famine, now, in the 20th century.' Apart from the facts that it was dawn and there was a famine, nothing in what Buerk said was right. It was precisely not a biblical famine, in the locusts/great flood/visitation-from-God sense that Buerk was evoking. It was, rather, a man-made famine – the direct and, in all likelihood, inevitable result of deliberate policies in Addis Ababa by the Stalinist government of Mengistu Haile Mariam. That is to say, it was a famine that was more likely to occur in the 20th century – the heyday of man-made famines – than at any other time in human history.
>
> Peter Gill, *Famine and Foreigners: Ethiopia since Live Aid*

Witness

- Aid used for projects that harm the environment
- Aid used for projects where most of benefits go to highly paid advisers from abroad with no local knowledge.

Achieving any cohesion in the design and management of aid programmes has also been a problem. A regular complaint from those who are evaluating the effectiveness of aid projects is that different agencies have overlapping and unco-ordinated approaches that diminish their overall effectiveness. Failing to involve the state sufficiently in the planning and implementation stages may also handicap efforts to build participation and develop active citizenship.

The famine in Ethiopia in 1984 was the subject of a massive global fundraising campaign led by the rock star Bob Geldof and featured the first globally televised concert. This raised $144 million and was hailed as a great achievement by millions of people all over the world. In the last few years some people have criticized the long-term impact of that aid effort and questioned its real value, claiming that there has been no real benefit to the country.

Large amounts of aid risk distorting the relationship between the state and its population in much the same way as windfall oil revenues. Civil rights may become a low priority in an oil-rich state where wealth is concentrated in the hands of a few people. Aid-dependent governments may also be inclined to respond more to the interests and desires of donors than to those of their citizens. One study claimed to have found a 'robust statistical relationship between high aid levels in Africa and deteriorations in governance', arguing that 'political élites have little incentive to change a situation in which large amounts of aid provide exceptional resources

'Large amounts of aid risk distorting the relationship between the state and its population in much the same way as windfall oil revenues.'

for patronage and many fringe benefits' (Brautigam & Knack, 2004). One possible way out of this problem is to fund organizations within the country that hold the aid recipients accountable for the aid they receive. Some economists, including many in the IMF, also argue that large aid inflows cause economic problems in recipient countries, such as rising inflation, an artificially high and damaging exchange rate and other effects that undermine economic competitiveness.

The case for aid

Even those who support aid provide widely divergent explanations for doing so. Some see aid as a generous gesture from people in the developed world attempting to rebalance the inequalities in the global distribution of income. Others see it as minimal reparation for problems caused by the rich countries through colonialism and unfair terms of trade. Still others argue that it is necessary for the promotion of human rights and democracy.

Aid was meant to help the poor living in developing countries break out of the cycle of poverty. It could be argued that not much has been achieved in the last 50 years and that this is proof that aid is not working. One estimate of growth in the developing world claims that, in the last 30 years, aid has added one percentage point to the growth rates of the poorest countries. This does not sound much but even at this low level it does suggest that aid can make a difference.

Some conclude from this that aid needs to be given in far larger amounts. Jeffrey Sachs argues this case and presents it as a moral alternative to neoliberal views of non-interference. As far as Sachs is concerned, those who are born in developing countries do not have the same life chances as people born in the developed world. He argues that the richer countries should provide much larger-scale aid programmes to lift people out of poverty and equalize their life chances (J Sachs, 2008).

Other proponents of aid, such as William Easterly, reject this analysis and argue that providing aid in this way will mean top-down and inappropriate programmes that are bound to fail. What is needed, he argues, is more small-scale, home-grown initiatives that are sustainable because they offer genuine local participation and involvement. For Easterly, it is the quality of the aid projects that is the problem at the moment and not the amounts of money given by donor countries.

Critics of both these approaches claim that they take little account of the influence of politics and the role of the state in creating the conditions for the success of aid programmes. Sachs' proposed interventions are also limited to agriculture, basic social services and basic rural infrastructure. The assumption is that combating poverty will enable economic growth whereas evidence from countries such as China,

> ## Sachs and Easterly – contrasting perspectives
>
> ### Jeffrey Sachs
>
> #### The problem
> Aid has not been successful in eradicating poverty because it has not been given on a large enough scale. Poverty itself leads to underinvestment in basic services (such as health and education) and leads to deeper poverty.
>
> #### Solutions
> Massive injection of aid by rich countries. Target basic services (agriculture, education, health, water and sanitation, communication and transport) to unlock the poverty trap. Then poor people will be able to save, invest and prosper on their own.
>
> ### William Easterly
>
> #### The problem
> Aid has failed because it is planned from the top down, without accountability structures and without feedback from the people served.
>
> #### Solutions
> In contrast with top-down measures, bottom-up programmes find out what local people want, and supply it using market mechanisms.
> Make aid agents individually accountable. Evaluate aid programmes more thoroughly, based on feedback from the intended beneficiaries.
> Reward success and penalize failure.

Vietnam and South Korea suggests that this is not necessarily the case – in these countries, industrialization came before a reduction in poverty, implying that a change in the economic structure is needed. In contrast, Easterly's views are criticized for being over-reliant on market solutions in places where the people are too poor to generate market demand – he insists, for example, that 'the parts of the world that are still poor are suffering from too little capitalism.'

The aid debate continues, though few would dispute that in emergencies it is essential for the immediate survival of many of those involved. The earthquake crisis in Haiti in January 2010 and the floods in Pakistan in August 2010 emphasized aid's importance at the same time as they underlined the extreme difficulties that may be encountered in providing the right sort of assistance.

Effective aid
It is not difficult to find examples of aid programmes that have been effective in promoting development. The box opposite provides some

details of a scheme supported by the British voluntary organization
ActionAid in the Rumphi district of northern Malawi.

Recognizing that there are problems with the design and
implementation of some aid programmes is important but that
awareness has to be balanced by understanding how successful well
planned and carefully constructed aid projects can be in promoting
development. Participation and empowerment of individuals and
communities is increasingly recognized as a vital ingredient in
successful aid programmes.

Life after divorce

Most of the people in the
district are poor and live by
farming. Most of the farming
is done by women – but
women have no rights to
own or inherit the land. It
is very difficult for a woman
to provide for a family if
she is by herself and unjust
land rights that discriminate
against women are the
main reason that families
go hungry in the Rumphi
district. The aid project
aims to educate women and
men about women's rights
and tries to persuade tribal
leaders to allow women to
own and inherit land.

Thadu Chidimba (photographed) was divorced by her husband
and left with five children and 12 nephews and nieces to look after
because three of her sisters had died. She had no way of supporting
them and they often went without food. After meetings were
held in the village, the chief was persuaded to give a plot of land
to a group of women farmers, including Chidimba. The women
have been very successful and grow maize, cassava, groundnuts,
vegetables and herbs all year round. With the profit from the
surplus, Chidimba has also been able to buy pigs and cattle. She is
now able to feed all her family and send them to school.

From *Fertile Ground*, ActionAid, 2010

Feature

Participation

A Participatory Poverty Assessment (PPA) is a tool that allows NGOs and governments to consult the poor directly; the findings are transmitted to policymakers, allowing the poor to influence their decisions.

Unlike a household survey, which consists of a predetermined set of questions, a PPA uses a variety of flexible participatory methods that combine visual techniques (mapping, matrices, diagrams) and verbal techniques (open-ended interviews, discussion groups) emphasizing exercises that facilitate information sharing, analysis and action.

It has been recognized that an approach dominated by economic analysis fails to capture the many dimensions of poverty, while a multidisciplinary approach can deepen understanding of the lives of the poor. PPAs, with their focus on well-being and quality of life, have consistently shown that the poor are not only affected by low income but also by such problems as vulnerability, physical and social isolation, insecurity, lack of self-respect, lack of access to information, distrust of state institutions and powerlessness.

PPAs have grown in importance. This is because the World Bank has started requiring all countries to have Poverty Reduction Strategy Papers (PRSPs) and part of the information that forms the basis of these documents has to come from PPAs.

How does participation fit with development theories?

Although participation as a way of helping to reduce the effects of poverty is not a new development model, it does not fit with all theories of development. Both modernization and neoliberal theorists share the belief that the traditional values operating at community level are 'non-economic barriers to development'. They believe that local communities are 'backward' and that they can offer no useful approach to improving economic conditions.

Some argue that these negative perceptions of local communities have dominated mainstream development thinking and Wolfgang Sachs and Arturo Escobar believe that they ignore the positive side of local cultures and the value systems that they invariably contain. These academics believe that there are indigenous cultural practices that share assets at a community level and reduce people's exposure to risk in times of hardship. An example might be the Hindu *jajamni* system where all castes within a village provide goods and services for each other in return for a share of the harvest.

Why is participation important?

Participation involves people pooling their efforts to attain their objectives. The cartoon opposite demonstrates why participation needs

everyone to be included because everyone experiences poverty differently.
Among the benefits of grassroots participation are that it:
* Delivers change and improvement to people's lives and environments
* Gets more individuals and communities active and engaged
* Fosters understanding of how local action connects to global issues
* Builds ownership and responsibility for the longer term
* Helps to establish and meet local targets that complement national ones
* Lessens hostility to environmental change.

The Paris Declaration on Aid Effectiveness

All aid organizations are becoming more accountable for the quality of their aid programmes – both to the recipients of the aid and to the donating public. Major events that highlighted the aid-giving process such as the Drop the Debt and Make Poverty History campaigns of the late 1990s and early 2000s led to a search to find ways to make aid more effective. The Paris Declaration on Aid Effectiveness in 2005 emerged from a conference attended by representatives from all the countries, agencies and regional and international banks that participate in the aid process. It was agreed that, wherever possible, developing countries should formulate and implement their own development plans according to their own priorities.

The Paris Declaration is a multi-layered commitment to improve aid to developing countries but is focused on five key principles:
1. **Ownership**: Developing countries must lead their own development

policies and strategies, and manage their own development work
on the ground. The target set by the Paris Declaration was for
three-quarters of developing countries to have their own national
development strategies by 2010.

2. **Alignment**: Donors must structure their aid programmes so that
   they are aligned with the priorities outlined in developing countries'
   national development strategies. They must use local institutions
   and procedures for managing aid wherever possible in order to build
   sustainable structures. They also promised to 'untie' their aid from
   any obligation that it be spent on donor-country goods and services.

3. **Harmonization**: Donors must co-ordinate their development
   work better to avoid duplication and high transaction costs for
   poor countries. They agreed on a target of providing two-thirds
   of all their aid via 'programme-based approaches' by 2010. This
   means that aid is pooled in support of a particular strategy (such as
   universal primary education) rather than fragmented into multiple
   individual projects.

4. **Managing for results**: Agencies involved in the aid process must
   improve their means of monitoring the impact of aid schemes and
   the impact they make on poor people's lives.

5. **Mutual accountability**: Donors and developing countries must
   account more transparently to each other for their use of aid funds,
   and to their citizens and parliaments for the impact of their aid. The
   Paris Declaration says all countries must have procedures in place by
   2010 to report back openly on their development results.

Debt relief

Measuring the flows of money into and out of developing countries
does help to give a clearer picture of the relevance of aid to poorer
countries. According to the IMF and World Bank, sub-Saharan Africa
has over $231 billion in external debt (2010) and though the region
receives $10 billion in aid per year, it loses more than $14 billion in
debt payments annually. In other words there is a net flow of capital in
favour of the rich countries. Relieving the countries of their high debt
levels would do more to help development than can be achieved with
current aid levels. Improvements in their relative terms of trade could
make even more of a difference.

The Jubilee Drop the Debt Campaign leading up to 2000 was, in
some ways, one of the most successful international initiatives ever.
Its aim was to campaign for the abolition of unfair debt in developing
countries. It organized a campaign in 166 countries and 28 million
people signed the world's largest petition. To publicize the initiative,
mass participation events were held – for example, the human chain of

70,000 people in Birmingham, England, in 1998. Awareness was raised by using celebrities like Brad Pitt.

The campaign has been partly successful. By 2010, 30 of the poorest countries in the world had benefited from $88 billion in debt cancellation and there is evidence that spending on public services has risen across these countries. In 10 African countries where debt has been cancelled there has been an increase in spending of around 40% on education and 70% on healthcare.

Campaigners against debt march during the World Social Forum in Nairobi, Kenya, in 2007.

Other impacts of debt relief

- When primary school fees in Uganda were removed, partly as a result of debt relief, the number of children enrolled in primary schools more than doubled (to more than 5 million) over the next four years. Enrolments increased by another 50% (2.7 million more children) in the four years after that
- Over 2,000 new schools and nearly 32,000 new classrooms were built in Tanzania in three years
- In 2003, Zambia spent twice as much on debt repayments as on healthcare. Now, thanks to debt cancellation, it has abolished user fees at rural clinics to give citizens free basic medical services
- 3,600 new teachers are being trained each year in Malawi
- A free childhood immunization programme has been introduced in Mozambique; so far, almost a million children have been vaccinated against killer diseases

- In Uganda, debt relief led to 2.2 million people gaining access to clean water.

Notwithstanding these successes, the debt relief given to poor countries is still very small compared to the $222 billion still owed by the poorest 48 countries – let alone to the $3.4 trillion owed by the poorest 128 countries.

The long delay in making debt relief available to countries is another problem. The HIPC (Heavily Indebted Poor Country) initiative was launched by the IMF in 1996. Countries on the list have to complete a two-stage process before any debt relief is given.

The process has taken over 10 years for some of the 28 countries

---

The IMF two-stage process

First step: decision point. To be considered for HIPC Initiative assistance, a country must fulfil the following four conditions. It must:

- be eligible to borrow from the World Bank's International Development Agency, which provides interest-free loans and grants to the world's poorest countries, and from the IMF's Extended Credit Facility, which provides loans to low-income countries at subsidized rates
- face an unsustainable debt burden that cannot be addressed through traditional debt relief mechanisms
- have established a track record of reform and sound policies through IMF- and World Bank-supported programmes
- have developed a Poverty Reduction Strategy Paper (PRSP) through a broad-based participatory process in the country.

Once a country has met or made sufficient progress in meeting these four criteria, the Executive Boards of the IMF and World Bank formally decide on its eligibility for debt relief, and the international community commits to reducing debt to a level that is considered sustainable. This first stage under the HIPC Initiative is referred to as the decision point. Once a country reaches its decision point, it may immediately begin receiving interim relief on its debt service falling due.

Second step: completion point. In order to receive full and irrevocable reduction in debt available under the HIPC Initiative, a country must:

- establish a further track record of good performance under programmes supported by loans from the IMF and the World Bank
- implement satisfactorily key reforms agreed at the decision point
- adopt and implement its PRSP for at least one year.

Once a country has met these criteria, it can reach its completion point, which allows it to receive the full debt relief committed at decision point.

Feature

List of countries that have qualified for, are eligible or potentially eligible for HIPC relief (as of 1 July 2010)

Post-Completion-Point Countries

Afghanistan	The Gambia	Mozambique
Benin	Ghana	Nicaragua
Bolivia	Guyana	Niger
Burkina Faso	Haiti	Rwanda
Burundi	Honduras	São Tomé & Príncipe
Cameroon	Liberia	Senegal
Central African Republic	Madagascar	Sierra Leone
Congo	Malawi	Tanzania
Democratic Republic of Congo	Mali	Uganda
Ethiopia	Mauritania	Zambia

Interim Countries (Between Decision and Completion Point)

Chad	Côte d'Ivoire	Guinea-Bissau
Comoros	Guinea	Togo

Pre-Decision-Point Countries

Eritrea	Kyrgyzstan
Somalia	Sudan

that have been given debt relief. Critics attack the HIPC Initiative for the stringent conditions imposed on countries, which include following the IMF's rigid economic policy prescriptions. They also point out that the process is limited to only a few countries and does not include all debt in the cancellation agreement. Critics further claim that this is because the process of debt relief is controlled by the creditors – who do not accept any responsibility for their part in creating and maintaining the debt crisis. The debt cancellation also does not apply to money owed to private banks.

Nevertheless, the gains for those countries that have made it to the end of the process are very real – and are borne out by the concrete evidence from villages and city streets. For example, before 2006, when Malawi was granted debt relief by the IMF, 25% of its budget was spent on foreign debt repayment. In the year following debt relief Malawi was able to increase its spending on agriculture, health and education by 25%, 83% and 56% respectively (see box overleaf).

It is indisputable that debt relief is desperately important to poor

A clinic that works

Forty-year-old Limbikani Simbota, his wife Linile and their six children live in Kauma village, just on the outskirts of Malawi's capital, Lilongwe. Limbani works as a security guard, earning 5,000 kwacha ($35) a month, while Linile is a housewife. With their meagre financial resources, life has been hard for the family, but access to public services, especially health, education and clean water, is a must for their survival.

Limbikani remembers how difficult it used to be to get medical care at the nearest health centre. After travelling five kilometres to the understaffed clinic, he would spend hours queuing, only to be told in the end that there was no medicine available and that he would have to buy drugs from a private hospital or pharmacy instead. The long waits and lack of medicines at the clinic meant that, within Limbikani's community, working hours were often wasted and sicknesses left untreated.

However, from 2006 Malawi began to receive help from the Heavily Indebted Poor Countries (HIPC) initiative, which releases countries from their foreign debts. Before then, Malawi was creaking under $3 billion of debt, with a quarter of the national budget going towards foreign debt repayment. Now, Malawi is able to spend more money on essentials like health, education and agriculture.

Linile confesses that she does not really know the meaning of external debt cancellation. However, she can see that the clinic is much better now than four years ago, as there are adequate amounts of medicine and enough medical personnel to attend to patients. In the past, most people opted to bypass the clinic and go straight to the referral hospital, about eight kilometres away. This created heavy congestion at the referral hospital, which often lacked medical supplies itself.

UK Department for International Development 2009

Witness

countries. The extra national income gained by not having to repay debt is money spent by the government of that country and not by a foreign agency. The extra money has to be allocated on agreed reforms and poverty reduction strategies but the process can also benefit governance and improve participation in the development process. The potential long-term gain from debt relief is worth more than just the money.

Key statistics on Haiti	
Total external debt	$1.2 billion
Total external debt payments	Haiti gave $92 million to the rich world in 2007 in debt payments.
Population	10.0 million
Poverty	75% of people live on less than $2 a day
Average life expectancy	61 years
HIV prevalence rate	1.9%

Debt relief in Haiti

Haiti is the poorest country in the western hemisphere and is ranked 145th (out of 169) in the HDI rankings. The IMF had previously refused to consider it for entry to the list of HIPC countries until it finally changed its mind in October 2006. In July 2010 the IMF announced the cancellation of all debts owed to it (see the Jubilee Debt Campaign box overleaf).

Queuing for food aid in Port-au-Prince in front of a building devastated by the 2010 earthquake.

Jubilee Debt Campaign view

Why should the debt be cancelled?

This money was used to prop up a corrupt and oppressive regime and should not be repaid at the expense of those who have already suffered at the hands of this regime. The Haitian people should not have to pay for the crimes of their past leaders. Not only did these loans fail to benefit the Haitian people, the consequent debt service payments continue to cost the country millions of dollars that could be better spent on education and health. For example, less than one quarter of children aged between 6 and 12 living in rural areas are enrolled in school. Haiti is one of the countries worst affected by the recent huge increase in food prices, which has led to riots and social unrest. The devastating earthquake in January 2010 and the humanitarian disaster it brought renewed the urgency for total debt cancellation to aid its recovery.

Debt cancellation

Haiti finished the HIPC programme by meeting the conditions set by the IMF. It subsequently had $1.2 billion of its debt wiped off. However, as of 2010, interest on its remaining debts, and debts that were not included under the HIPC scheme has meant it still faces a massive $1 billion debt that needs to be serviced to the rich world. This debt is even more abhorrent if we now consider the devastation caused in early 2010 by an earthquake in one of the poorest countries in the world. The Jubilee Debt Campaign calls for further debt cancellation that will allow the Haitian government and people to cope with the aftermath of such a tragic event.

Witness

7 Trade & Development

How fair is global trade?

* *Trade has increased significantly since globalization but the least developed countries are still those which are the least involved in the global trade system.*
* *Developing countries often rely on single commodities for a large share of their trade, which makes them very vulnerable.*
* *Fluctuations in the price of commodities adversely affect the terms of trade of the poorest countries. Even a small increase in the developing world's share of world trade could bring major benefits.*
* *There are disagreements about whether or not the liberalization of trade benefits the least developed countries.*
* *Individual countries have joined together to form large trade blocs so as to promote and protect their trading interests.*

Key points

Global trade

All measures of the value and volume of trade since the early 1990s have shown a large increase. It is clear that this increased trade has benefited richer nations far more than it has poorer countries. Although the ratio of exports to GDP has risen for most countries over the last 50 years, even in developing countries, the 49 poorest countries only have a total global share of trade of 0.6% (2008) compared to the 37% of the top five exporting countries (the US, France, Germany, Japan and the UK). The poorest countries' share of global trade has halved since the 1980s.

The nature of the goods traded by these two groups is also completely different. For the majority of the poorer, smaller, countries the main exports are crops or raw materials that are exported to a limited number of countries, often former colonial powers. For example, copper accounts for 70% of Zambia's export trade and coffee for 73% of Burundi's export trade. This exceptionally high reliance on a single

'The world's

49

poorest countries account for 0.6% of global trade.

The top 5

exporting countries account for 37%.'

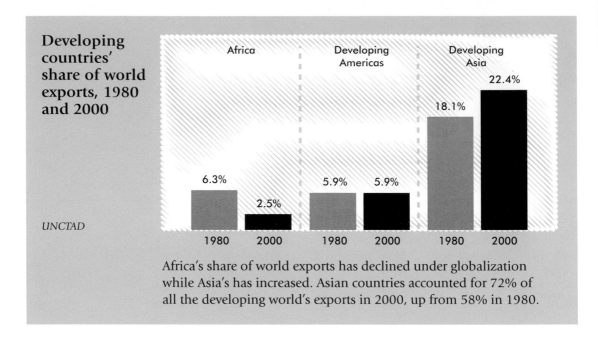

Developing countries' share of world exports, 1980 and 2000

UNCTAD

Africa's share of world exports has declined under globalization while Asia's has increased. Asian countries accounted for 72% of all the developing world's exports in 2000, up from 58% in 1980.

commodity makes the country very vulnerable to fluctuations in prices for minerals or weather conditions for crops. There are other factors such as taste and fashion trends in rich countries that may also adversely affect producers in developing countries.

Terms of trade

'Terms of trade' refers to the cost of goods that a country has to import compared with the price at which they can sell the goods they export.

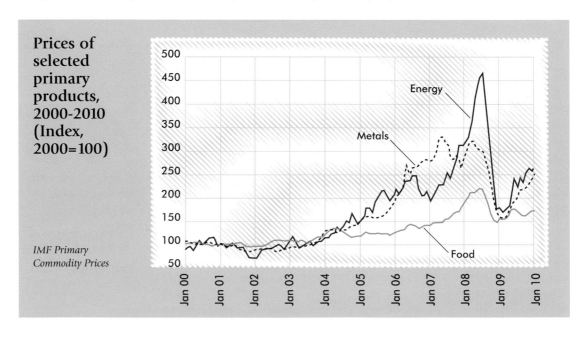

Prices of selected primary products, 2000-2010 (Index, 2000=100)

IMF Primary Commodity Prices

The majority of goods exported by the richer countries are manufactured goods, which have high added value. The price of these goods has tended to rise steadily over a period of time.

The price of the crops and minerals exported by most developing countries, on the other hand, follows a much less predictable path, fluctuating erratically. In recent years manufactured goods have become more expensive in relation to primary products. In real terms, this means that poorer countries have to sell more of their main exports if they are to purchase the manufactured goods that they need, such as medical equipment or agricultural machinery. These deteriorating terms of trade have led directly to increased poverty in some developing countries.

Occasionally developing countries may benefit from changes in the price of commodities or changes in the pattern of world trade. Oil prices rose sharply at the start of 2008 and this meant that African oil producers, such as Nigeria, could substantially increase their export earnings. The increased earnings have been estimated as approximately $30 billion a year, which is more than the whole of Africa receives in aid. In the same period there was a major increase in trade between many African countries and China as a result of China's continued global search for raw materials needed for its rapid industrial expansion. This increased demand from China has pushed up the price of many minerals and benefited some African economies. At the same time the lower price of many Chinese goods also helped consumers in Africa and other developing countries.

Different perspectives on global trade

Dependency theorists see trade as another opportunity for the rich Global North to continue the exploitation of poorer countries that started in the colonial period. Rich countries dominate world trade because of their

Campaigners for trade justice marching in London in 2004.

economic power, their control of the World Trade Organization (WTO) and their manipulation of commodity prices. The relatively low incomes from trade for developing countries do not allow them to improve their levels of wealth and social development.

Neoliberals, on the other hand, believe that trade restrictions cause distortions in world trade. They argue that the opening of national markets to international competition would allow the markets to operate fairly and effectively and to ensure that countries will prosper by using their 'comparative advantage' to produce goods at a price that others are prepared to pay. They believe that all countries, rich and poor, would benefit from the resulting increase in international trade.

The indisputable reality is that most developing countries have opened up their national markets to foreign companies and international trade because they have no other choice. Rich countries, meanwhile, continue to impose protectionist policies, including tariffs and quotas

---

World trade talks fail

The most recent talks on the liberalization of world trade, held in Doha in 2008, failed to reach an agreement that would have improved trading opportunities for the poorest countries. The main stumbling block to progress was the protection that the developed world wanted to continue to give its own farmers through farm subsidies, although there was also a failure to agree on the extent of liberalization of services such as banking and telecommunications. Most countries agreed on the notion of a 'safeguard clause' that would allow a country to impose tariffs on imported goods if there was a big drop in the price of an agricultural product within that country or a large increase in imports but the US argued that the level of the safeguard had been set too low and intense negotiations with India and China failed to reach an agreement.

The failure of the talks was seen as a big blow to the expansion of global trade but some people feel that it is easy to exaggerate the impact of the failure of the talks. Some of the measures discussed at the talks had implementation periods of up to 14 years and therefore it is unlikely that there will be any immediate global impact. However some economists see the talks as a major failure of the multilateral approach to negotiations concerning world trade and predict that it is much more likely to lead to a series of agreements carried out on a regional or bilateral basis because they are much easier to negotiate. If this does happen it will put the smaller and poorer countries at a disadvantage when they are negotiating with richer and more powerful countries.

BBC news, 28 August 2008

Witness

Seven deadly WTO rules

1 WTO limits protection against cheap food imports

Developing countries are restricted from intervening and raising barriers against cheap food imports, while export food subsidies by rich countries are allowed to continue.

The outcome is a flood of food imports that undermines local producers and threatens the lives of many poor people.

2 WTO limits government regulation of services

Countries which agree to sign up must open up their services sectors to foreign suppliers by abolishing restrictions on access to those markets.

The outcome may be that services such as health, education and water supply are run and controlled by profit-driven foreign companies.

3 WTO limits regulation of foreign investment

There is a ban on policies and regulations favouring the use of domestic over foreign products.

The outcome is the denial of some ways that a poor country may support the development of local industries over foreign producers.

4 WTO limits the use of agricultural subsidies

Some of the poorest countries are limited in their ability to increase subsidies to agriculture and some subsidies may be banned altogether. Meanwhile the US and EU are permitted to spend huge amounts of money on agricultural subsidies.

The outcome is to reduce the level of food security of many poor people by restrictions on subsidies and deny poor countries an important development tool.

5 WTO puts limits on industrial subsidies

Governments are prevented from using industrial subsidies to promote the manufacture of domestic products over imported alternatives. Some subsidies of special use to rich countries are permitted.

The outcome is the taking away of a critical policy tool which may help poor countries develop their own industrial sector.

6 WTO blocks exports from developing countries

Rich countries can retain high import barriers or other restrictions against exports from developing countries.

The outcome is a loss of much-needed export revenues and a negative impact on the economic growth rate of many poor economies.

7 WTO gives business rights over knowledge and natural resources

The WTO requires countries to introduce effective patenting laws, including plant varieties and seeds, which can give TNCs rights over those products for 20 years.

The outcome is effectively to legalize biopiracy of natural resources and knowledge.

Christian Aid

Witness

Rigged rules

'World trade has the potential to act as a powerful motor for the reduction of poverty as well as for economic growth, but that potential is being lost. The problem is not that international trade is inherently opposed to the needs and interests of the poor, but that rules that govern it are rigged in favour of the rich.'

Oxfam

Witness

as well as technical regulations to stop imports on health and safety grounds. Developed countries also subsidize agriculture to protect their own farmers. The US subsidizes cotton, corn, wheat and rice production, while the EU subsidizes dairy and meat production.

World Trade Organization

The World Trade Organization (WTO), which now has 146 member countries, implements and advances global trade agreements and resolves trade disputes between nations. It was established in 1995 with the aim of enforcing the free trade of manufactured goods, services and intellectual property amongst its member countries. Its importance in the governance of world trade is not disputed but the impartiality of its rules is not accepted by everybody.

For many observers and campaigning organizations, the WTO has presided over the spread of neoliberal economic policies associated with free trade and has made workers much more vulnerable to the whims of transnational corporations (TNCs) seeking the cheapest places in which to produce their goods. This 'race to the bottom', they maintain, shows the power of TNCs to manipulate global trading conditions and make use of the 'comparative advantage' (cheap labour) offered by developing countries. National governments compete to encourage investment from TNCs and so the price is driven even lower.

The power that rich countries and TNCs have over the nature of their trade with developing countries has undoubtedly led to abuses of poor workers in those countries. Aid organizations and the media have highlighted some of the injustices and it has led to the growth of 'kitemarking' to denote that the product has been produced under conditions where workers are given a fair wage and work under acceptable conditions. The most important of these ethical trade kitemarks is the Fairtrade label.

The growth of Fairtrade

Alternative Trading Organizations (ATOs) have existed since the 1940s and 1950s, mostly organized by religious groups or NGOs. Initially they

Fatuma, a worker with the community organization Just Change India, in their shop in Nettikulam.

focused on giving handicraft producers from the developing countries an opportunity to sell their goods in developed countries. The movement was very small scale until 1988 when the Fairtrade certification movement was created in the Netherlands. It allowed goods produced in developing countries access to the normal distribution channels. The Fairtrade certification of a product guaranteed that it had been produced according to some key principles:

- Environmental sustainability
- Workers allowed to organize democratically and trade unions recognized
- A premium paid to improve social conditions
- No child labour
- Good working conditions and pay
- A long-term relationship between producers and purchasers where prices covered the cost of production and there was usually a guaranteed minimum price.

Starting from products such as coffee and tea, consumers have shown that they are prepared to pay a premium price to guarantee a fair trading relationship with producers in the developing world. The Fairtrade symbol can now be seen on a range of products from bananas to footballs. In 2008, Fairtrade-certified sales amounted to approximately $3.8 billion worldwide, a 22% year-on-year increase. Even in 2009, in the depths of a global recession, Fairtrade sales rose by 10% compared to the previous year. As of December 2008, 746 producer organizations in

58 developing countries were Fairtrade-certified. More than 7.5 million people – farmers, workers and their families – across 59 developing countries benefit from the international Fairtrade system.

Opposition to Fairtrade

The response to the growth of Fairtrade has been mixed. There have been concerns expressed by some that the organization has been unable to monitor the conditions of workers adequately and that some producers have abused the Fairtrade label. Fairtrade's increasing popularity has drawn criticism from the political left and right. The Adam Smith Institute sees Fairtrade as a type of subsidy or marketing ploy that impedes growth. Segments of the left have criticized Fairtrade for not adequately challenging the current trading system – and for certifying products by big companies with questionable credentials, such as Nestlé (see the case study of Fairtrade bananas in the Windward Islands on page 137).

Trade blocs

Another upshot of the increasing globalization over the last 50 years is the gathering together of groups of countries to form trading associations. On the simplest level, these associations exist as free-trade areas within which there are no internal barriers to trade between member countries. An example of this is the North American Free Trade Area (NAFTA). Some groups of countries have gone much further along this road and moved towards full political integration, such as the European Union. Unusually, the European Union also recognizes the free movement of labour as part and parcel of its commitment to free trade. In other trade groups there is a political and cultural resistance to freeing up the movement of labour because to do so would inevitably mean an end to immigration restrictions.

As well as increased integration amongst members of a trading bloc, it is argued that trading blocs help globalization through making global negotiations easier. For example, in the case of trade negotiations the EU will negotiate as a single trading bloc, making it easier to push through new policies or rules. However, there are some economists who feel that the growth of trade blocs encourages regionalism and that the restrictive trade practices that exist within the blocs hinder the movement towards global free trade.

African land grab

For many people interested in global development issues the news that very large areas of land in Africa have been sold or leased to foreign governments and companies is a big concern. The driving force is the increase in global food prices and the increased production of biofuels to

Major trade blocs

European Union

The EU has expanded to incorporate 26 countries and has a combined population of 356 million. Within the EU, there has been a marked integration of the national economies. Trade among member states has increased. There has also been greater movement of capital and labour (notably the movement of migrant workers from Poland to the UK and Ireland). Within the EU, there has also been a single currency and single monetary policy adopted by 11 members.

NAFTA

NAFTA is a treaty between Canada, Mexico, and the US that was designed to foster greater trade between the three countries. NAFTA has been in effect since 1994.

The key goals of NAFTA were:

- to reduce barriers to trade
- to create an expanded and safe market for goods and services produced in North America
- to establish mutually advantageous trade rules
- to help develop and expand world trade and provide a catalyst to broader international co-operation.

Critics have argued that creating the trade bloc only served business interests in the US and ignored the negative social and environmental impacts of free trade on the smaller economies of Mexico and Canada.

MERCOSUR

The Mercosur (formed 1991) trade bloc's purpose is to allow for free trade between member states and counteract the dominant trading influence of the US in the region. Its ultimate goal is full South American economic integration. Mercosur's full members include Argentina, Brazil, Paraguay, Venezuela and Uruguay. Brazil is the region's largest economy with a gross domestic product (GDP) of over $1.6 trillion in 2008. The population of Mercosur's full members totals more than 270 million people. It is the world's fourth-largest trading bloc.

ASEAN

ASEAN stands for the Association of Southeast Asian Nations. It was founded in 1967 in Bangkok, Thailand. Its original charter counted five member-countries: Indonesia, Malaysia, the Philippines, Singapore, and Thailand. Since then, five other nations have joined up: Brunei in 1984, Vietnam in 1995, Burma and Laos in 1997, and Cambodia in 1999. China joined as a Free Trade Partner in January 2010.

Feature

> ### How food and water drive a new foreign land grab in Africa
>
> *The farm manager shows us millions of tomatoes, peppers and other vegetables being grown in 500-metre rows in computer-controlled conditions. Spanish engineers are building the steel structure (for the greenhouses), Dutch technology minimizes water use from two boreholes and 1,000 women pick and pack 50 tonnes of food a day. Within 24 hours, it has been driven 200 miles (320 kilometres) to Addis Ababa and flown 1,000 miles (1,600 kilometres) to the shops and restaurants of Dubai, Jeddah and elsewhere in the Middle East.*
>
> *Ethiopia is one of the hungriest countries in the world, with more than 13 million people needing food, but paradoxically the government is offering at least three million hectares of its most fertile land to rich countries and some of the world's most wealthy individuals.*
>
> *Leading the rush are international agribusinesses, investment banks, hedge funds, commodity traders, sovereign wealth funds as well as UK pension funds, foundations and individuals attracted by some of the world's cheapest land.*
>
> *Together they are scouring Sudan, Kenya, Nigeria, Tanzania, Malawi, Ethiopia, Congo, Zambia, Zimbabwe, Mali, Sierra Leone, Ghana and elsewhere. Ethiopia alone has approved 815 foreign-financed agricultural projects since 2007. Any land which investors have not been able to buy is being leased for approximately $1 per year per hectare.*
>
> *Saudi Arabia, along with other Middle Eastern emirates such as Qatar, Kuwait and Abu Dhabi, is thought to be the biggest buyer. In 2008 the Saudi government, which was one of the Middle East's largest wheat-growers, announced it was to reduce its domestic cereal production by 12% a year to conserve water.*
>
> John Vidal, *The Observer*, 7 March 2010

Witness

try to reduce dependence on oil. The EU will need to grow crops on over 17.5 million hectares (over half the size of Italy) if it is to meet its 10% biofuel target by 2015. European energy companies have acquired about 3.9 million hectares in Africa to help them achieve the target. The World Bank has defended the large-scale buying of land in developing countries by companies from the Global North, claiming that it can facilitate the transfer of technology and technical know-how, and ultimately have positive impacts on local populations. However, the displacement of farmers in countries such as Ethiopia remains problematic (see box above).

It is almost certain that there will be global food shortages in the future. Improving agricultural technology cannot keep pace with the threat to food supplies posed by population increase, climate change, environmental degradation and political instability. Agricultural land in Africa will come under even greater threat from foreign buyers who want to produce the fruit and vegetables needed in wealthy countries. Some argue that this is a repeat of the way that the old colonial powers grabbed African resources 200 years ago but there are others, such as the World Bank, who believe that this new invasion will actually benefit the African continent because of the advantages it will derive from the huge investment in the new agricultural technology brought by agribusiness.

Transnational corporations (TNCs)

A TNC is a business that manages production or delivers services in more than one country. Each TNC has a management headquarters in its home country and operates in several other countries. The largest TNCs have budgets that are much bigger than the annual GNI of many developing countries and for this reason they have considerable international and local influence. Of the 100 largest economies in the world, 52 are corporations and 48 are countries.

The table below shows the world's 10 largest TNCs ranked by the

'Of the 100 **LARGEST** ECONOMIES in the world,

CORPORATIONS

are COUNTRIES.'

Largest TNCs measured by value of foreign assets (2008)

Rank & Name	Home economy	Industry	Value of foreign assets, millions of dollars	Value of total assets, millions of dollars	TNI % (A)	TNI Rank /100 (B)
1 General Electric	US	Electrical & Electronic	401,290	797,769	52	75
2 Royal Dutch/ Shell Group	UK	Petroleum	222,324	282,401	73	32
3 Vodafone	UK	Telecommunications	201,570	218,955	88	6
4 BP	UK	Petroleum	188,969	228,328	81	20
5 Toyota	Japan	Motor Vehicles	196,569	296,249	53	74
6 Exxon	US	Petroleum	161,245	228,052	68	42
7 Total	France	Petroleum	141,442	164,662	75	27
8 E.On	Germany	Utilities	141,168	218,573	56	67
9 Electricité de France	France	Utilities	133,698	278,759	42	90
10 ArcelorMittal	Luxembourg	Metal & metal products	127,127	133,088	87	10

UNCTAD

A – Transnationality Index, calculated as the average of the ratios of foreign assets to total assets, foreign sales to total sales and foreign employees to total employees.
B – Transnationality Index rank within top 100 TNCs ranked by value of foreign assets.

No-one elects the owners and directors of these companies, but they often play a more powerful part in our lives than governments. Increasingly, governments are not even able to control the actions of TNCs, because this is seen as contravening the principles of 'free trade'. A typical TNC operates in many countries. Its head office, where major decisions are taken, will be in one country, but its manufacturing operations may take place in many other countries. Typically, a TNC will find countries with the cheapest labour, and the most relaxed environmental and labour laws, to keep down its costs. If a government tries to impose stricter laws, the TNC can threaten to relocate to another country. This intimidates poorer countries into accepting lower standards, because they do not want to risk losing the jobs and investment the company brings.

Governments and corporations sometimes seem to have a very close relationship. For example, corporations may fund presidential election campaigns, and then wait to be rewarded in return by beneficial government policies. Rich-country governments may force poor countries to accept particular trade deals, or give contracts to particular companies, by threatening to remove or reduce their aid if they do not comply. In this way, corporations manage to influence or even dictate government policy.

Many poor countries have been forced to privatize their services as part of structural adjustment conditions. This means private companies (often TNCs) move in to run services at a profit, such as water systems, railways, and telephone companies. The IMF believes government intervention should be reduced to a minimum. The problem is that, unlike governments, private companies have no obligation to look after the poorest people.

Global Village 2006

Witness

value of their foreign assets. There are many other ways to compare TNCs. In the table the TNI (Transnationality Index) is calculated by averaging the ratio of foreign and total values in assets, sales and employment for each company. A measure that used the total annual sales turnover would have ranked the US company Wal-Mart first in 2008. Financial institutions, such as banks and insurance companies, are usually excluded from TNC league tables because the way they operate makes it difficult to calculate their assets and their turnover would be distorted.

However we measure the size of TNCs, it is clear that they are the most powerful participants in the globalization of the world's economy. Even a brief analysis confirms that their home bases are in the core areas of Europe, North America and the tiger economies of the Far East.

Why are TNCs such an important part of the globalization process? There is no doubt that the location of TNCs in developing countries may

This 'Big Bad World' cartoon by Polyp appeared in *New Internationalist* magazine no 327.

bring many advantages to that country. These may include:
- Employment and training of local labour that can have external benefits for the host country and economy
- Increased growth rate for the host nation because of the introduction of new investment and new technology
- Increased revenue from taxation
- Development of supporting or complementary industries
- Increased tax contributions and foreign exchange that can be used to purchase key imports.

Whilst there is little doubt that international trade has the potential for vast wealth creation for all parties, the evidence that economic growth is not an effective means of poverty reduction is also conclusive. The 40% of the global public who survive on less than $2 a day have received little additional income from economic growth over the past 20 years. Improvements in poverty levels have been isolated to a few regions such as China and East Asia. Most other regions, particularly sub-Saharan Africa, have experienced an increase in poverty levels over the same period. In addition, the inequality of income distribution from growth continues to grow.

The evidence suggests that it is crucial to address inequality if poverty is to be reduced. The reason why trade is unable to deal with inequality is the high concentration of trade that is controlled by transnational corporations. Some 70% of world trade is controlled by just 500 of the largest industrial corporations. The privatization of the majority of goods and services traded has meant that senior management and major shareholders of these corporations are the main beneficiaries of international trade. The benefits are also minimal for the employees of these corporations. In 2002, the top 200 corporations had combined sales equivalent to 28% of world GDP, whilst employing less than 1% of the global workforce.

Rajesh Makwana, Share the World's Resources, 2006

Witness

There are also disadvantages:
- TNCs may have competitive advantages over local firms that destroy local competition
- They may cause environmental damage through lack of production controls and cost cutting
- They may out-source their components from abroad and undermine local business
- They may avoid tax in one country by remitting profits to other countries with lower rates of taxation
- They may 'blackmail' governments and workers in negotiations by threatening to relocate to lower-cost locations.

Given their international reach and mobility, prospective countries, and sometimes regions within countries, must compete with each other to have TNCs locate their facilities (and subsequent tax revenue, employment and economic activity) within their region. To compete, countries and regional political districts offer incentives to TNCs such as tax breaks, pledges of governmental assistance or improved infrastructure, or lax environmental and labour standards. Transnational companies account for all foreign direct investment (FDI) and 70% of world trade is controlled by 500 of the largest industrial corporations. It is difficult to overestimate their influence on the development of global trade.

There are some who believe that the high concentration of power in transnational enterprises is a major problem in the fight against poverty and that increasing levels of trade with developing countries is not necessarily going to benefit the poor. Is trade or aid the better solution to raising levels of development? The answers are never simple.

Coca-Cola CASE STUDY

Global fizz

Coca-Cola is the biggest soft-drinks manufacturer in the world and its headquarters is in Atlanta, Georgia. It employs 92,000 people globally and 86% of those are employed outside the US. It claims to sell its soft drinks in over 200 countries – more than the number of countries in the United Nations. It sells nearly 400 different products and approximately 70% of its sales are generated outside the US. Its total global sales turnover was $31.94 billion in 2009 and its profits were $5.81 billion. It is one of the key sponsors of the FIFA World Cup.

Coca-Cola does not actually make its drinks. The actual production and distribution of Coca-Cola follows a franchising model with over 900 bottling plants around the world. Bottlers buy the concentrate from Coca-Cola in the US; they then mix it with water and sweeteners and bottle the finished product. As the bottler adds sugar and sweeteners, the sweetness of the drink is said to differ in various parts of the world, in order to cater for local

Street rubbish in the Nepalese capital, Kathmandu, beneath a Coca-Cola ad depicting an idealized countryside.

taste. Each of the bottling companies has exclusive rights to a region of the world and, although Coca-Cola owns shares in some of the bottling companies, the majority are independent. Bottlers are in charge of distributing the products to the retailers and they are also normally responsible for all advertisements and other sales initiatives within their areas.

The presence of Coca-Cola in a country can bring some benefits but it has also been the subject of a considerable amount of criticism from environmentalists and other groups in recent years. The company is aware of the need to create a positive image and participates in many community schemes in Africa and Asia. For example, it started a microfinance start-up scheme to provide 4,000 Vietnamese women with the merchandise, training and basic equipment to start a business selling Coca-Cola and invested $1.5 billion dollars in Russia for the construction of manufacturing plants and improvements to local infrastructure. The company claims that studies in Asia, Africa and eastern Europe have consistently shown that, for every job in the Coca-Cola system, an average of 10 more jobs is supported in local communities.

The production process is a thirsty business. The corporation's own figures say that it may use up to 35 litres of water to make one half-litre bottle of Coca-Cola and the potential impact on the environment is clear. In 2009 it 'pledged to return to communities and to nature an amount of water equivalent to what it uses in beverages and their production. This means reducing the amount of water used to produce beverages, recycling water used for manufacturing processes so it can be returned safely to the environment, and replenishing water through locally relevant projects.'

The company has been criticized for depleting groundwater levels in India as a result of the high water consumption in its bottling plants. In Kerala and Uttar Pradesh, local people linked the drying up of wells and scarcity of drinking water to the presence of bottling plants. In the same states, scientists found toxic levels of cadmium, lead and chromium in the waste sludge from the production process that Coca-Cola were 'giving away for free' to farmers as fertilizer. Both episodes have caused considerable damage to the company's reputation but not really affected its profitability or position as a major transnational corporation. ∎

Caribbean CASE STUDY

Bananas and fair trade in the Windward Isles

Banana growing was established in the Windward Isles – a group of islands in the Caribbean – by British colonists to supply the home market over 50 years ago. When the UK joined the EU in 1973, bananas from the islands were allowed tariff-free entry to European markets in recognition of their historical links to the UK and as recognition of the importance of bananas to the Windward Isles' economies. Bananas accounted for up to 50% of the islands' export revenues.

Banana growing on the Windward Isles is labour intensive and conducted by small-scale farmers who produce a very small proportion of the world's banana output.

A farmer in St Lucia preparing Fairtrade bananas for the European market.

By contrast, banana production in Latin America is typified by large-scale plantations and extensive farming techniques. Large US companies, such as Dole and Chiquita, dominate banana production in the region, which is responsible for over 30% of the world's output.

Banana production in the Windward Isles went into decline after Latin American exporters, encouraged by US-based banana corporations, complained to the WTO about the unfair treatment of their bananas from Latin America through the imposition of tariffs and quotas by the EU. The WTO ruled in favour of the big banana exporters and the Windward Isles' share of the UK market dropped from 45% in 1992 to less than 9% in 2009, forced out by cheaper bananas from Latin America and West Africa. British supermarkets also entered a banana price war that further pushed down the price of bananas.

The impact on the Windward Isles was very serious. The number of banana farmers dropped from 27,000 to 4,000 and the result was high unemployment, youth unrest and increasing poverty. The Fairtrade Foundation has been working with the banana growers since 2000 and exports have subsequently increased each year, reaching 42,000 tonnes in 2009. Over 90% of the growers on the island are now part of the Fairtrade network in 48 groups across Dominica, St Lucia and St Vincent. The growers won an important legal battle in 2008 to win the right to sell their bananas directly to the export company rather than the banana companies and make more profit as a result.

The Windward Islands Farmers Association (WINFA) is responsible for the banana supply chain up to export and provides services to farmers such as the supply of fertilizer, pest and disease control, and agricultural advice, at a significantly reduced cost. Over 100 new staff have been hired in the islands, technical staff trained, and payment and pest control departments created. The challenge for the Fairtrade movement in the Windward Islands is to diversify into other products such as mangoes and coconuts and to involve itself in the local processing of products such as fruit juices. Like many small, poor countries, these islands are very dependent on one commodity and very vulnerable to changes in market conditions. ■

Health & Development

h & Health &
ent Development De

How does the health of the population affect development?

✱ *People have basic human needs. These include access to healthcare and a healthy, safe environment.*

✱ *The health of a population is integral to its sustainable development. It is also a reliable indicator of the levels of poverty and inequality in a society.*

✱ *Improved health enables society and individuals to make use of available resources and fully exploit their own capacities.*

✱ *Health programmes run by the government, institutions or agencies can promote progress towards development.*

Key points

Health and development – isn't it obvious?

Improving the standards of healthcare enjoyed by people is one of the primary aims of any development programme. There is a general correlation between the wealth of a country (as measured in GNI per capita) and its levels of health (using measures such as life expectancy, infant mortality and incidence of infectious diseases). This correlation is easily explained: individual wealth makes it easier for people to access healthcare and national wealth makes it more likely that decent levels of nutrition will be available to the population, as well as sanitation and clean water. While it is true that there has been a big improvement in global health over the last 30 years, this is not true of all countries – in some, life expectancy is now much lower.

The optimism of the 1970s

People in sub-Saharan Africa suffer a lower standard of healthcare than in any other region of the world. Some historical perspectives place the blame for this situation upon the Western world. This is because the healthcare systems inherited by most African countries after the colonial

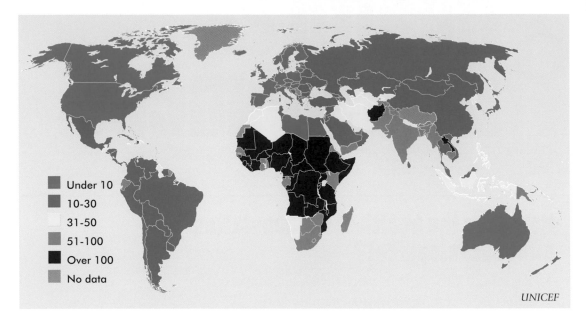

UNICEF

Under-5 mortality rate per 1,000 live births, 2009.

period focused on providing care for the privileged in urban areas. Many newly independent African governments recognized this imbalance and attempted to extend the range of their provision, emphasizing primary care and a community-based approach. Measurable progress, although uneven, was made in many countries and was recognized by the World Health Organization (WHO) at the Alma Ata Conference in 1978. This conference in Kazakhstan was attended by virtually all of the member nations of the WHO and UNICEF. The declaration agreed there (Health For All by the Year 2000) was seen as a major milestone in the promotion of global public health. Its broad definition of health ('a state of complete physical, mental, and social well-being, and not merely the absence of disease or infirmity') was enlightened, and its emphasis on the importance of primary healthcare (PHC) as an essential part of an integrated health system was also well received by health professionals working in the developing world.

The declaration was optimistic that the glaring inequalities in health status between people in the developed and developing worlds could be addressed by a better use of the world's resources, mostly achieved by reducing conflict and thereby releasing money spent on armaments. That optimism now seems very misplaced. The rich aid-giving countries decided that the full implementation of health systems based on PHC would be too expensive. A watered-down version, 'selective primary health care' – focused on some specific health issues – was introduced in many countries and was subsequently derided by critics as 'Health for Some by the Year 2000'.

The debt crisis

There was progress in some countries, but the global economic crisis of the 1980s undid a lot of that work as indebted states were forced to seek the 'help' of the World Bank and the IMF. Many countries in the developing world had borrowed money to help fund development projects; when interest rates started to rise, paying back that money became increasingly difficult. The Bank and the IMF offered access to emergency funds but often insisted on public spending cuts in return, including cuts in healthcare and public services – this was called 'structural adjustment'. These adjustment programmes increased levels of poverty and helped to create conditions that encouraged the spread of diseases. During the 1990s healthcare services continued to disintegrate in many countries and resources were still siphoned off to pay foreign creditors. In 1997 sub-Saharan African governments were transferring four times what they were spending on the health of their people to Northern creditors. In 1998, Senegal spent five times as much repaying foreign debts as on health.

Declining life expectancy

An example of declining public health as a result of the loss of healthcare services can be found in Zimbabwe, where life expectancy at birth for males has dramatically declined from 60 years in 1990 to 37 in 2008, among the lowest in the world. Life expectancy for females is even lower at 34 years. In the same period the infant mortality rate climbed from 53 to 81 deaths per 1,000 live births. The high incidence of HIV and AIDS has been a major cause of the decline in the health of the Zimbabwean population but not all the countries in the region with a high incidence of HIV have been affected so badly. There is a wide range in the extent and standards of public healthcare provision – even between countries at similar stages of economic development.

The table below shows some health-related indicators for seven African countries. The statistics show some obvious similarities but also some significant differences. Is health expenditure in each country the key factor?

Health indicators for selected tropical African countries (2008)

Country	HDI Ranking/182	Death Rate/ 1000	Annual health expenditure per capita ($)	HIV prevalence (% of pop)	Mortality rate <5 years /1000
Dem. Rep. of Congo	176	17	9	3.5	199
Kenya	147	12	34	7.8	128
Malawi	160	12	17	11.9	100
Rwanda	167	14	37	2.8	112
Tanzania	151	11	22	6.2	104
Uganda	157	13	28	5.4	135
Zambia	164	17	57	15.2	135

World Health Organization

Developed and developing countries
– different health priorities

There are major differences in the health priorities of developed and developing countries. In developing countries the emphasis is on combating infectious diseases and issues associated with birth and maternity. In developed countries the emphasis is on lifestyle factors associated with smoking and diets that have high levels of fatty foods, such as heart disease and cancer. These are much more likely to occur the longer a person lives and as a result a lot of healthcare resources are allocated to caring for the elderly. In developing countries the biggest problem is viral and bacterial communicable diseases such as cholera, hepatitis, polio and typhoid, and airborne diseases such as whooping cough, diphtheria, tuberculosis and pneumonia. In developed countries these diseases are sometimes encountered but can usually be treated effectively. Other diseases in developing countries may be transmitted by insects, including malaria, bilharzia and sleeping sickness. There is a higher prevalence of these diseases amongst the young in developing countries because they are often weakened by malnutrition. The situation is often worse in rural areas where access to healthcare, sanitation and clean water is more difficult. In sub-Saharan Africa today, two-fifths of the population still lack access to safe water and two-thirds do not enjoy adequate sanitation.

Can changes in health patterns as a country develops be predicted? Logic would suggest that there should be a relationship between the general health of the population and a country's level of development. Omran's epidemiological transition model attempts to do this by linking disease patterns over a period of time to changing social, economic, demographic and environmental conditions.

According to this model, the most pronounced positive changes in

Percentage of population with access to:

	Improved drinking-water, 2008			Improved sanitation, 2008		
	Total	Urban	Rural	Total	Urban	Rural
Sub-Saharan Africa	60	83	47	31	44	24
Middle East & North Africa	86	93	76	80	90	66
Asia	87	96	82	49	63	40
Latin America & Caribbean	93	97	80	80	86	55
Industrialized countries	100	100	98	99	100	98

UNICEF

Key features of Omran's transition model (1971)

First phase: subsistence agriculture, high fertility rate, high infant death rate, low life expectancy; infectious diseases are the main cause of death.
Second phase: improvements in agriculture, sanitation and nutrition and reduced death rate.
Third phase: intensive agriculture and industrialization, lower fertility rate, longer life expectancy; non-communicable degenerative diseases become the main cause of death.

Feature

health and disease patterns take place amongst children and mothers. The result is a sharp decline in the mortality of these groups and, because of the improved survival rates and other social and economic factors, a declining birth rate. The model has obvious similarities to the better known demographic transition model of population growth and is often referred to by those who support a modernist perspective on development.

The cost of healthcare

Providing a programme of healthcare for all is a very expensive proposition for any government but is a particularly heavy burden in developing countries. All the richer countries spend at least 5% of their gross national income on public healthcare, and some countries spend much more. In developing countries the figure is much lower: Sierra Leone spends 0.9% and Bangladesh 1.7%. In some parts of the world, notably in sub-Saharan Africa, missionaries still play a significant part in healthcare provision alongside contributions from various NGOs. Where some form of public healthcare programme does exist, it often follows outdated, inappropriate colonial methods that are top down and urban based. Much of the healthcare budget is frequently concentrated in a few key hospitals and there is little left to provide for the poor in rural areas. As a result access to essential drugs for basic treatment is low. Even in Brazil, one of the wealthier developing countries, only 35% of the population have access to the drugs they might need.

Many essential medicines remain inaccessible to those most in need. This is due to poverty and impoverished healthcare systems but also to the international commercialization of health. Drugs and medicines are disproportionately developed for rich country populations and the pharmaceutical companies concentrate on the development of 'lifestyle drugs' such as Viagra and Prozac. Of the 1,393 new drugs or medicines developed by the companies between

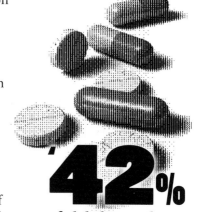

'42%

of global expenditure on medicines is spent on 5% of the world's population living in North America, while only 20% is spent on the majority of the world's population with the highest burdens of disease in Africa, Asia, the Middle East and Latin America.'

Global Health Watch 2008

1975 and 1999, only 16 were for 'tropical diseases'. There is a critical shortage of effective drugs for the treatment of the diseases of the poor such as malaria, leishmaniasis, sleeping sickness and tuberculosis. One explanation for this may be that poor communities offer pharmaceutical companies reduced opportunities to make a profit.

An unfair trade in health workers

Another problem for governments trying to provide healthcare services in developing countries is training and retaining workers. In Malawi, for example, there is one doctor for every 88,000 people, the worst ratio in the world. This compares to one per 300 in the UK, one per 400 in Australia and one per 470 in Canada. To make matters worse, countries with a high disease burden, like Malawi, have to watch as the health workers they train leave to work in developed countries. According to one researcher: 'The predominant flow of health professionals is from developing countries, where they are scarcest relative to needs, to developed countries, where they are more plentiful.' The number of non-European nurses registering with the Irish Nursing Board, for example, rose from less than 200 per year to more than 1,800 per year between 1990 and 2001. In contrast, it is estimated that 550 of the 600 doctors trained in Zambia since independence (1964) have moved to developed countries.

A number of issues help to drive this trend. There is an increasing demand for health workers to look after the ageing populations that are a demographic feature of the rich world and there is active recruitment in poorer countries by agencies working for the rich world health providers. In addition, the internet makes information on job vacancies available

Nancy Wambui Itotia is a Kenyan nurse working in a British care home to send home money for her family.

'In Kenya I could not make ends meet on a nurse's salary. The nurses I saw in Kenya are so demoralized they are not working properly. So much is needed. When everything is in such a mess, where do you start? If the government cared for nurses and gave them some incentives then they would be willing to work.

'I have seen it happen gradually. When I first qualified as a nurse in 1978 we had a really good health service in Kenya. The standard of care was good. But it deteriorated throughout the Moi period and now it is very poor. You can see that for yourself. Before, people were treated as people. Now they are treated like rejects.'

New Internationalist 379, June 2005

Witness

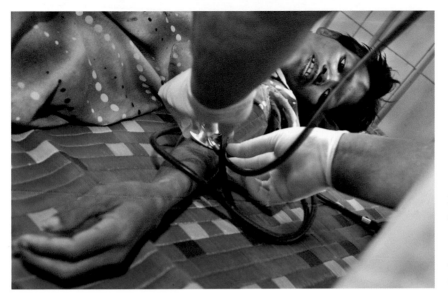

Poeum Pech, a 29-year-old mother of two who is HIV-positive, has her blood pressure taken in Siem Reap, Cambodia.

internationally and health workers who are often witnessing the collapse of health systems in their own countries are inevitably attracted by prospects overseas.

Profiting from health

In recent decades, the World Bank has made it a policy to promote the privatization of the health sector, internationally and in developing countries. In Africa the privatization of healthcare has reduced access to services for huge numbers of poor and sick people. When infectious diseases are the major health issue, public health services are essential. Private healthcare cannot make the necessary interventions at community or village level. The introduction of the market has transformed healthcare from a public service, designed for all, to a private commodity, available only to those who can pay. Those that are poor are effectively denied access to basic healthcare as a result. The introduction of payment for treatment has succeeded in driving the poor away from healthcare in many countries. Privatization often means the promotion of medical insurance schemes which are totally unsuited to an African context where less than 10% of the labour force is formally employed.

> '[M]any people, most of them in tropical countries of the Third World, die of preventable, curable diseases.… Malaria, tuberculosis, acute lower-respiratory infections – in 1998, these claimed 6.1 million lives. People died because the drugs to treat those illnesses are non-existent or are no longer effective. They died because it doesn't pay to keep them alive.'
>
> **Ken Silverstein, 'Millions for Viagra, Pennies for Diseases of the Poor',**
> *The Nation,* 19 July 1999

Witness

The influence of the pharmaceutical industry

The power and influence of the pharmaceutical industry has also become a source of concern for many people interested in development issues. The combined annual turnover of the world's top five drug companies is twice the gross national income of all sub-Saharan countries combined.

The top 10 pharmaceutical companies in the US's Fortune 500 (the country's 500 most profitable companies) earned $269 billion in sales in 2008 and made combined profits of $49 billion. They also spent $83 billion on sales and administration – more than twice the amount they spent on research and development. Their wealth makes it possible for them to influence the rules of world trade through their close relationships with Western governments and this does not always benefit the world's poorest or least healthy. The influence of the companies is particularly strong in the US where there are six pharmaceutical lobbyists for each of the 535 members of Congress. Rules on drug patents in the European Union are subject to the same sort of pressure.

There are some signs of changing attitudes amongst the pharmaceutical companies, which have come under economic pressure to find new markets for their drugs and also public pressure for them to show more corporate responsibility. One of the potential impacts of President Obama's attempt to bring in healthcare legislation is a lowering of the prices that pharmaceutical companies are allowed to charge for their drugs

'The combined annual turnover of the world's top five drug companies is

twice

the gross national income of all sub-Saharan countries combined.'

For the first time in a half-century, sales of prescription drugs are forecast to decline this year in the US, historically the industry's biggest and most profitable market. The Obama administration and Congress's attempt to pass legislation overhauling the healthcare system, including provisions that could lower the cost of medicine, could put drug makers' US businesses under further pressure.

As a result, developing countries like Venezuela have begun to look more attractive to the industry. Sales of prescription drugs in emerging markets reached $152.7 billion in 2008, up from $67.2 billion in 2003, according to IMS Health.

Pfizer (pharmaceutical company) is benefiting from a belief in Venezuela and in much of the developing world that branded medicines are worth paying a premium for because they're safer and more effective than generics. Pfizer's prices in Venezuela tend to be about 30% under US prices, but are still 40% to 50% more than generics, which are widely available here since patents aren't usually enforced.

Wall Street Journal, July 2009

Witness

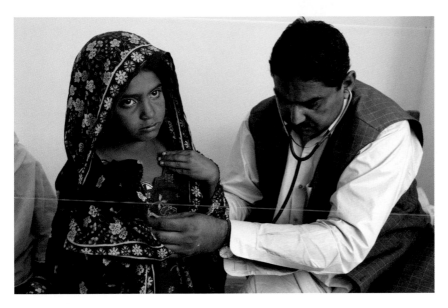

Six-year-old Amira Maqsi is examined by a doctor at a clinic for people displaced by the severe flooding in Pakistan in 2010.

in the US. This is forcing companies to re-assess the value of markets in the developing world. Pfizer is one of the large companies which has started selling branded drugs in poorer countries even though these are more expensive than the generic drugs that are also available (see box opposite).

The impact of generic drugs

A 2003 agreement brokered by the WTO concerning the selling of cheaper generic drugs in developing countries was initially greeted as a step forward but has also been criticized because of the protection it continues to give the big pharmaceutical companies in the developed world. Under the agreement, developing countries are allowed to export home-produced generic drugs to other countries where there is a national health problem as long as the drugs are not part of a commercial or industrial policy. The drugs have to be packaged or coloured differently to prevent them from prejudicing markets in the developed world. Cheaper generic drugs have been very important in making anti-retroviral treatment available for larger numbers of AIDS sufferers in developing countries, particularly in Africa.

Developing countries paid a high price for this agreement. But what have they received in return? Drug companies spend more on advertising and marketing than on research, more on research on lifestyle drugs than on life-saving drugs, and almost nothing on diseases that affect developing countries only. This is not surprising. Poor people cannot afford drugs, and drug companies make investments that yield the highest returns.

Joseph Stiglitz, 'Scrooge and intellectual property rights', *British Medical Journal*, 23 December 2006, Volume 333, pp. 1279-128

Witness

How should public healthcare be funded?

India has one of the fastest-growing economies in the world but how it looks after the health of its population causes considerable controversy within the country. The government spends less on public healthcare as a percentage of gross domestic product (GDP) than almost all other countries and there is a high dependency on the private sector (see box opposite). There are many issues which are raised by such a policy and it is worth spending some time thinking about the advantages and disadvantages of a public healthcare system with these characteristics.

The tension between public and private provision of healthcare is the subject of heated debate in both developing and developed countries. In

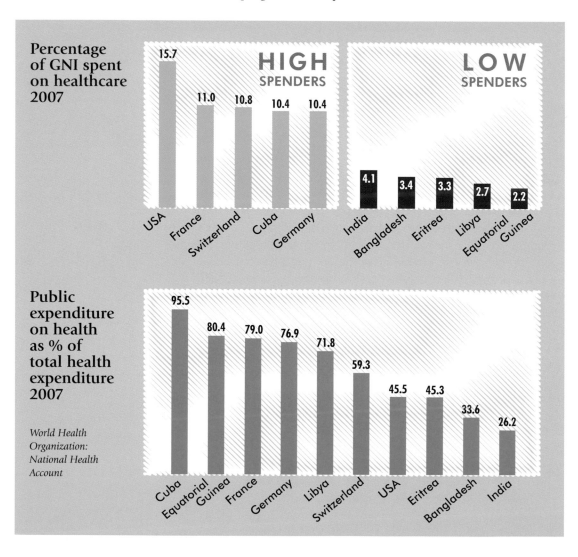

Percentage of GNI spent on healthcare 2007

HIGH SPENDERS

USA	France	Switzerland	Cuba	Germany
15.7	11.0	10.8	10.4	10.4

LOW SPENDERS

India	Bangladesh	Eritrea	Libya	Equatorial Guinea
4.1	3.4	3.3	2.7	2.2

Public expenditure on health as % of total health expenditure 2007

World Health Organization: National Health Account

Cuba	Equatorial Guinea	France	Germany	Libya	Switzerland	USA	Eritrea	Bangladesh	India
95.5	80.4	79.0	76.9	71.8	59.3	45.5	45.3	33.6	26.2

India ranks 171 out of 175 in public health spending

India ranks 171 out of the 175 countries in the world in public health spending. The country spends less than some sub-Saharan African countries, according to the World Health Organization. India spends 5.2% of its GDP on healthcare – but only 0.9% comes from government spending on public health.

Said Dr H Sudarshan who was part of WHO Commission on Macro Economics and Health: 'There has been a marginal increase in public health spending with the National Rural Health Mission, but there is a need for increasing the health budget and also simultaneously to build the capacity of the state to use the allocated budget efficiently in public health.'

Dr N Devadasan, Director of Institute of Public Health, Bangalore, said: 'There is growth in GDP but there has been no increase in healthcare spending. This inadequate public health spending has forced the public to depend on the private sector.'

Times of India, 11 August 2009

Feature

---

the UK in July 2010, the Health Secretary of the coalition government, Andrew Lansley, announced the transfer of £80 billion ($130 billion) from the annual healthcare budget to general practitioners (GPs) to give them responsibility to make decisions about patient care. The administration of such huge sums of money would require assistance, almost certainly from the private sector, and the move is widely seen as a way of increasing private sector involvement in the NHS.

The proportion of healthcare costs paid for by the government varies a lot from one country to another. The models that countries have adopted are the result of many economic, cultural and political factors but more countries seem to be turning to a model that requires private health insurance from potential patients – regardless of whether they can afford it or not.

There is much more that needs to be said about global health issues. Child and maternal health issues play a vital part in development and these are discussed in more detail in Chapter 14 on the Millennium Goals, while issues related to HIV, AIDS and malaria are treated in Chapter 9. For many people, nothing epitomizes the need for greater equality in global wealth more than the gulf between rich and poor in terms of health.

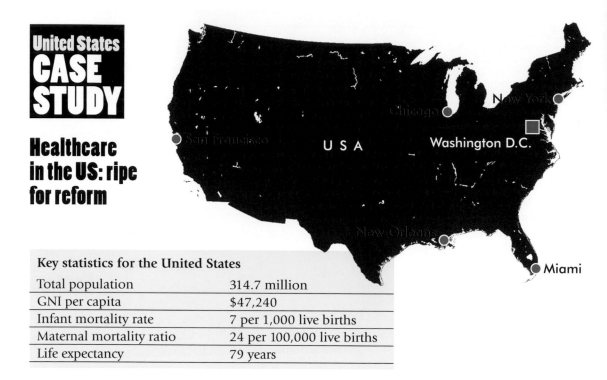

United States CASE STUDY

Healthcare in the US: ripe for reform

San Francisco

Chicago

New York

USA

Washington D.C.

New Orleans

Miami

Key statistics for the United States	
Total population	314.7 million
GNI per capita	$47,240
Infant mortality rate	7 per 1,000 live births
Maternal mortality ratio	24 per 100,000 live births
Life expectancy	79 years

There is no universal system of healthcare in the US and it is easier to understand its structure if you are acquainted with some of the basic premises of American politics. Any provision of services by the state is associated with 'socialism' – seen by many in the US as verging on communism – and virtually impossible to get through Congress. There are federally funded programmes for some of the poor (Medicaid) and those over 65 (Medicare) as well as other schemes for the disabled and war veterans but generally it is up to individuals to obtain health insurance. Most are covered through their employers, but others sign up for private insurance schemes.

Under the terms of most insurance plans, people pay regular premiums, but sometimes they are required to pay part of the cost of their treatment (known in the US as a deductible) before the insurer covers the expense. The amount paid into the insurance plan each month varies according to their plan. At least 15% of the population (over 46 million people) are uninsured and a further 35% are 'under-insured', meaning that the terms of their insurance plans do not cover the cost of their treatment.

Ownership of healthcare facilities in the US is also mainly in private hands, although federal, state, county and city facilities also exist. Many hospitals (about 70%) are owned by non-profit organizations but there are also a significant number of 'for profit' hospitals. There is no nationwide system of government-owned hospitals but there are some medical facilities owned by local government that are open to the general public. Those without insurance are treated in emergency rooms at some locally run hospitals.

An expensive system

The US spends more on healthcare per person ($7,681) and also more of its total national income (16.2% in 2008) than any other nation. Although most of its citizens rely on private health insurance, the US government still spent $800 billion on the Medicare and Medicaid programmes in 2008, and that amount increases each year. The high cost of medical care is reinforced by the fact that medical debt is responsible for over 50% of all bankruptcies in the US.

There are many reasons for the high cost of healthcare in the US but one of the main reasons is the high cost of drugs purchased from the pharmaceutical companies. The high revenue generated by the sale of drugs has meant that 82% of the world's facilities for research and development in biotechnology are based in the US. The patents available on new drugs allow the companies to charge high prices for drugs for a 20-year period during which other companies are banned from producing the same drug. This allows the companies to recover the very high costs of research and development – and also to make very large profits.

What are the problems with the US system?

The huge amounts of money spent on healthcare in the US do not result in positive achievements on some important health indicators. Average life expectancy is 79 years, which is good in global terms but places the US behind 21 other countries.

How the US pays for healthcare: private health insurance costs are soaring

US national health expenditure 1960-2007

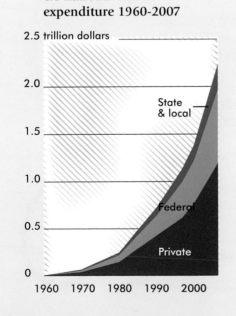

Breakdown of US federal health expenditure, 2007

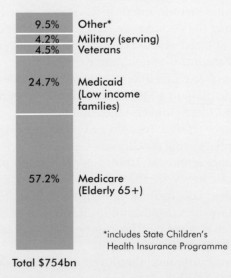

*includes State Children's Health Insurance Programme

US Department of Health and Human Services

High cost, poor access: an emergency room in Massachusetts.

Infant mortality (7 per thousand births) is also higher than in most other rich countries and the US is only ranked 43rd in the world – behind even its socialist bugbear Cuba. The probable explanation for this is the unequal distribution of wealth in the US and the number of people living in extreme poverty – often illegal immigrants.

President Obama promised the reform of healthcare in his presidential campaign but it has been difficult to achieve because of the vested interests of the health insurance and pharmaceutical companies. The ever-rising burden of the cost of healthcare on the US economy eventually allowed a bill

Key features of the Healthcare Reform Bill

Cost: $940 billion over 10 years; this would reduce the budget deficit by $143 billion.

Coverage: Expanded to 32 million currently uninsured Americans.

Medicare: Prescription drug 'coverage gap' will be closed – meaning the poor do not have to pay high 'deductible' costs; those affected who are over 65 will also be helped with rebates and discounts on brand-name drugs.

Medicaid: Expanded to include families under 65 with a gross income of up to 133% of federal poverty level ($30,000 for a family of four) and childless adults.

Insurance reforms: Insurers can no longer deny coverage to those with pre-existing conditions.

Insurance exchanges: Uninsured and self-employed will be able to purchase insurance through state-based exchanges.

Subsidies: Low-income individuals and families wanting to purchase their own health insurance will be eligible for subsidies.

Individual mandate: Those not covered by Medicaid or Medicare must be insured or face a fine.

High-cost insurance: Employers can offer workers pricier plans subject to tax being paid on the excess premium.

Data

Infant mortality rates: how the US is lagging behind

Countries with the lowest infant mortality rates, 2008

1 per 1,000 San Marino

2 per 1,000 Iceland, Liechtenstein, Luxembourg, Singapore

3 per 1,000 Andorra, Austria, Czech Rep, Finland, France, Greece, Ireland, Italy, Japan, Monaco, Norway, Portugal, Slovenia.

4 per 1,000 Belgium, Cyprus, Denmark, Estonia, Germany, Israel, Netherlands, Spain, Switzerland.

5 per 1,000 Australia, Croatia, Cuba, Hungary, New Zealand/Aotearoa, South Korea, UK.

6 per 1,000 Brunei, Canada, Lithuania, Malaysia, Malta, Poland, Serbia.

7 per 1,000 Chile, Montenegro, Slovakia, United Arab Emirates, **United States**.

Data

to be passed by Congress on 21 March 2010. It was opposed by all Republican members of the House of Representatives and by 34 Democrat members. It will allow healthcare to be extended to tens of millions of poorer US citizens who were previously uninsured. ■

Uganda CASE STUDY

Healthcare – a major challenge for Uganda

Key health statistics for Uganda	
Total population	32.7 million
GNI per capita	$460
Infant mortality rate	79 per 1,000 live births
Maternal mortality ratio	430 per 100,000 live births
Life expectancy	53 years

Despite a lot of investment in recent years, Uganda has one of the worst healthcare records in the world and is ranked 186th out of the 191 nations. Healthcare funding is the most obvious problem. The Ministry of Health had a budget of $210 million in 2008 and 60% of the money came from overseas donors. By comparison, the province of Quebec in Canada spent $17,850 million on 7 million people – equivalent to $2,550 per capita spent on healthcare compared with just $7 per capita in Uganda.

Organizing healthcare on such a limited budget is obviously difficult. There are not enough doctors for health centres to function properly and there is only one doctor for every 20,000 people in the country. Only 38% of healthcare posts are filled in Uganda and health workers have little incentive to work in poor rural areas. Some 70% of Ugandan doctors and 40% of nurses and midwives are based in urban areas, serving only 14% of the Ugandan population.

Only 50% of the population lives within five kilometres of a health centre, a problem caused by the overwhelmingly rural nature of the population distribution in Uganda (86%). The challenges for healthcare are massive; from an inadequate infrastructure that makes travelling to health centres very difficult, to a population where malaria is the biggest cause of death and 7% of the

Health facilities in Uganda are arranged in a linear hierarchical manner:

Health centres – this is the lowest level, serving a population of 30,000-100,000
District general hospitals – serving 500,000
Regional referral hospitals – serving 2 million
National referral hospital – serving 32 million

Data

population are HIV-positive. Around 60% of mothers still deliver their babies at home, mostly because transport difficulties make it impossible to refer them to health centres. When people who are seeking medical attention do make it to a health centre or hospital there is a very high chance that they will be unable to see a doctor or to obtain the medicines they need.

There have been some successes. The number of deaths from common measles has been reduced by more than 95% in the last 10 years and the prevalence of HIV reduced from 30% in the mid-1990s to 7% in 2008. In addition, over 80,000 people are receiving anti-retroviral treatment for AIDS. There have been no cases of polio for the last 10 years and the model of successful vaccinations carried out by primary healthcare workers and other trained volunteers is an example of what can be achieved with very few resources. The wider implementation of basic PHC measures such as hand washing, improved sanitation, wearing shoes and improved nutrition could prevent 90% of diseases, while improved personal and social education in schools could lead to healthier behaviour and eventually reduce the fertility rate. ■

A vicious circle

How underfunding and understaffing afflict poor countries such as Uganda.

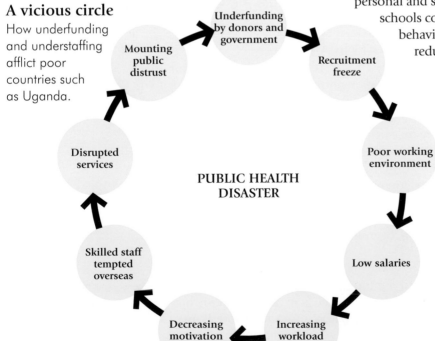

9 HIV, AIDS & Malaria

How do HIV, AIDS and malaria affect development in Africa?

✳ *There are wide variations in the incidence of HIV and malaria in African countries and regions.*

✳ *The high incidence of the diseases in some countries has a significant negative impact on development.*

✳ *The role of women in African society has made them more vulnerable to HIV and AIDS.*

✳ *A range of strategies is needed to combat the spread of the diseases and the support of richer countries is essential.*

Key points

The impact of HIV and AIDS in Africa

The human immunodeficiency virus (HIV) and the fatal condition that develops from it (AIDS) were first reported in 1981 in the US city of Los Angeles, although they had almost certainly been present before then. In the 30 years since HIV and AIDS were first recognized they have spread to every country on earth and caused untold human misery and economic damage. Sub-Saharan Africa is more heavily affected than any other region of the world. An estimated 22.4 million people are living with HIV in the region – around two-thirds of the global total. In 2008 around 1.4 million people died from AIDS in sub-Saharan Africa and 1.9 million people became infected with HIV. Since the beginning of the epidemic more than 14 million children have lost one or both parents to AIDS.

The high prevalence level means that the number of people dying from AIDS will continue to rise for some years to come. Its social and economic consequences are already widely felt, not only in the health sector but also in education, industry, agriculture, transport, human resources and the economy in general. In some parts of sub-Saharan Africa, AIDS has devastated whole communities and destroyed years of development progress. For the 11 countries in Africa with prevalence rates

Prevalence of HIV and AIDS in selected African countries

Country	Adult (15-49) HIV prevalence rate %	People living with HIV	Women with HIV	Children with HIV	AIDS deaths	Orphans due to AIDS
Swaziland	26.1	190,000	100,000	15,000	10,000	56,000
Botswana	23.9	300,000	170,000	15,000	11,000	95,000
Lesotho	23.2	270,000	150,000	12,000	18,000	110,000
South Africa	18.1	5,700,000	3,200,000	280,000	350,000	1,400,000
Namibia	15.3	200,000	110,000	14,000	5,100	66,000
Zimbabwe	15.3	1,300,000	680,000	120,000	140,000	1,000,000
Zambia	15.2	1,100,000	560,000	95,000	56,000	600,000
Mozambique	12.5	1,500,000	810,000	100,000	81,000	400,000
Malawi	11.9	930,000	490,000	91,000	68,000	560,000
Kenya	7.1-8.5	1,500,000-2,000,000	800,000-1,100,000	130,000-180,000	85,000-130,000	990,000-1,400,000
Uganda	6.7	1,000,000	520,000	110,000	91,000	1,000,000
United Rep. of Tanzania	5.4	940,000	480,000	130,000	77,000	1,200,000
Nigeria	3.1	2,600,000	1,400,000	220,000	170,000	1,200,000
Total sub-Saharan Africa	5.0	22,000,000	12,000,000	1,800,000	1,500,000	11,600,000

Children are defined as people under the age of 15; the HIV prevalence rate is among adults aged 15-49.

UNAIDS Report 2009

above 13%, the average life expectancy is 47.7 years – 11.0 years less than would have been expected without HIV and AIDS.

Combating the disease was made much more difficult by the 2007-08 global financial crisis. Already very short of funding, African countries have had to make cuts in the amount of money they spend on healthcare. Donor countries are also finding it very difficult to meet their pledges to fund the fight against HIV and AIDS.

Countries in sub-Saharan Africa face a triple challenge:
- Providing healthcare, anti-retroviral treatment, and support to an increasing number of people with HIV-related illnesses
- Reducing the annual toll of new HIV infections by enabling individuals to protect themselves and others
- Coping with the impact of over 20 million AIDS deaths, on orphans and other survivors, communities, and national development.

The high incidence of HIV and AIDS has a profound impact on

Two-thirds of Africans with HIV go untreated

Already, large percentages of households in sub-Saharan Africa are poor, and the large number of people on treatment means ever-increasing treatment programme costs.

Yet sub-Saharan Africa only accounts for 1% of global health expenditure and two per cent of the global health workforce. Currently, only one third of HIV-positive Africans in need of anti-retroviral (ARV) treatment can access it…

Dr Bactrin Killingo, chairperson of the Nairobi-based Collaborative Fund for HIV Treatment Preparedness [says] 'If current cost constraints faced by HIV treatment programmes are not addressed, while the demand for expensive second-line treatment increases, we will soon find ourselves in a situation similar to the 1990s, where millions of lives were lost unnecessarily because people could not afford the treatment they needed to stay alive.'

Kristin Palitza, 'Health-Africa: Global Financial Crisis Leads to HIV Budget Cuts', Inter Press Service, 18 May 2009

Witness

---

development and an immediate impact on business. Productivity rates have lowered, absenteeism has increased and so has labour turnover, with the loss of experienced workers a frequent problem. The increased turnover puts more pressure on recruitment and raises training costs. Larger companies also face increased costs for the healthcare and death benefits they offer staff. In addition there are a smaller number of skilled people in an already reduced workforce. As the disease attacks mainly young adults who are economically active, it reduces the taxable population and therefore the amount of money the government can spend on health and education.

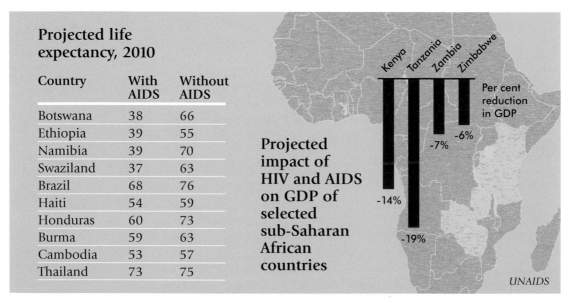

Projected life expectancy, 2010

Country	With AIDS	Without AIDS
Botswana	38	66
Ethiopia	39	55
Namibia	39	70
Swaziland	37	63
Brazil	68	76
Haiti	54	59
Honduras	60	73
Burma	59	63
Cambodia	53	57
Thailand	73	75

Projected impact of HIV and AIDS on GDP of selected sub-Saharan African countries

Kenya   Tanzania   Zambia   Zimbabwe

Per cent reduction in GDP

-7% -6%

-14%

-19%

UNAIDS

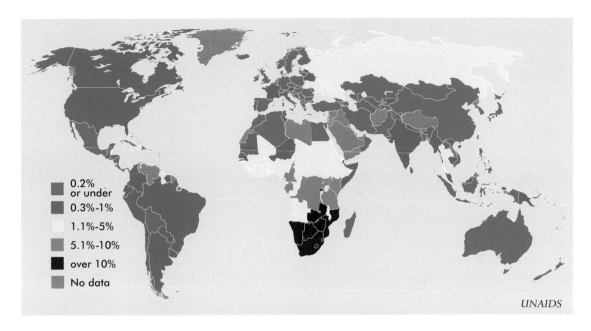

UNAIDS

How are different countries in Africa affected by HIV and AIDS?

Estimated HIV prevalence rate (aged 15-49), 2009.

There is a large variation in the HIV prevalence rates and the number of people dying from AIDS in African countries. In Somalia and Senegal the HIV prevalence is under 1% of the adult population, whereas in Namibia, South Africa, Zambia and Zimbabwe around 15-20% of adults are infected with HIV. In three southern African countries (Swaziland, Lesotho and Botswana), the national adult HIV prevalence rate now exceeds 20%.

In Nigeria, HIV prevalence is low (3.1%) compared to the rest of Africa but its large population (it is the most populous country in sub-Saharan Africa) means that around 2.6 million Nigerians are living with HIV. Adult HIV prevalence in East Africa exceeds 5% in Uganda, Kenya and Tanzania.

AIDS denial

Fighting the spread of HIV and AIDS in Africa is a complicated story and there are many problems to overcome. Recognizing possible causes of the rapid spread of the disease is a necessary step in attempting to reduce its impact. For many Africans there is a stigma attached to admitting to HIV infection and to using condoms. In addition, many have refused to recognize that HIV causes AIDS. Thabo Mbeki, former President of South Africa, and Robert Mugabe, current President of Zimbabwe, have both suggested that AIDS stems from poverty rather than from HIV infection. The power they wield within their own countries to influence people and deny attempts to provide appropriate health resources has done enormous damage. The use of condoms to protect against the transmission of HIV during sex has been a cultural problem. Some people see the introduction of condoms as part of a conspiracy seeking to limit the growth of the African population or to stifle the traditional power of men.

Around 60% of the population who are infected with HIV in sub-Saharan Africa are women and this high incidence is exacerbated by the transfer of the disease during pregnancy and birth. The higher incidence among females may in part be caused by cultural reluctance to discuss the virus or the use of preventive methods.

Combating HIV and AIDS

Lack of money to help fight the spread of the disease is an obvious problem, although a great deal of aid is distributed throughout developing countries with high HIV rates. Even with a relatively high level of funding it may be hard to implement programmes. Potential problems may occur because of inadequate infrastructure, corruption within both donor agencies and government agencies, or a lack of co-operation between foreign donors and local government.

There have been some successes, though, as governments, aid agencies and pharmaceutical companies have spent increasingly large amounts of money in their attempts to stop the spread of the disease. Anti-retroviral drugs (ARVs) that slow down the progression from HIV to AIDS were initially so expensive that they were mostly unavailable to the majority of HIV sufferers in the developing world. Generic forms of the drug, often produced in India and China, have reduced the cost and about 3.9 million people in sub-Saharan Africa had access to such treatment in 2009 compared with 2.9 million in 2008. However, this still only represents 37% of the HIV-infected population and access to the drugs is still impossible for many people. Even the greatly reduced cost of the drugs is beyond the poor who make up the majority of the population affected by the disease and who have to rely on free drugs that the government may make available. Even if a country has the drugs available to treat HIV sufferers, distribution may be impossible because of the rural location of a large part of the population and the lack of the healthcare workers needed to make sure that the drugs are used effectively.

There is little possibility that an AIDS vaccine will be developed in the near future but some scientists believe that more extensive use of ARVs could help to reduce the spread of the disease. This is because the drugs reduce the 'viral load' of the patient by up to 2,000 times and make

'Around 60% of the population who are infected with HIV in sub-Saharan Africa are women.'

them less infectious. At the moment the drugs are often only available to people in the later stage of disease progression when it is too late to stop them infecting other people. The most recent report from the United Nations offers some encouragement that the Millennium Development Goal of halting the spread of HIV and AIDS by 2015 may be achievable; this is discussed in Chapter 14.

Impact on households

The impact of AIDS on households where poverty rates are already high is disastrous. Many families lose their income earner and other families have to provide home-based care for sick relatives, reducing their ability to earn money. Many of those who die leave partners who are themselves infected and in need of treatment and care while there are over 12 million orphans in the region as a direct result of the epidemic. Even the cost of funerals adds an additional burden to the poorest of families.

The demand for care for those living with HIV is difficult to meet, not only because of the cost, but also because of the high proportion of healthcare workers who are themselves affected by the disease. Schools are also hit by the high incidence of the disease amongst students and teachers, which reduces their ability to provide HIV education and support for the community.

The ABC controversy

In the late 1990s a roadside sign appeared in Botswana: 'Avoiding AIDS as easy as... **A**bstain, **B**e faithful, **C**ondomise'. The message was not particularly controversial. It has been known since the 1980s that individuals could act to reduce the personal risk of contracting HIV through sex. The risk can be removed altogether by avoiding any sexual activity or reduced considerably by only having sex with one faithful partner. It can also be reduced by using a condom. The message was simple and apparently unarguable but it is the emphasis that was placed on the three elements that has caused controversy.

A roadside sign in Botswana (see The ABC controversy).

Under the US-funded PEPFAR (President's Emergency Plan For AIDS Relief) initiative, countries that accepted funding had to place far more emphasis on abstinence and the importance of maintaining monogamous relationships than on the use of condoms. Young people were to be encouraged to abstain from sex until marriage. Only high-risk users (prostitutes, drug users and those already infected by HIV) were to be encouraged to use condoms and there was no general education of young people in the use of condoms so as to reduce infection rates. Pope Benedict XVI stirred up the controversy even more by saying that 'the scourge [of HIV] cannot be resolved by distributing condoms; quite the contrary, we risk worsening the problem'.

Critics of the PEPFAR interpretation have argued that the emphasis on abstinence has had a negative impact on attempts to reduce transmission rates. In countries with high infection rates, it is of course preferable to delay participation of young people in sexual activity for as long as possible – but that is not practical when millions of girls and young women may be in abusive relationships. Moreover, even marriage offers no protection from infection if you are not sure about the HIV status of your partner.

Any successes in lowering rates of transmission of the disease have come from multi-layered approaches that involve all parts of society. These will probably include a media campaign involving posters, radio messages and rallies and the training of teachers to deliver effective HIV and AIDS education. Community leaders and heads of churches are important in encouraging the candid discussion of HIV and AIDS with the aim of reducing any stigma attached to the virus and the condition. Improving the status of women, providing adequate testing facilities and offering ARV treatment to those already infected are also necessary steps in fighting the spread of the disease.

The history of HIV and AIDS in Malawi provides plenty of evidence of the issues many countries face in trying to reduce transmission rates (see case study, page 165).

Progress towards meeting the Millennium Development Goals target for reducing the spread of HIV and AIDS is discussed in Chapter 14.

'Condoms, when distributed with educational materials as part of a comprehensive prevention package, have been shown to significantly lower sexual risk and activity, both among those already sexually active and those who are not.'

UNAIDS, October 2004.

Malaria

Many of the diseases which are such a problem in developing countries have been found in developed countries in the past but have been controlled, and in some cases eliminated, by improved nutrition, hygiene and sanitation. Malaria is usually considered as a tropical disease and it poses one of the greatest threats to world health. Over three million people die from the disease each year, with 80% of malaria cases – over 200 million – occurring in Africa. The disease is transmitted by mosquitoes, which breed in stagnant or slow-moving water. The parasites that cause malaria are spread through the bites of infected mosquitoes. The disease is debilitating and makes sufferers more vulnerable to a wide range of other infections.

Malaria transmission rates can differ depending on local factors such as rainfall patterns (mosquitoes breed in wet conditions), the

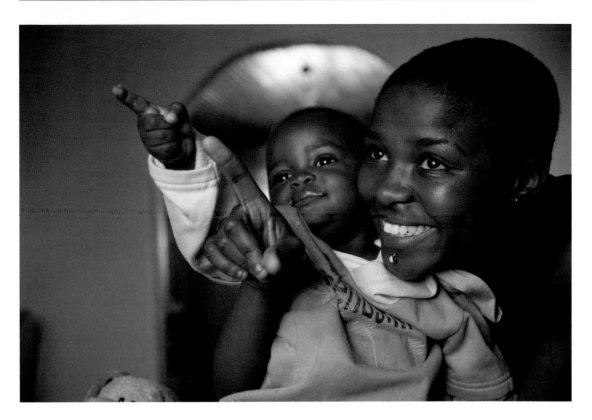

proximity of mosquito breeding sites to people, and the types of mosquito species in the area. Some regions have a fairly constant number of cases throughout the year and these countries are termed 'malaria endemic'. In other areas there are 'malaria seasons' usually coinciding with the rainy season.

Epidemics can be triggered by wet weather conditions and further aggravated by floods or mass population movements driven by conflict. Most cases of and deaths from malaria occur in sub-Saharan Africa. However, Asia, Latin America, the Middle East and parts of Europe are also affected. In 2008, malaria was present in 109 countries.

Thembi with her 16-month-old daughter in New Crossroads, a poor area of Cape Town, South Africa. Thembi is HIV-positive but she took ARV medication while pregnant so her daughter is not.

Controlling the disease

Many researchers argue that the prevention of malaria may be more cost-effective than treatment of the disease in the long run, but the money required is out of reach of many of the world's poorest people. It is estimated that malaria could be controlled at the cost of $3 billion in aid per year. Vector control (eradication of mosquitoes), indoor residual spraying (spraying interior walls with insecticide) and the use of insecticide-treated mosquito nets and bedclothes have all been used successfully in different parts of the world. There are also ongoing attempts to perfect a vaccine for malaria although nothing is currently available – Western pharmaceutical companies have not made research into this a priority because the market for such a vaccine in rich countries would be limited. Prophylactic drugs are available to prevent people contracting the disease but these are usually only available to short-term visitors and not to residents because of their cost and potential negative side-effects.

Impacts of malaria

The economic impact of a high incidence of malaria can be profound. It has been estimated that countries with a high incidence of malaria may suffer a fall of up to 1.3% in GDP and the losses accumulate over time to make a substantial difference between those countries that experience high rates and those that do not. It is estimated that malaria costs African countries alone $12 billion a year in lost output. In some heavy-burden countries, the disease accounts for:

• up to 40% of public health expenditures
• 30% to 50% of inpatient hospital admissions
• up to 60% of outpatient health clinic visits.

Malaria disproportionately affects poor people who cannot afford treatment or have limited access to healthcare, and traps families and communities in a downward spiral of poverty. Malaria sufferers are not able to work effectively or carry out many of the essential food-producing jobs that are needed by poor families. Attempts to diversify the economy to include tourism are doomed to failure because tourists are less likely to visit malaria-prone areas (see the case study on Uganda's attempts to combat malaria on page 168).

How has Malawi coped with its AIDS crisis?

Key statistics on Malawi	
Total population	15.3 million
GNI per capita	$280
Life expectancy	54 years
HIV prevalence rate	11%
Number living with HIV	920,000
Children orphaned by AIDS	650,000

The AIDS epidemic is responsible for eight deaths every hour in Malawi. Out of a population of nearly 14 million, almost one million people in Malawi were living with HIV at the end of 2007. AIDS is the leading cause of death amongst adults in Malawi, and is a major factor in the country's low life expectancy of just 53 years.

Malawi's first AIDS case was reported in 1985. Malawi was then under the dictatorial rule of President Hastings Banda and his puritanical beliefs made AIDS education very difficult as public discussion of sexual matters was generally banned or censored. Between 1985 and 1993, HIV prevalence amongst women tested at urban clinics increased from 2% to 30%.

In 1994, following the first multi-party elections, President Muluzi took office and acknowledged that the country was undergoing an AIDS epidemic. By this stage AIDS had already caused severe damage to Malawi's social and economic infrastructure. Farmers could not provide food, children could not attend school and workers could not support their families, either because they were infected with HIV or because they were caring for someone who was. In 2002, Malawi suffered its worst food crisis for over 50 years, with HIV one of the factors that contributed most significantly to the famine. About 70% of hospital deaths at that time were AIDS related.

The government response was to try to increase awareness of the disease. Malawi's first National AIDS Policy was launched in 2004. The policy was intended to improve the provision of prevention, treatment, care and support services. HIV prevalence has stabilized at between 11% and 17% since the mid-1990s, and prevalence amongst women attending antenatal clinics has fallen slightly. Several urban areas, including the capital, Lilongwe, have witnessed a decline in HIV prevalence, although some rural areas have seen prevalence increase. The diversity of languages and culture within Malawi has increased the difficulty in spreading AIDS education.

The AIDS crisis has affected all sectors of society in Malawi, but certain patterns have emerged as the epidemic has progressed:

- The majority of HIV infections in Malawi occur through heterosexual sex. Homosexuality is illegal though, as in most African countries, it is probably more common than is officially acknowledged
- There is a higher rate of infection amongst women than men. Around 60% of adults living with HIV in Malawi are female
- Young people between the ages of 13 and 24 have the highest rates of infection
- By the end of 2007 over half a million children had been orphaned by AIDS
- HIV prevalence is almost twice as high in urban areas as it is in rural areas but is declining in urban areas and rising in rural areas.

Persuading women to have HIV tests at antenatal clinics was difficult because they feared that a positive result would lead to discrimination but in 2007 the government introduced mandatory testing alongside a voluntary counselling programme. In 2008 around 68% of pregnant women received VCT (Voluntary Counselling and Testing), compared with just 8% in 2004.

Various NGOs have promoted the use of condoms in Malawi. Between 1992 and 2004 the percentage of married women using contraception increased from 7% to 28%. However, further progress has been more difficult with condom use well below the target of 55%. The influence of religious leaders is important and has probably adversely affected the wider acceptance of condoms in Malawi. A 2008 UN-funded project distributed female condoms through specially trained staff in beauty salons.

In 2004 only 13,000 Malawians infected with HIV were receiving anti-retroviral therapy. This rose to 146,657 by the end of 2008. However, there are still many people living with advanced HIV who are currently not receiving ARV treatment. Access to treatment is particularly limited in rural areas, as problems such as a lack of transportation prevent many people from reaching health services. These areas have been heavily affected by food shortages in recent years. Malnutrition is now endemic, meaning that even in cases where treatment is available, lack of food means the drugs are not as effective.

Attempts to increase access to HIV testing and treatment have been hindered by a severe shortage of staff. Malawi has just one doctor per 50,000 people – one of the lowest levels in the world. Around 60 nurses are trained every year, but at least 100 others leave the country annually to seek employment in other countries. While the shortage of medical staff in Malawi has partly been caused by factors such as migration and a lack of access to education, it has also been directly aggravated by AIDS: in 2008 four nurses were lost to HIV and AIDS-related illness every month.

Women in Malawi are socially and economically subordinate to men. This fuels HIV infection, as traditionally men are allowed to have sex with a number of partners and women are powerless to prevent unprotected sex. Many women are taught never to refuse sex with their husbands, and sexual abuse and coerced sex are common. In some communities a widow is married to a relative of her husband upon his death. There is a risk of HIV transmission, particularly in cases where AIDS was the cause of death of the woman's previous husband.

Get with it! Dancing is the order of the day at this AIDS club meeting in a Malawi school.

HIV infection in Malawi is disproportionately female, and younger women are particularly affected. AIDS affects more than four times as many women as men amongst the 15-19 age group in Malawi, and about a third more women than men amongst the 20-25 age group. However, amongst those who are over 30 the trend reverses, as more men than women are affected. This pattern reflects the fact that younger women are often married to older men, or coerced into having sex with them. Promoting gender equality is key to anti-AIDS strategy: the spread of the disease will be halted if women do not have to stay in abusive relationships and can insist on the use of condoms. Child mortality will also be reduced if pregnant women who are HIV-infected receive ARV therapy to reduce the chances of transferring the infection to their new-born child. In South Africa 43% of deaths of children under five are due to AIDS and babies who are HIV-positive are 15 times more likely to die within the first six months of life than uninfected babies. ∎

Combating malaria in Uganda

Key statistics on Uganda	
Total population	32.7 million
GNI per capita	$460
Life expectancy	53 years
HIV prevalence rate	6.5%
Households with at least one insecticide-treated bednet	16%
Under-fives receiving anti-malarial drugs	61%

Uganda has one of the highest incidences of malaria in the world, compounded by high rates of HIV and tuberculosis. Reducing the incidence of these diseases is vital for development but attempts to fight malaria have met many problems.

Background

Clinically diagnosed malaria is the leading cause of deaths in Uganda, accounting for 25-40% of outpatient visits at health facilities, 15-20% of all hospital admissions, and 9-14% of all hospital deaths. Nearly half of inpatient deaths among children under the age of five are attributed to malaria. A contributing physical factor is that, in most parts of Uganda, temperature and rainfall allow stable, year-round malaria transmission at high levels with relatively little seasonal variability.

The President's Malaria Initiative (PMI)

Uganda is one of 15 countries participating in PMI, which was launched in 2005 and is led by the US Agency for International Development. The goal of PMI is to work with partners to halve the incidence of malaria in sub-Saharan Africa and promote general development. PMI works with organizations such as the Roll Back Malaria Partnership; the World Health Organization; the World Bank; the Bill and Melinda Gates Foundation; NGOs, including faith-based and community groups; and the private sector.

Strategy

PMI supports four key interventions to prevent and treat malaria:
- Insecticide-treated mosquito nets (ITNs). Sleeping under a long-lasting ITN provides protection from malaria-carrying mosquitoes. The nets are non-toxic to humans, but can repel and kill mosquitoes for up to three years
- Indoor residual spraying (IRS). IRS involves the spraying of the inside walls of

PMI strategy progress 2006-09

	2006	2007	2008	2009
IRS: Houses sprayed	103,329	446,117	575,903	567,035
ITNs: Distributed	305,305	683,777	999,894	651,203
SP Treatments	-	-	2,556	45,780
ACTs: Procured	261,870	-	1,140,840	-

Uganda Malaria Operational Plan 2010

houses with insecticides. Mosquitoes are killed when they land on these sprayed walls, reducing malaria transmission
- Intermittent preventive treatment for pregnant women (IPTp). IPTp is a means of reducing the consequences of malaria in the pregnant woman and her unborn child. It consists of the administration of at least two doses of the anti-malarial drug sulfadoxine-pyrimethamine (SP)

- Diagnosis and treatment. Effective management of malaria depends on early, accurate diagnosis and prompt treatment with an effective drug. Artemisinin-based combination therapies (ACTs) are the recommended first-line treatment.

Collecting a free insecticide-treated mosquito net from the NGO Malaria Consortium in northern Uganda.

Reported malaria cases in Uganda 2002-08

Year	Reported malaria cases All ages	Reported malaria cases <5 years
2002	7,536,748	3,900,000
2003	9,657,332	4,400,000
2004	10,717,076	4,700,000
2005	9,867,174	5,800,000
2006	10,168,389	3,857,916
2007	12,038,438	4,528,442
2008	11,029,571	8,656,327

WHO World Malaria Report 2009

Despite the evidence that more people are protected or treated, the incidence of malaria in Uganda is increasing. The country still has the third highest number of deaths each year in Africa and some of the highest recorded malaria transmission rates in the continent, particularly in the areas around Lake Kyoga. On average, a person in the Apac district near Lake Kyoga will receive more than 1,500 infectious bites each year.

Doubts have been raised about the government's commitment to the anti-malaria strategy after indoor spraying of houses was stopped in 2008 because of a High Court injunction from a politician who claimed that the spray contained DDT and could cause cancer. There are also allegations of corruption and in 2010 three officials from the Malaria Control programme were arrested for illegally selling anti-malarial drugs for personal gain. Insecticide-treated nets have been distributed but they are not being properly used by those most at risk and an education programme is needed to maximize their effectiveness.

One positive sign is the agreement between Indian pharmaceutical giant Cipla and Afro-Alpine Pharma to produce artemisinin powder at a factory in western Uganda. The domestic production of an important anti-malarial drug is very good news for the region's poor who bear the brunt of the disease – and it is also good news for the small-scale farmers who have been contracted to grow the *artemisia annua* shrub from which the artemisinin is extracted. ■

Gender & Development

How does the role of women in society affect development?

* *Gender inequality affects all societies at every stage of development.*
* *Inequalities experienced by women have a negative effect on the development process.*
* *In many societies women have a significant role in income generation as well as in household management and child-rearing.*
* *Discrimination against women has its roots in traditional culture and is sometimes reinforced by legislation.*
* *Improvements in gender equality have a profoundly positive effect on human development across the board.*

Key points

Why is gender equality a vital development issue?

The decision by the United Nations to include gender equality, the empowerment of women and improvement in maternal health among its targets for the Millennium Development Goals was based on overwhelming global evidence of inequality, discrimination and abuse of female rights.

Gender and poverty

In most of the poorest countries it is women who carry out the hard physical labour involved in subsistence farming, including weeding and tilling the land, grinding the grain, carrying water and cooking. However, 75% of the world's women cannot get bank loans because they have unpaid or insecure jobs and they are not even entitled to own property in many countries. It is estimated that women only own 1% of the world's wealth. The preference for male children (not least because they are traditionally more likely to earn money that will benefit the family) has

- Of the world's one billion poorest people, 60% are women and girls
- Two-thirds of the 960 million adults in the world who cannot read are women
- The majority of children who are not in primary school are girls
- Women make up, on average, only 16% of parliamentarians worldwide
- Women everywhere earn less than men because they are concentrated in low-paying jobs and because they earn less for doing the same work
- The typical women's role as unpaid carers of family members is unrecognized for its contribution to the global economy
- Up to half of all adult women have experienced violence at the hands of their intimate partners
- Systematic sexual violence against women has characterized almost all recent armed conflicts and is used as a tool of terror
- In sub-Saharan Africa, 57% of those living with HIV are women, and young women aged 15-24 are at least three times more likely to be infected than men of the same age
- Each year, half a million women die and 18 million more suffer chronic disability from preventable complications of pregnancy and childbirth.

Taking Gender Equality Seriously, UNDP 2006

Data

resulted in sex-selective abortions or even infanticide of girls in India and China on such a scale that it has led to a population imbalance. In countries where males are valued more than females, girls and women receive less food and healthcare when resources are short and are less likely to be able to attend school.

Modern approaches to gender and development

Recognition of global inequality as a factor in development and a human rights issue has a relatively short history and has evolved from 1970s demands for women to be included in development programmes to, more recently, a wider recognition that the social and cultural factors that create gender inequality have to be changed, including laws that discriminate against women. Three approaches can be identified.

1970s Women in Development (WID)
This approach recognized gender inequalities and made demands for women's inclusion in development programmes and issues. Its weakness lay in its failure to tackle the underlying social, cultural, legal and economic factors that cause inequality.

1980s Women and Development (WAD)
This model recognized that both men and women were disadvantaged by global economic structures, including class and wealth distribution. According to this thinking, women have always been part of the development process but their participation has been to their disadvantage and worsened their chances of equality. The situation will only improve for

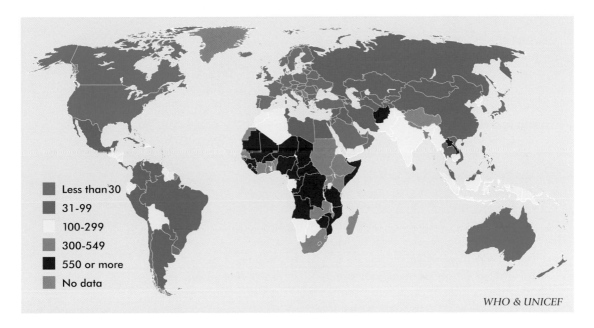

WHO & UNICEF

women when international structures are more equitable.

Late 1980s/1990s *Gender and Development (GAD)*

Although this approach was based on feminist ideas, it did consider the impact of development on both sexes. Here development was recognized as a complex process influenced by political, social and economic factors. A country is not in a particular state or stage of development – it is much more complicated than that – and the important thing is to empower the disadvantaged in communities to improve and enhance their lives. The state also needs to support the social reproduction role of women in society.

2000s

More recently, the focus has been on a rights-based approach and the need to change laws that discriminate against women. The Convention on the Elimination of All Forms of Discrimination against Women (CEDAW), which was adopted by the UN General Assembly in 1979, has been seen as increasingly important.

Maternal mortality ratio, 2008 – deaths per 100,000 live births.

The importance of gender equality

Addressing the inequality between men and women actually makes good economic sense. When women have equal access to education, and go on to participate fully in business and economic decision-making, it makes a huge difference in the fight against poverty. Empowering women means that they will be better educated and likely to be healthier. Improving their access to financial resources and jobs translates into increased earning power and a rise in household incomes. Women's autonomy

The myriad benefits of girls' education

Among the many long-term benefits of educating girls are:

- *Enhanced economic development*. Decades of research provide substantial evidence of the link between the expansion of basic education and economic development – and girls' education has an even more positive effect. Countries that fail to raise the education level of women to the same as that of men increase the cost of their development efforts and pay for the failure with lower growth and reduced income
- *Education for the next generation*. If educated girls become mothers they are much more likely to send their children to school, thereby passing on and multiplying benefits both for themselves and society in a positive intergenerational effect
- *Protection*. [Educated] children are less likely to be trafficked or exploited as labourers, and less vulnerable to abuse and violence; and since girls are more likely to suffer these assaults, education is especially important to their protection
- *Healthier families*. Children of more educated women tend to be better nourished and get sick less often. The effect of a mother's education on her child's health and nutrition is so significant that each extra year of maternal education reduces the rate of mortality for children under the age of five by between 5 and 10%
- *Fewer maternal deaths*. Women who have been to school are less likely to die in childbirth. The effect of schooling in reducing the number of births means that, for every 1,000 women, every additional year of education will prevent two maternal deaths.

UNICEF, *The State of the World's Children 2004*

Feature

– the ability to participate in decision-making – is closely associated with improved child nutrition. According to UNICEF, there is a 'double dividend' to gender equality – not only does it improve women's own lives but it furthers the cause of child survival and development. The children of educated, empowered women also tend to be more healthy and to have a much better chance of breaking out of the cycle of poverty.

Although gender equality and women's empowerment is central to achieving the Millennium Development Goals and there are some positive trends in gender equality, there are still many areas of concern. Girls account for the majority of children not attending school and almost two-thirds of women in the developing world work in the informal sector, where they are much more vulnerable to job availability and low pay, or as unpaid workers in the home. The promotion of equal rights in the developing world is very uneven and some countries have made much quicker progress than others. There are many examples where culture and religion have prevented progress and the fight for global gender equality will be a long, hard battle.

Sustainable development is not possible without greater gender equality and there are examples of successful projects run by the state, NGOs, UN and other organizations which see improving the lives of women as their primary aim. Most women in developing countries are unable to access finance because they lack collateral and steady employment. To overcome this problem, many development schemes concentrate on offering microcredit. This involves very small loans being given to people in poverty who would normally not be able to access credit. The intention is to help them set up small businesses and to encourage entrepreneurship. The box below describes an example of a micro-loan scheme for women in Liberia that was set up with funds from the UN.

'The fight for global gender equality will be a long, hard battle.'

The impact of globalization on gender inequality

Globalization has had a mixed impact on gender equality. In the developed world, one of the impacts of globalization has been that more women have the opportunity to go out to work and are unable to spend as much time

---

Micro-loans boost women's empowerment in rural Liberia

For the women of the Mandel-Mel Women's Union in Gbarma, Gbarpolu County, in the northern part of Liberia, agriculture production is gradually taking on a new face as microfinance schemes boost farming projects, generating thousands of dollars in revenue.

Established in April this year, the 25-member local women's union was the first organization to benefit from micro-loans given by the Village Savings and Loan Association (VSLA). Since then, the women have cultivated 10 hectares of land for pineapples, cassava and eddoes, with hopes of introducing other crops as production expands.

The project, which began with an initial micro-loan of $7,200, jointly funded by the United Nations Development Programme (UNDP) and the United Nations Capital Development Fund (UNCDF) through the VSLA, has so far accumulated $162,955 in revolving funds.

The microfinance scheme managed by the VSLA is just one of the many ongoing small loan initiatives in various parts of the country. Although not every case turns out as successful as the Mandel-Mel women's pineapple project, micro-loans have helped secure sustainable access to financial services and improve the livelihoods of many low-income people of Liberia.

United Nations Liberia News, 24 December 2009

Feature

Women protesting against their low pay and poor working conditions in Ciudad Juarez, Mexico. They work in a factory assembling parts for the US market.

bringing up and caring for their families as in previous generations. One of the consequences of this has been the use of women from developing countries as cheap labour to fill this caring gap; this may have a knock-on effect in terms of a family care deficit in those developing countries.

Many observers, including feminists, believe that there have been other negative impacts from the growth of a global economy. Transnational corporations (TNCs) based in the rich world have increasingly moved their operations overseas looking for the cheapest sources of labour. The low status of women in many developing countries means that the cheapest labour available is female. Young females in particular are particularly at risk of exploitation because they have no experience of the workplace and no knowledge of how

> *The International Labour Organization says there are at least 850 EPZs (Export Processing Zones) in the world, but that number is likely much closer to 1,000, spread through 70 countries and employing roughly 27 million workers... Regardless of where the EPZs are located, the workers' stories have a certain mesmerizing sameness: the workday is long –14 hours in Sri Lanka, 12 hours in Indonesia, 16 in southern China, 12 in the Philippines. The vast majority of workers are women, always young, always working for contractors or subcontractors... The management is military-style, the supervisors often abusive, the wages below subsistence and the work low-skill and tedious... Fear pervades the zones. The governments are afraid of losing their foreign factories; the factories are afraid of losing their brand-name buyers; and the workers are afraid of losing their unstable jobs.*
>
> **Naomi Klein, *No Logo*, Knopf 2000**

Witness

'When you are financially independent, you are also independent in other ways,' says Vinutha, who works for a software company in Banglaore, India. Her friend Lakshmi agrees. She is quite clear about the kind of marriage she wants. She will continue working and have one or at most two children (whatever the sex), and if her husband treats her badly then she will 'have to look elsewhere'.

International Socialism Journal, Autumn 2001

to defend themelves in the workplace. The long hours they work mean that they are cut off from their normal social support structures and stereotyped as a docile and nimble workforce. Much of the work done by women, particularly in the recently industrialized countries – in the Special Economic Zones of China, for example, or the *maquiladoras* of Mexico – is repetitive assembly work in strictly regimented conditions. Lives outside the factory are also often affected by the long hours and the intrusive impact of the large corporations on local life.

TNCs have been strongly criticized for their treatment of workers in developing countries and many have become sensitive to the impact such negative publicity can have on their brand images. It is not difficult to compile a long list of famous companies that have been accused of abusing the rights of workers in developing countries and female workers are particularly vulnerable.

Other observers identify more positive impacts of globalization. They cite evidence that many women are liberated from their previous lives of drudgery by the experience of going to work and having the opportunity

Overcoming Purdah

The participation of women in the workforce in Bangladesh is a relatively new phenomenon. Apart from domestic work, there was little public space for women in an atmosphere of Purdah, or veiling, in this primarily Muslim country. Rural schoolteachers have always been men and the urban health sector, which hires female nurses, is extremely small and serves less than 5% of the population.

The great majority of Bangladesh's 130 million people continue to live in rural areas and rely on agriculture for their income. Garment work – which employs around one million people, 90% of them female – has therefore been a novelty and it is no wonder that many economic experts have applauded this new development. Along with their sisters who have entered financial markets by receiving microcredit loans, found employment in NGOs and public and private organizations, or migrated to other countries as domestic workers, these women have lifted their veils and come out of their homes in larger numbers than ever before.

Farida Khan, *Open Democracy*, 14 April 2004

Some benefits from focusing on gender in development

- Positive changes in gender relations and more respectful social attitudes towards women
- More decision-making and political participation by women in the community
- Women's increased knowledge of their legal rights
- Greater likelihood that girls will stay in school
- Reduced violence against women
- Improved communication and mutual support between men and women on family planning, HIV and other sexually transmitted infections
- Increased knowledge by men of women's healthcare issues
- Shifts in attitudes about shared roles and responsibilities between men and women in child-rearing, labour and reproductive health issues.

State of the World Population 2005, UNFPA

Feature

to meet other women and develop relationships. One study found that women factory workers in Southeast Asian countries had more personal freedom, including more choice in marriage, than those who remained in rural areas.

The evidence concerning the impact of globalization on gender equality will need to be constantly reviewed as the process has an ever-changing impact on millions of lives in the developing world.

There are clearly very marked contrasts between the experiences of women in different countries. This is a dynamic issue which is undergoing constant changes, some for the better and some for the worse. More evidence on the recent global progress towards achieving gender equality is considered in the review of the Millennium Development Goals in Chapter 14.

The two case studies provide a marked contrast to each other. Kenya is an example of a developing country in which social and cultural factors have to be overcome in order for women to benefit from more equal relations between the sexes. Traditional Japanese society, meanwhile, was also patriarchal but economic and social change over the last 30 years has had a profound impact on the way in which Japanese women perceive their role in society.

Breaking with tradition

Key statistics on Kenya	
Total population	39.8 million
GNI per capita	$770
Lifetime risk of maternal death	1 in 39
Contraceptive prevalence	46%
Female literacy rate as % of male	92%

Kenya still retains the characteristics of a traditional, patriarchal society, where the husband is the head of the household and women often have little influence in decisions affecting their lives. Only 5% of women own property or the land they work on – this is a primary cause of economic hardship and increases their dependence on men.

Tradition and culture frequently combine to make life very difficult for many Kenyan women. It is hard for a woman to refuse to have sex with her husband. In some communities, the relatives of a man who dies will disinherit his widow and children, leaving them without the means to sustain themselves. Producing proof of marriage is another problem for widows who are trying to reclaim property from their husband's family. Forced marriage is also a custom in some communities. On the death of her husband, a woman may be 'inherited' by his brother or close relative. The woman's consent to this new marriage or to sexual relations is not sought. Violence is a feature of many women's lives.

For many of the women who are forced into a new marriage there is the added worry of the health risks associated with marriage. They may become infected with HIV and eventually die of AIDS. The high levels of HIV in the population mean that sexual violence against women and children carries a significant risk of transmission of the virus and of subsequent illness and death. The practice of Female Genital Mutilation (FGM) is widespread. About 50% of females nationwide have suffered FGM.

Access to land and labour rights

In most rural areas of Kenya, access to land provides the basis for economic survival. It ensures security and can lead to higher investment and increased productivity. Although under official law women have the right to inherit land from their fathers and deceased husbands, in practice cultural and institutional barriers often prevent women from claiming their rights. As a result, women are increasingly marginalized and pushed into extreme poverty. Restricting women to a domestic role also makes it

Women in Marakwet district returning home with firewood.

their country. They make up only 30% of the public-sector workforce and only 22 out of the 220 elected members of parliament are female.

Rural land management

More than half of the rural population in Kenya are female and they are primarily responsible for family food production. They commonly provide over 80% of the labour involved in food production as well as collecting wood for fuel, water for domestic use and cooking. Development schemes in Kenya that focus on land management have to recognize the importance of female participation if there is to be any hope of success. Women are mainly responsible for remedial action that might be needed if the soil becomes exhausted and yields decline and this could mean changing farming practices or providing manure to replenish the soil.

Urbanization means that many men will be away in urban areas and it is rural women's groups who are most likely to be involved in projects to improve water supply or fight against deforestation by starting tree seedling nurseries. Recognizing the importance of the role of women in rural areas and raising their status through education and participation in projects has become a priority for most NGOs. ■

difficult for them to be aware of their rights in any dealings with the outside world. The institutions they engage with also have deeply embedded traditional cultures that reinforce the marginalization of women and make the problem worse.

In such a patriarchal society, women have little control over the governance of

Key statistics on Japan	
Total population	127.2 million
GNI per capita	$37,870
Lifetime risk of maternal death	1 in 12,200
Contraceptive prevalence	54%
Female enrolment in secondary school	100%

Women's transformation

The high growth rate of the Japanese economy in the 1960s brought rapid changes, such as an improved standard of living and scientific and technological innovation. The increased national wealth helped in bringing about longer life expectancy, a lower birth rate, and higher educational standards. Family life was affected, and particularly the lives of women. They began to participate in much greater numbers in economic and social activities but the traditional idea that women were to stay at home was still deeply rooted.

The Asian financial crisis of the mid-1990s resulted in Japanese employers, particularly in the service sector, employing women as a cheaper source of labour to reduce their costs. The result of this was that women became much more established in the Japanese labour market. In 2008 the percentage of women in the workforce was 40.8%, compared to 35.9% in 1985.

Although more women went out to work they were still expected to carry out their domestic role as they always had done. Government research in 1995 suggested that

on average a working man spent 26 minutes each weekday on domestic chores compared to over three hours by full-time working women. Marriage did not appear an attractive package for many young women as a result

Teenagers in Tokyo displaying their distance from the traditional female role.

of this and other factors such as the long hours worked by most men and the limited availability of childcare.

This helps to explain why for the last two decades more and more young women have not been getting married. One in four women in their thirties and one in 10 women in their forties is unmarried and their numbers are rising. To remain single in Japan also means that it is likely they will not have children because to be a single parent or a child of a single parent still carries a social stigma in Japanese society.

The increasing number of women who choose to stay single is an indication that a major change has taken place. By 2020, almost 30% of Japanese households will be headed by singles. In Tokyo the number is more than 40%, according to government statistics. About 43% of Japanese men in their early thirties are unmarried, double the rate in 1980.

One of the inevitable results of this is that women are having children much later, if at all. Japan's birth rate dipped to 1.29 children per woman in 2008, one of the lowest in the developed world, from 1.54 in 1990. Japan's population is expected to peak at an estimated 128 million in 2010 and after that, the population is projected to decrease, dropping to 120 million by 2026 and to 100 million by 2050. The high life expectancy in Japan causes its own problems. The average life expectancy for women is 86 years and for men 79 years. With fewer workers paying into it, the national pension system is on the verge of bankruptcy – increasing proportions of the

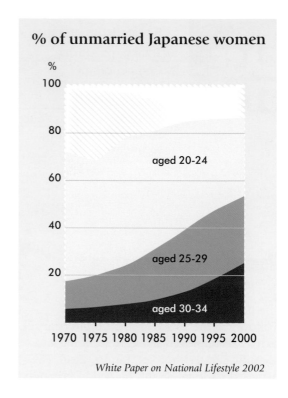

% of unmarried Japanese women

aged 20-24

aged 25-29

aged 30-34

White Paper on National Lifestyle 2002

population are of pensionable age and receive their pensions for a longer period.

Some Japanese political leaders have criticized single women who have refused to retain their traditional roles in the home. Yoshiro Mori, Japan's former prime minister, insisted that women who did not give birth should not receive pensions. 'Welfare is supposed to take care of and reward those women who have lots of children,' he said. 'It is truly strange to say that we have to use tax money to take care of women who don't even give birth once, who grow old living their lives selfishly and singing the praises of freedom.' ∎

Does migration have a negative impact on development?

* *Migration usually reflects inequalities in levels of development.*
* *Economic, social, political and environmental factors may lead to migration.*
* *Migration is often the result of conflict. Conflict has a negative impact on development.*
* *Internal and international migration may encourage or hinder development in those areas where it is taking place.*

Key points

Human migration has a very long history and has been an important factor in shaping the cultures and societies we know today. Countries such as Australia, Canada, New Zealand and the US have effectively been formed by successive waves of migration over the last few centuries. Migration may be over a short or long distance, within a state or to another country, voluntary or forced. Migratory movements have varied characteristics and the reasons for migrations are also very diverse. The most common migratory movement in the world is internal, from rural areas to urban areas in the same country, particularly in the developing world. The phenomenon of urbanization has seen hundreds of millions of people seeking to improve their lives. The result has been the creation of vast cities faced with the challenge of providing the services needed for such a large population influx. The rapid growth of cities in the developing world is one of the dominant issues in modern human geography.

* It has been estimated that approximately 740 million people are internal migrants – almost four times as many as those who have moved between nations
* Among people who have moved across national borders, just over a third moved from a developing to a developed country – fewer than 70 million people

- Most of the world's 200 million international migrants moved from one developing country to another or between developed countries.

Why do people migrate?

One of the main contemporary forms of migration involves millions of migrant workers who move temporarily to find jobs in countries where wealth levels and job opportunities are higher. It is estimated, for example, that there are 300,000 young women from countries such as Bangladesh and the Philippines who are employed as maids in Kuwait, while large numbers of young Pakistani males are employed in the construction industry in Saudi Arabia. The Arab states of the Persian Gulf – including Qatar, Bahrain and United Arab Emirates – are the largest employers of temporary migrant workers because of their relative wealth and low population. In most Arab Gulf countries the labour force consists of up to 80% migrant workers. The workers mostly come from the Philippines, Indonesia, Sri Lanka, Nepal and Bangladesh. About 10% of the population of the Philippines (8 million people) are migrant workers.

Conflict in different parts of the world, including Iraq, Afghanistan, Somalia, the Balkan states and central Africa, has forced many people to flee their countries because of the violence that surrounds them. In many of the receiving countries a tension has developed between those immigrants who have a genuine fear for their lives and those who are fleeing from poverty and seeking a better quality of life – economic

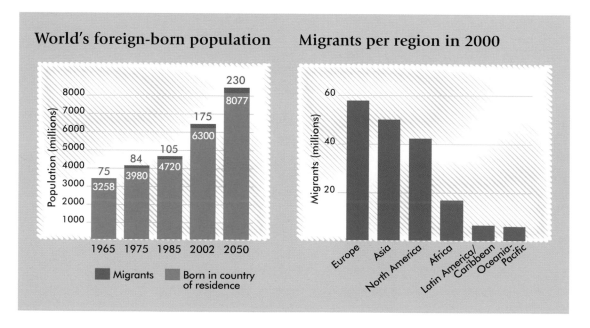

'Refugee' – a legal definition

Refugee is a legal term used to describe a person who fulfils the definition set out in the Geneva Convention of 1951 relating to the status of refugees. The Geneva Convention contains the internationally recognized definition of a refugee, and this definition is applied by all countries which have signed the Convention, including the UK.

The Convention says that in order to be recognized as a refugee a person has to show that: *'Owing to a well-founded fear of being persecuted for reasons of race, religion, nationality, membership of a particular social group or political opinion, is outside his country of nationality and is unable or, owing to such fear, is unwilling to avail himself of the protection of that country; or who, not having a nationality and being outside the country of his former habitual residence as a result of such events, is unable or, owing to such fear, is unwilling to return to it.'*

This definition can be broken down into various parts. In order to make a successful asylum application you will need to show that each of the parts applies to you. If you cannot show that all the different parts apply to you then you will not be able to make a successful application.

Well-founded fear – This means that you must be genuinely afraid of return to your country of nationality or habitual residence, and that fear must be what any ordinary person would fear when considering the information available about the situation in the country of origin. The fear must be viewed in context.

Persecution – There is no definition of 'persecution' in the Convention itself, but we understand it to mean a threat to the person's life or freedom, or other serious human rights violations. It can also be the result of a series of less serious elements which, taken together, form a pattern of treatment which amounts to persecution. Discrimination alone will not necessarily amount to persecution, but if the discrimination makes it very difficult, or even impossible for you to earn a living, practise your religion or access normally available benefits such as education, then it *may* amount to persecution.

For reasons of race, religion, nationality, membership of a particular social group or political opinion – These are known as the 'Convention Reasons'. Unless the persecution suffered falls within one of these definitions, you are not a refugee, even if you have been persecuted or severely ill-treated.

Is outside the country of nationality – This is a vital ingredient. You cannot be a refugee while still in your country of origin. You have to escape your country and apply for asylum in another country in order to fall within the definition in the Geneva Convention.

Is unable or, owing to such fear, is unwilling to avail himself of the protection of that country – For you to be **unable** to obtain protection from your country of origin, there has to be something beyond your control which prevents you from doing this, for instance civil war or other disturbance, or because the authorities of the country of origin have refused your request for protection. If you are **unwilling** to avail yourself of the protection of your country of origin you must be unwilling as a result of your well-founded fear of persecution for a Convention reason, and so this refers back to the earlier part of the definition. In order to be successful you will have to show that the danger to you exists everywhere in your country, and that there is nowhere safe for you to go.

Islington Law Centre 2008

Feature

migrants. The distinction is often very difficult to make and the term 'asylum seekers' has been frequently used in recent years to describe both groups. The UK, like many other countries, does not make it easy for a migrant to be granted refugee status and allowed to stay in the country. The box on page 185 contains advice given to migrants who are seeking refugee status in the UK.

Theories of migration

Migratory patterns are complex but there are theories that have been proposed to help us understand more about the reasons why they occur. They offer a simplification of the process as a way of clarifying general principles and even older theories such as Ravenstein's (1889) have some relevance to the modern world.

Ernest Ravenstein is usually regarded as the earliest migration theorist; he used the census information from England and Wales to develop his 'Laws of Migration'. In his theory, migration is governed by a push/pull process. Push processes are unfavourable conditions in one place that tend to push people out, such as oppressive laws, persecution or high levels of taxation. Pull processes are favourable external conditions that tend to pull people from where they live, such as better healthcare or more employment opportunities.

His law stated that:

- The primary cause of migration is better external economic opportunities
- The volume of migration decreases as distance increases

Observation	Explanation
Most migrants only go a short distance	Limited technology, transport and poor communications. People know more about local opportunities
Migration occurs in stages	Typically from rural to small town, to large town or city in steps. People become locked into the urban hierarchy
There is movement away from large cities as well as movement into it	The rich move away from the urban areas and commute from nearby villages and small towns
Long-distance migrants are more likely to move to large cities	People who are far away will only know about the opportunities in large cities
Urban dwellers are less migratory than rural dwellers	There are fewer opportunities in rural areas
Women are more migratory than men over short distances	This is because of marriage and the low status of women in some societies
Migration increases with advances in technology.	Improved transport, communications and easier access to information have an effect.

- Migration occurs in stages rather than in one big move
- Factors such as gender, age and social class influence a person's ability to migrate.

Theorists that followed Ravenstein mostly offered variations on his model of migration. Stouffer's theory of intervening opportunities proposed that the volume of migration between two places depends not so much on the distance between the places and the population size but the perceived opportunities that exist in those two places and between them. The Gravity Model of the 1960s stated that the volume of the migration is inversely proportional to the distance travelled by the migrants and directly proportional to the populations of the source and destination.

Everett Lee's model amended the push/pull mechanism slightly and proposed the idea of intervening obstacles that have to be overcome before migration takes place. It is more of a behavioural model, with the source and destination having a range of attributes that potential migrants will perceive differently depending on their personal characteristics such as age, sex and marital status.

As far as Lee was concerned, although variables such as distance and physical and political barriers can impede migration, the migration

A migrant worker from Nicaragua picks coffee beans in Monteverde, Costa Rica.

process is selective because things such as age, sex, level of education and social class will affect how a person can respond to these intervening obstacles.

Theories on international patterns of migration are also variants of the push/pull model.

- Neoclassical economic theory states that nations with scarce labour supply and high demand will have high wages that pull immigrants in from nations with a surplus of labour
- Segmented labour-market theory is more complex and argues that 'developed' economies require a certain level of immigration because they have a primary market of secure, well-paid work and a secondary market of low-wage work. The theory argues that immigrants are recruited to fill the jobs that are necessary for the overall economy to function but are avoided by the home-bred population because of the poor working conditions
- World-systems theory argues that international migration is an inevitable outcome of global capitalism. There are structural problems caused by industrial development in the rich countries which result in migration from the periphery (poor nations) to the core (rich nations). This migration occurs due to 'push' factors that are created in the poor nations by the way that core nations have made themselves wealthy – for example, by growing cash crops in developing countries and displacing subsistence farmers.

A key modern example of mass migration is that within China, where millions are leaving the rural areas to seek work in the booming cities (see the case study opposite).

The migration of refugees fleeing conflict or environmental catastrophe is clearly rather different in character. In Africa in the 1970s there were only 700,000 refugees and internally displaced people (IDPs); today there are 7 million. Conflict is the major cause of this huge increase. The common notion is that refugees are a temporary problem and that they return home within a relatively short period. However, more often than not, refugees are a long-term issue in terms of the pressure they put on resources. Governments often only plan for the short term when there is a refugee influx and fail to take account of the longer-term social and environmental problems a longer stay may cause.

The migratory experience of many Tutsi people from Rwanda in 1994 was a case in point. The forced migration of refugees into neighbouring countries – caused by ethnic genocide – had a devastating environmental and social impact and has left a lasting legacy. Hundreds of thousands of people were forced to seek shelter in areas that were ill-equipped to cope with such large numbers (see the case study on page 193).

China
CASE STUDY

Key statistics on China	
Total population	1,345.7 million
Population annual growth rate	0.8%
GNI per capita	$3,620
Life expectancy	73 years
Urbanized population	46%
Average annual growth of urban population	3.5%

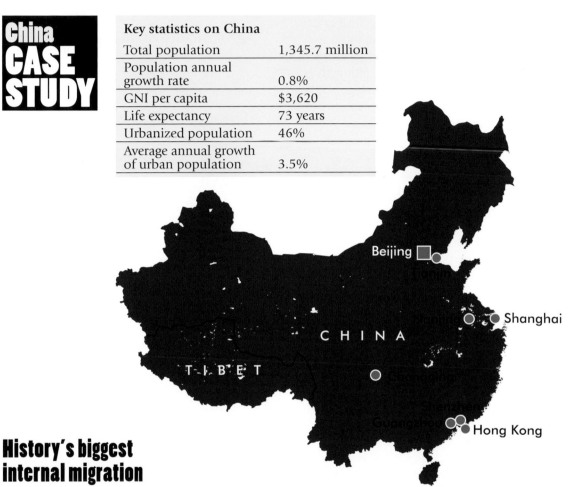

Beijing
Tianjin
Nanjing   Shanghai
CHINA
T I B E T
Chengdu
Shenzhen
Guangzhou   Hong Kong

History's biggest internal migration

China is experiencing the biggest internal migration in history. An estimated 230 million Chinese people have left the countryside and migrated to the cities in recent years. They have become known as the 'floating workers'. About 13 million new migrants are added to this number every year. So many migrants leave their homes looking for work that the rail system cannot cope. In Hunan province, 52 people were trampled to death in the late 1990s when 10,000 migrants were herded onto a freight train. At Chinese New Year and other holiday times when workers try to return home to their families, public transport systems are completely overwhelmed. These labour flows are basically directed from the interior to coastal areas; people tend to move from the central and western regions to the eastern areas.

The reasons for this mass migration are not difficult to understand. Many farmers and farm workers have been made obsolete by modern agricultural practices – involving greater use of machinery – and average rural incomes are only 20% of average urban incomes. Most of the migrants are from the provinces of Sichuan, Hunan, Henan, Anhui and Jiangxi. Their destinations are usually cities like Beijing, Shanghai, Shenzen and other coastal conurbations, although increasing numbers are also making for cities in the interior where there is less competition for employment.

They work for low pay, often under horrendous conditions, in factories, at construction sites, in mines and on railways and roads. Women are mostly employed in low-paying factory jobs or service jobs. The average migrant earns $100 a month and sends about a third of it home. Families with at least one migrant worker are almost automatically lifted above the poverty level of $1 a day.

There have been restrictions on movement in China for many years as part of the centrally planned economy and the need to maintain rural populations for food production. A strict registration system was devised to classify people as either rural or urban residents. Only registered city dwellers were allowed to live in urban areas and unregistered rural migrants could be imprisoned if caught. The *hukou* is the name of the official household registration card; this records people as living where their families are originally from. Migrant workers without an urban permit have a very difficult time. They face discrimination from urban dwellers because of their lack of education and lack of social skills. They are paid less than other

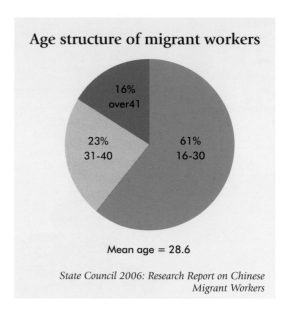

Age structure of migrant workers

16% over41

23% 31-40

61% 16-30

Mean age = 28.6

State Council 2006: Research Report on Chinese Migrant Workers

workers and are denied the basic services enjoyed by permanent urban residents such as subsidized housing, subsidized medical care and schooling for their children. Some cities are becoming more flexible in granting urban residence to migrants but, in general, migrant workers have a very hard life.

The southern province of Guangdong is one of China's fastest-growing industrial areas and is one of those planning to end the hukou permit system. One third of its population of 110 million are migrants but economic growth has been so fast that it has struggled to attract as many migrant workers as it needs to fill its factories. The largest concentration is in the Pearl River Delta,

'Scrapping the [hukou] system will be helpful in the long term, but it will be hard to eradicate deep-rooted prejudices against those from the countryside. Some people say there's no way they should live in the city, because of their low education and bad habits.'

Ren Li, resident of Chongqing

> 'Country people stand out in the urban crowd. Their hands and faces are more weathered, their clothes simpler and more ragged. Often they move about town lugging unwieldy bundles of bedding and belongings, wrapped in plaid-patterned woven-plastic fabric that somehow has become the standard for such purposes in poor countries around the world.'
>
> James Fallows, *The Atlantic*, April 2009

Witness

where there are an estimated 10 million migrants, including half a million child labourers.

China's government has indicated that it wants to improve the rights and working conditions of its migrant workers and there are many who have predicted that the large migrant workforce will pose a major threat to China's security in the future if their standard of living is not significantly improved. China is hoping to pay for this improvement using the income from a continued expansion of its exports. Having such a large 'floating workforce' has its advantages and disadvantages for the Chinese economy and social structure.

In February 2009 the Chinese government

Assembling toys in a factory in Shenzhen Special Economic Zone.

Benefits of large migrant workforce:

- A large supply of labour in urban areas
- Although the work is low paid, it does reduce poverty levels
- Better access to education opportunities for migrant workers and their children if they are allowed urban benefits
- An increase in remittances by migrants to families in rural regions. Migrants send home around $45 billion a year. On average, 80% of their incomes go to their families. This money is vital to keeping the rural economy going, allowing families to move into better homes, send their kids to school, and buy things like livestock, home additions, or even a plough or tractor
- Migrant workers help to increase the local demand for services.

Disadvantages of large migrant workforce:

- The large numbers of migrants moving into cities causes overpopulation and the development of migrant suburbs with no access to healthcare or education
- The increasing size of cities leads to an increased demand for water, electricity, sanitation and other services
- Migration away from rural areas leads to rural depopulation and a distorted population profile as younger people form the majority of migrants
- Police officials have warned that rapid changes to the residency system could lead to social chaos and soaring crime. Monitoring of targeted individuals such as dissidents would also become harder
- The increased industrial activity possible because of migrant workers will lead to more environmental degradation and pollution.

Feature

announced that 20 million migrant workers had lost their jobs or could not find one because of the economic crisis. The figure was triple the 6 million figure it had released just a month before. In some villages, most of the workers that had left returned home. However, in 2010 economic growth in China returned to its pre-crisis level and the demand for migrant labour increased again. ∎

Rwandan refugee crisis, 1994

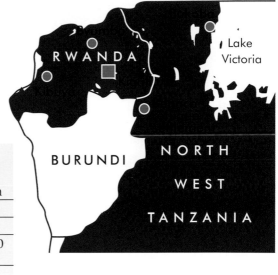

Key statistics on Tanzania and Rwanda		
	Tanzania	Rwanda
Total population	43.7 million	10.0 million
GNI per capita	$500	$460
Life expectancy	56 years	51 years
Infant mortality rate	68 per 1,000 live births	70 per 1,000 live births
Urbanized population	26%	19%

In 1994, the most systematic and organized genocide since the Nazis' 'final solution' was committed in Rwanda. From the beginning of the genocide on 6 April to the beginning of the humanitarian relief programme on 12 July, around 800,000 Rwandans were killed.

From 1993 'hate' broadcasts on the radio were the central mechanism used to incite fear and hatred between the Hutu and Tutsi ethnic groups. The beginning of the genocide was signalled by the shooting down of President Habyarimana's plane. The Hutu population were urged to take up arms because it was suggested that Tutsi groups were responsible. Within hours, thousands had already been killed. It was later discovered that the shooting was organized by a group of radical Hutus led by the President's wife, Agathé Habyarimana, and had been planned for over two years.

The international community did nothing to stop the genocide, believing it to be a civil war for the first three weeks. Less than a year before the genocide started, the US had failed in its attempt to intervene in Somalia and it was unwilling to get involved in another African venture.

As the genocide spread across Rwanda, Tutsis who were close enough to the border fled into neighbouring countries. Over two days in April 1994, 250,000 Rwandan refugees fled across the border – at the time, it was the biggest and fastest refugee movement the UN High Commissioner for Refugees (UNHCR) had ever witnessed.

The growth and impact of Benaco refugee camp

Many of these refugees arrived in Benaco, a small town in the northwest corner of Tanzania. The movement of so many people into such a small area put a huge pressure on the local environment and meant that the carrying capacity was exceeded to such an extent that many aid and government officials were worried it could force the local community to become IDPs. The term 'carrying capacity' describes the largest population that the resources of a given environment can support.

The 250,000 refugees that moved into the area brought with them 50,000 cookers. These cookers used large amounts of fuel and consequently produced vast amounts of air pollution. With such large numbers of refugees requiring fuel to cook, approximately 1,000 tonnes of wood (equivalent to 20 hectares of forest) were needed in the camp every day. When the refugees first moved into the area it was a one-hour walk to get wood but as the forest was denuded it took much longer.

In an attempt to protect the nearby Kusulo town, refugees were shuttled to a forest 15 kilometres away from the camp. The refugees had to walk back on foot with the wood they needed. Over a period of time the supply of wood from this forest was used up, spreading the environmental impact of the camp.

Whole maize and beans were provided to refugees as food aid. The maize had to be boiled for six hours for it to be nutritious and the stoves were very inefficient. This increased pressure on wood supplies and by December 1994 there were no forests left in the area.

The poor carrying capacity of the area for the new refugee camp was possibly illustrated best through the water supply. In the camp, the Rwandan refugees were receiving just 5-6 litres a day because of the pressure on the local water source. In the nearest village, Kusulo, water started to be sold, where once it was free, because

the village had to share the aquifer with the Benaco camp. Although the camp was set up next to a small lake, the lake could only supply a quarter of the water needed for both the camp and the town. The lake was fed by a swamp which ran through Benaco camp and this meant that there was more water getting to the refugee camp than to the local population. Boreholes were drilled to pump water from the aquifer below. After six months of the Benaco camp using the boreholes, they ran dry.

It was obvious that the land around it could not cope with the sheer numbers of people in the camp and it was agreed that it had to be broken up. However, this did not happen for another two years and in that time Benaco became the second-largest city in Tanzania, after Dar es Salaam. The table below shows the population density in Benaco compared with Tokyo and Mexico City as of 1996.

After 1996 most of the Tutsis returned to Rwanda. The situation the Rwandan government faced appeared hopeless. The civil war had ended with over 130,000 people in prison suspected of war crimes. Those crimes ranged from organizing the genocide and participating in mass murder and sexual violence to the destruction of property. The Rwandan justice system was totally overwhelmed and making the situation worse was the fact that during the genocide judges and lawyers were targeted by the Hutus.

	Population	Area (hectares)	Density (people per hectare)
Benaco	159,879	586	273
Tokyo	8,400,000	57,800	145
Mexico City	10,300,000	150,000	69

Prisoners (in pink) attend a Gacaca trial in Rwanda.

Working through the normal processes of law would have taken over 25 years and it would have been impossible to begin the process of national reconciliation. The solution adopted was to make use of *Gacaca* courts.

Gacaca courts, an example of participation in development

Gacaca is a traditional model of dispute resolution. It simply means 'judgement on the grass', as all Gacaca hearings take place outside. Traditionally, household heads are the judges and serve as both sentencers and mediators in order to resolve disputes at community level. The system is based on voluntary confessions and apologies by wrongdoers and offers a pragmatic and community-based approach.

Rwandan 'organic' law was set up in 1996 to facilitate the prosecution of those suspected of community acts of genocide. The new law applied to both Gacaca and national courts. The law stated that there were four categories

of crime, based on their level of seriousness.
- Category 1: The most serious crimes. These are tried by the national and international courts. They have the power to hand out punishments upon conviction, including imprisonment and the death penalty. This category targets the planners and organizers, notorious murderers, perpetrators in religious or political authority and those who committed acts of sexual violence.
- Categories 2-4 are considered less serious crimes, ones that could be dealt with by Gacaca courts. Although the range of punishments does not include the death penalty, it includes every other kind of sentence, ranging from community service through to life imprisonment.

What level of participation is there?

The reintegration of suspects back into the community and the truth-telling nature of their confessions to the Gacaca courts offer hope of reconciliation. Gacaca's positive attributes lie in its characterization as a model of restorative justice. Around 250,000 community members have been trained to serve in Gacaca courts all over Rwanda. These members are drawn from both the Hutu and Tutsi ethnic groups.

How are Gacaca courts helping?

Gacaca courts help the most vulnerable. As women are the heads of tens of thousands of households and the producers of up to 70% of the country's agricultural output, they are overwhelmingly responsible for the livelihood and stability of their community. Rwandan women have to live in the same communities as those who assaulted them or killed their family members and, as judges and witnesses, women have the responsibility for determining punishments or deciding on the desirability of the suspect's reintegration. The community basis of Gacaca allows women to participate on various levels, recognizes their role in the reconciliation process and establishes their identity beyond that of just being a victim.

Many women have sought to hear the confessions of the accused and an admission of guilt. As reconciliation for Rwandans represents an act between two people where one confesses and the other forgives, the confession is a necessary first step for regeneration. Most of the victims also want to know how their people died. If the perpetrators are ready to tell them the stories of their dead relatives, and tell them where they are, they can bury them in dignity. This is the beginning of healing and reconciliation.

'A pill that is bitter is sometimes the one that heals.'
Charles Katiyama

Rwandan women have a lot invested in the success of the Gacaca courts in terms of their economic status. Some women will receive compensation from the government or from reintegrated perpetrators if their property was destroyed or the breadwinners in their family were killed by the accused.

Has Gacaca led to a growth and development of civil society?

The Gacaca courts were based on respected traditional methods that have taken the attitudes and values of Rwandan society to heart. They have allowed a healing process to begin for both the perpetrators and the victims.

Although the Gacaca courts were not established until around 10 years after the genocide, the majority of the population feel that they have helped many in overcoming the memories that haunt the country. It has enabled the victims to see that the crimes that were committed against them are not accepted by the community. The suspects, meanwhile, have understood that, once they have served their sentence and confessed, they may be accepted back into the community.

How has this growth in civil society helped the development of Rwanda?

Rwanda has made outstanding strides in the gender equality arena. For example, it is the only country in the world whose parliament has a majority of women MPs. Key ministries such as Foreign Affairs, Education and Infrastructure are led by women. In terms of economic development since the genocide, in 2008 the country's GDP grew by 6%. Rwanda has also joined the East African Community (EAC) in an attempt to consolidate its development initiatives and promote inter-regional co-operation. ∎

Environment & Development

Does development inevitably lead to environmental decline?

* *The poor are most at risk from environmental decline but the underlying problem is overconsumption in the rich countries.*
* *Current global food production methods are environmentally unsustainable.*
* *Sustainable agriculture could reduce damage to the environment but there are arguments about its impact on total food production.*
* *There has been no agreement to limit the carbon emissions that cause climate change even though there is a consensus that a warmer climate will be devastating to the environment and threaten the survival of many.*
* *Maintaining biodiversity has economic as well as environmental benefits for humans.*
* *The over-exploitation of natural resources can have long-term regional consequences.*

Key points

The desire to eradicate poverty and simultaneously promote the need for a healthy planet can sometimes appear to be contradictory. The poor countries are often those with the highest levels of population growth and the most fragile environments. They also have limited means (financial, political and managerial) to deal with these major challenges and the battle for existence in these circumstances only appears to result in a further decline in the quality of life and more damage to the environment.

It is not, however, the poor who are primarily responsible for the deterioration in our environmental conditions. The wealthiest and most powerful nations are those most responsible for the exploitation of the earth's natural resources: its forests, land, mineral reserves, fresh water

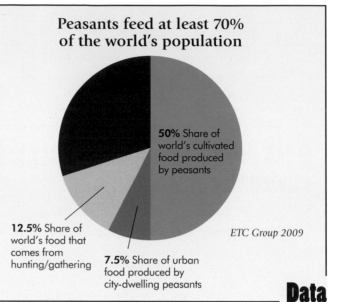

Half of the people in the world are peasants

There are 1.5 billion peasants on 380 million farms; 800 million more growing urban gardens; 410 million gathering the hidden harvest of our forests and savannas; 190 million pastoralists and well over 100 million peasant fishers. At least 370 million of these are also indigenous peoples. Together these peasants make up almost half the world's peoples and they grow at least 70% of the world's food.

Peasants feed at least 70% of the world's population

50% Share of world's cultivated food produced by peasants

ETC Group 2009

12.5% Share of world's food that comes from hunting/gathering

7.5% Share of urban food produced by city-dwelling peasants

Data

and oceans. All of these have suffered an alarming decline over the last 50 years. Environmental crises, including those brought on by changing weather patterns, have the greatest impact on the poor in developing countries but they are only paying the bill for the actions of the developed world which have been the root cause of the problem.

Growing food for an expanding global population has an inevitable impact on the environment. In the rural environments of the developing world, the poor are mostly forced to cultivate marginal land with little productive capacity.

They are forced to subsist through low-input, low-productivity agriculture. They are unable to invest in fertilizers for their lands and without these inputs the soil becomes depleted or 'mined' of its natural fertility. As this 'soil mining' continues and the land becomes even more unproductive, they have to expand onto additional, even poorer land to meet their basic food needs, degrading those soils as well. Overgrazing and deforestation compound the problem, with land degradation the inevitable result of all these activities.

While world food production is projected to meet consumption demands for the next two decades, long-term forecasts indicate persistent and worsening food insecurity in many countries, especially in sub-Saharan Africa. The pressure on the land will become even more intense and sustainable land management is essential to break out of the cycle of increasing poverty and environmental deterioration.

Sustainable agriculture describes an approach to farming that maintains or enhances the land and its natural resources for future generations. Organic farming uses techniques that are sustainable environmentally although there are arguments about its ability to produce enough food to feed the global population. That argument could fill a book by itself but there are other methods that try to reduce the inputs needed to grow crops or use natural processes to control pests.

- Conservation tillage, whereby crops are grown with minimal cultivation of the soil. The stubble or plant residues are not completely incorporated and most of the crop remains on top of the soil rather than being ploughed into the soil. The new crop is planted into the stubble or small strips of tilled soil
- Polycultures require the growing of a mixture of crops. There are several advantages to this: it maximizes the use of light and water, provides several sources of income for the farmer and evens out the workload through the year
- Natural predators and plants like chilli and garlic can be used instead of chemicals to keep pests away
- Growing perennial plants, which need less fertilizer, can protect the soil and provide shelter all year round
- Drip irrigation reduces water loss through evaporation and maximizes the amount of water that gets to the plant
- Integrated pest management (IPM) uses information on the life-cycles of pests and their interaction with the environment to make the best use of pest-control methods. It reduces costs and minimizes the hazard to people and the environment.

An 'organoponico' or organic urban garden in Havana, Cuba. The flowers attract insects that would otherwise damage crops.

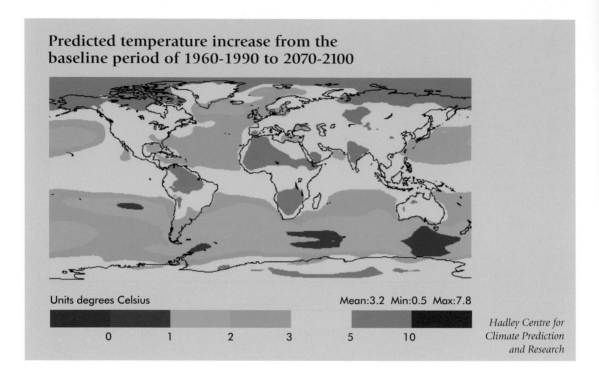

Predicted temperature increase from the baseline period of 1960-1990 to 2070-2100

Units degrees Celsius

Mean:3.2 Min:0.5 Max:7.8

0   1   2   3   5   10

Hadley Centre for Climate Prediction and Research

Producing our food in a more sustainable way is vital for the long-term health of the natural environment and for our own survival. It is just one of the challenges that we face. Climate change, access to water, and threats to biodiversity are other issues that are closely associated with human activity and its impact on the environment.

Climate change

The science surrounding the impact of rising carbon dioxide levels on the planet is contested. There are climate-change deniers who attempt to cast doubt on the extent of global warming, its significance, or its connection to human behaviour. The case for climate-change denial is often associated with the energy lobby (the oil companies and coal mining companies) and 'free market' thinktanks, often in the US.

In November 2009 a hacker illegally obtained emails and other documents from the University of East Anglia's Climate Research Unit that allegedly revealed misconduct amongst climate scientists who had deleted or manipulated data to make the case for global warming appear stronger than it actually is. The case was undoubtedly very helpful to climate deniers but the overwhelming scientific opinion on climate change remains that global warming is occurring and is mainly due to human activity. Some see it as the most significant threat to humankind and perhaps no other issue so clearly highlights the inequalities between nations and in the way they exploit natural resources.

The World Bank's *World Development Report 2010* says that human-induced climate change is expected to have a negative impact on agricultural productivity throughout the tropics and sub-tropics, decrease water quantity and quality in most arid and semi-arid regions, increase the incidence of malaria, dengue and other vector-borne diseases in the tropics and sub-tropics, as well as harming ecological systems and their biodiversity.

The polluters fail to pay

Increasing levels of carbon dioxide in the atmosphere are largely the result of industrial activity and the burning of fossil fuels. Carbon-dioxide levels in the atmosphere are the result of cumulative emissions over decades. Although China has recently passed the US in annual CO_2 emissions, the US bears by far the largest responsibility for the high levels of CO_2 currently in the atmosphere.

Some reasons for the US's high consumption of fossil fuels:

- The US originally had significant domestic reserves of oil in areas such as Texas which were easily exploitable; this led to the US economy being heavily based on oil
- The US economy is heavily industrialized, with a high use of fossil fuels in manufacturing and processing industries – and even in agriculture
- Oil is seen as part of the national culture – traditionally, for example, large fuel-hungry (gas-guzzling) cars have been seen as a status symbol

In this map the size of each country is proportional to its carbon emissions as of the year 2000.

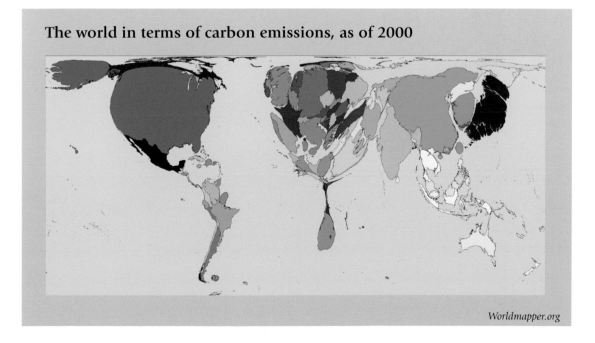

The world in terms of carbon emissions, as of 2000

Worldmapper.org

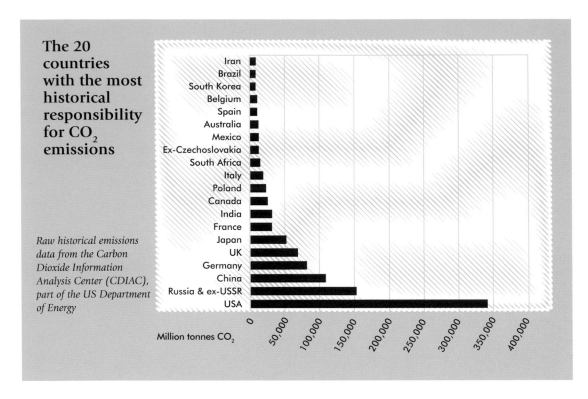

The 20 countries with the most historical responsibility for CO_2 emissions

Raw historical emissions data from the Carbon Dioxide Information Analysis Center (CDIAC), part of the US Department of Energy

- The energy lobby and the automobile industry are very powerful and have successfully influenced government policy, resulting, for example, in extremely low taxes on fuel. During the last presidential elections it is estimated that over $250 million was donated, either directly or indirectly, by the oil industry to the two main political parties
- In many southern states, such as Arizona, the high summer temperatures mean air conditioning is very widely used while in northern states, especially Alaska, the cold climate requires houses to be heated. Domestic energy use is very high.

Approximate energy use per person in selected countries and regions

Country/Region	Energy use per capita (KWh in 2008)
Canada	96,000
USA	89,000
Australia	75,000
EU	48,000
China	19,000
Average for Global South	5,500
Tanzania	4,000
Nepal	3,500

International Energy Agency (IEA), 2008

Sea-level rise

One of the key predicted effects of climate change is that sea levels will rise, threatening low-lying coastal regions and islands all over the world.

Sea levels have never been constant and have fluctuated significantly over the geological record at local and global levels. Localized sea-level rise is normally attributed to natural tectonic movements – leading to such features as the rias of southwest England and the raised beaches of Scotland, but it can also be related to changes in erosion or deposition along coastal regions.

More significant is the idea of eustatic sea-level change, which is a global issue. Eustatic sea-level changes can be caused by tectonic processes, but only on a geological time scale; changes in climate have a more immediate effect. Increased global temperatures due to climate change will increase sea levels in two ways:

- Thermal expansion: As the oceans warm due to climate change they expand
- Terrestrial ice melt: As glaciers and ice sheets on land melt, the water is added to the oceans, increasing their volume. The melting of sea ice has only a limited effect on global sea levels as the ice already displaces an equivalent volume of water, leading to no significant increase.

During the last century global sea levels rose by 0.1-0.2 metres. Current predictions for the coming century, however (see graph below), suggest

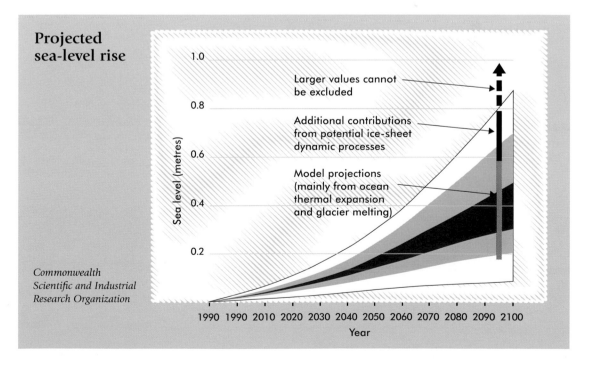

Projected sea-level rise

Larger values cannot be excluded

Additional contributions from potential ice-sheet dynamic processes

Model projections (mainly from ocean thermal expansion and glacier melting)

Sea level (metres)

Commonwealth Scientific and Industrial Research Organization

1990 1990 2010 2020 2030 2040 2050 2060 2070 2080 2090 2100

Year

a rapid increase in this rate, which will have significant consequences for coastal populations around the world.

The price of rising sea levels will be primarily paid by the citizens of the Global South. Although low-lying cities in the US, such as New York, are vulnerable to the effects of a rise in sea levels, the wealth of the US makes it likely that it will be better prepared to combat the impacts of sea-level rise than most other countries. To this end, for example, a task force has already been set up and charged with applying the best available science to evaluate ways to protect New York's remaining coastal ecosystems and natural habitats; and to increase coastal community resilience in the face of sea-level rise.

The prospects for the citizens of poorer countries, including small island nations, is much bleaker, as the case study opposite on the Pacific state of Tuvalu reveals.

The importance of maintaining biodiversity

The scientific evidence is that the current rate of extinction of species on earth is much higher than in the past and that the driving force behind the rapid rate of extinction is habitat loss as a result of human impact on ecosystems.

Biodiversity is important for other reasons as well. It is an indicator of the health of the environment and ecosystem. Changing the balance by removing some part of the ecosystem may cause feedback that threatens the ability of the ecosystem to survive. Many plants have medicinal properties that we have exploited to treat many diseases and illnesses, such as artemisia (for malaria) and Pacific yew for cancer research.

Some species have a cultural or artistic value that sets them apart from other species and can threaten their long-term existence. The tusks of elephants and rhinos and the pelts of tigers are much prized in some cultures and can be worth very large sums of money. As these animals are hunted and their numbers reduced, the value of their tusks and pelts becomes even higher, making it even more lucrative to hunt them and almost guaranteeing their extinction unless extraordinary measures are taken (see the case study on Africa's elephants on page 210).

At least 40% of the world's economy and 80% of the needs of the poor are derived from biological resources. In addition, the richer the diversity of life, the greater the opportunity for medical discoveries, economic development and adaptive responses to such new challenges as climate change.

Convention on Biodiversity

Data

Tuvalu CASE STUDY

Key statistics on Tuvalu	
Total population	10,530
Population annual growth rate	0.5%
Land area	26 square kilometres
Infant mortality rate	29 per 1,000 live births
Primary enrolment/attendance	100%

Death of a nation

Tuvalu is located in the Pacific Ocean between Australia and Hawaii. It is made up of nine islands, all of which are less than four metres above sea level.

Impacts of rises in sea levels on Tuvalu

Increased risk from cyclones: Tuvalu has always been vulnerable to flooding from cyclones. However, as sea levels rise, the risk of storm surges causing extensive damage to the islands increases significantly. It has been estimated that a 0.5-metre increase in sea level would double the chances of a major flood inundating the capital, Fongafale. These risks are exacerbated by climate change as increased global temperatures are likely to lead to more powerful cyclones and changes in sea temperature are believed to be degrading the world's coral reefs, which have acted as natural sea defences for island communities such as Tuvalu.

Loss of land: It has been estimated that an increase in sea level by 0.5-1 metre would lead to increased erosion of approximately one metre per year. This is critical given that

Adolescents on a coral beach in Funafuti Island, Tuvalu.

Tuvalu is only 400 metres across at its widest point. This erosion cannot all be blamed on climate change – the South Pacific Applied Geoscience Commission has also highlighted the impact of coral-reef blasting and extraction of sand for aggregate as important reasons for current rates of erosion.

Food security: Rising sea levels are likely to

The fate of my country rests in your hands

Ian Fry, the lead negotiator for the island nation of Tuvalu, speaking at the Copenhagen climate change conference in December 2009:

'The entire population of Tuvalu lives below two metres above sea level. The highest point above sea level in the entire nation of Tuvalu is only four metres.

'Madam President, we are not naive to the circumstances and the political considerations that are before us. It appears that we are waiting for some senators in the US Congress to conclude before we can consider this issue properly. It is an irony of the modern world that the fate of the world is being determined by some senators in the US Congress.

'We note that President Obama recently went to Norway to pick up a Nobel Prize, rightly or wrongly. But we can suggest that for him to honour this Nobel Prize, he should address the greatest threat to humanity that we have before us, climate change, and the greatest threat to security, climate change. So I make a strong plea that we give proper consideration to a conclusion at this meeting that leads to two legally binding agreements.

'Madam President, this is not just an issue of Tuvalu. Pacific island countries – Kiribati, Marshall Islands – Maldives, Haiti, Bahamas, Grenada, São Tomé in West Africa and all the LDCs – Bhutan, Laos, Mali, Senegal, Timor-Leste – and millions of other people around this world are affected enormously by climate change.

'This is not just Tuvalu.

'Over the last few days I've received calls from all over the world, offering faith and hope that we can come to a meaningful conclusion on this issue. Madam President, this is not an ego trip for me. I have refused to undertake media interviews, because I don't think this is just an issue of an ego trip for me. I am just merely a humble and insignificant employee of the environment department of the government of Tuvalu. As a humble servant of the government of Tuvalu, I have to make a strong plea to you that we consider this matter properly. I don't want to cause embarrassment to you or the government. But I want to have this issue considered properly.

'I clearly want to have the leaders put before them an option for considering a legally binding treaty to sign on at this meeting. I make this a strong and impassioned plea. We've had our proposal on the table for six months. Six months, it's not the last two days of this meeting. I woke this morning, and I was crying, and that's not easy for a grown man to admit. The fate of my country rests in your hands.'

Witness

lead to the salinization of the soil and this will have a significant impact on crops such as taro (pulaka) and other crops grown by the islanders which have a low salt tolerance.
Health: As domestic food supply becomes less abundant, many Tuvaluans, especially in the capital, are increasingly reliant on imported foodstuffs, which are significantly higher in fats, leading to lifestyle diseases such as diabetes.

'The industrialized countries caused the problem, but we are suffering the consequences... it is only fair that people in industrialized nations and industries take responsibility for the actions they are causing. It's the polluter-pays principle: you pollute, you pay.'

Panapase Nelisoni, from the government of Tuvalu, quoted in *New Internationalist* 419, Jan-Feb 2009

Witness

Fresh water: Tuvalu has limited supplies of fresh water and is almost entirely dependent on rainwater. During periods of relative drought, Tuvalu has been able to tap into a relatively small fresh-water lens located under the islands. As the sea level rises and storm surges become more powerful, it is likely that this fresh water will become contaminated by salt water, significantly reducing the water security of the islanders.

Migration: As sea levels rise, traditional economic activities such as farming are affected and if it continues both internal and international migration will increase. Already over 40% of Tuvalu's population live in the capital Fongafale, which covers an area of just 2.8 square kilometres. The worst outcome is the prospect of a complete forced international migration. Already 3,000 inhabitants have been evacuated to New Zealand/Aotearoa.

When Ian Fry made his appeal on behalf of the people of Tuvalu for a global agreement on carbon emissions (see box opposite), it was reported worldwide and he received a standing ovation from many delegates in the Copenhagen conference hall. Sadly, little was achieved apart from an agreement to continue talking and commitments from the major industrial nations that were far below the expectations of environmentalists. Most European nations committed themselves to reducing their emissions by 30% or more (from 1990 levels) by 2020. The US, however, was only aiming for a reduction of about 4% from 1990 levels, and China was reluctant to commit to any medium- or long-term reductions, although it is currently leading the world in renewable-energy generation.

In the final agreement the developed nations stated their aim of holding global temperature rise to 2°C. Before the conference, climate scientists had agreed that a rise of 1.5°C or less was needed to stop the inundation of small island states. The uneven distribution of a 2°C average global temperature rise could mean a catastrophic increase of 3-4°C in Africa. ∎

Aral Sea CASE STUDY

Key statistics on Kazakhstan and Uzbekistan		
	Kazakhstan	Uzbekistan
Population	15.6 million	27.5 million
GNI per capita	$6,740	$1,100
% below poverty line	3%	46%
Life expectancy	65 years	68 years
Adult literacy rate	100%	99%

An environmental tragedy?

Water demand in Central Asia already exceeds supply and, with the 48 million population of the Aral Sea region projected to rise to 75 million by 2025, the situation can only get worse. Around 60% of the population live in rural areas and practise irrigated farming, often with very inefficient water systems, and there is competition for the water sources that are available between Kazakhstan, Uzbekistan, Kyrgyzstan, Tajikistan and Turkmenistan. That is why the Aral Sea is so important.

Before the former Soviet Union diverted the Amudarya and Syrdarya rivers in the 1960s to enable extensive cotton production, the Aral Sea was the world's fourth-largest inland body of water. The sea lost more than 70% of its water as it was used to irrigate the thirsty cotton plants on arid farmland. The Aral Sea as a whole shrank in size from 66,400 km² in 1961 to 10,400 km² in 2008, exposing a barren sea bed of salt and sand with former sea ports stranded many kilometres from the water's edge and the rusting hulks of fishing boats scattered everywhere.

The scale of the change was so big that it caused local climate change, with reduced rainfall and increased temperatures. The remaining water became so unnaturally saline that most of the fish and fauna died. Drinking-water supplies became scarce, and tens of thousands of fishing, agriculture and service-sector jobs vanished. The chemicals that had been used as fertilizers and pesticides for the irrigated cotton crop were concentrated by the evaporating water and caused illness and birth defects.

By 1990, the Aral had shrivelled into a remnant northern sea within Kazakhstan and a southern one on the Kazakh-Uzbek border. Each sea was more than 20 metres lower than the original. UN Secretary-General Ban Ki-moon described it as 'clearly one of worst environmental disasters of the world'.

Things have changed a little in recent years, however. Between 2005 and 2007,

This satellite image shows all that now remains of the Aral Sea. The dotted line shows the original extent of the water.

*This human-engineered catastrophe of evaporating seas and small
unfishable patches of water is what the Small Aral Sea is fighting back
from. And curiously it is a large dam project – the Kokaral – made possible
by funding from the World Bank, a body not exactly renowned for its
environmental credentials, which is helping it to win the fight.*

   *Unlike many other dams which have caused environmental devastation,
such as India's Narmada dam which lost World Bank funding after
international furore, the Kokaral project is simply filling in an empty seabed
as locals wait for the fish and the jobs to return.*

   *Experts are not only amazed at how quickly the water has reached the
target depth of 42 metres, taking only a year after the 2005 completion of
the dam, but also how swiftly the native fish have restocked the sea.*

Paul Lauener, *New Internationalist* 437, November 2010

Witness

Kazakhstan and the World Bank funded restoration projects worth $86 million for the northern sea area. The 13-kilometre Kokaral dam was built to block the flow of water into the southern sea and work done on the Syrdarya River to increase its capacity and channel more water into the sea basin. A dam and canal were also built from the Syrdarya to restore fishing lakes to act as hatcheries for new fish populations.

   The northern sea has increased its surface area by 13% and its salinity has been reduced by more than two-thirds. Improved water-supply systems have brought drinking water to seaside villages and seven species of fish have returned, according to the World Bank.

The sea's recovery is also improving the local climate.

   Unfortunately the southern sea is still sinking and the European Space Agency predicts that it will dry out completely if it continues to shrink at its present rate. By 2009, the southeastern lake had disappeared and the southwestern lake had retreated to a thin strip at the extreme west of the former southern sea. There are claims that the southern sea's western side could be salvaged if engineers dammed it to prevent water draining away and the region's irrigation systems were reformed, but the outlook for this part of the Aral Sea is grim. ■

*'Even if agriculture and irrigation stopped – and you can imagine the social and
economic disaster – it would probably take 50 years for the sea to come back.'*

Joop Stoutjesdik, World Bank head of irrigation programmes, 2008

Witness

Africa's elephants: in the firing line

A British citizen who has studied African elephants for more than four decades, [Iain] Douglas-Hamilton spent much of the 1970s and 1980s piloting small aircraft over the continent to carry out the first modern elephant censuses. His data and eyewitness reports revealed that poaching had caused Africa's elephant population to crash, from an estimated 1.3 million in 1979 to fewer than 600,000 a decade later. His campaign to publicize the devastation and carnage caused by the ivory trade helped lead Kenya to burn more than 13 tons of government-stockpiled ivory to demonstrate its commitment to a global ivory ban. This multimillion-dollar sacrifice galvanized the 37 African elephant range states and led the Convention on International Trade in Endangered Species of Wild Fauna and Flora (CITES) to agree to a worldwide ivory ban that took effect in 1990. Initially, demand for ivory dropped, ivory prices plummeted, and vigorous anti-poaching policies in countries such as Kenya, Tanzania and Zimbabwe helped bring illegal hunting under control.

But today, a confluence of forces is causing a sudden spike in ivory poaching across Africa, threatening to wipe out elephants and, in turn, destroy tourism-dependent economies. Unlike the last poaching surge, the current one is being aided by cellphone networks and criminal syndicates that are providing some poachers with sophisticated equipment such as night-vision goggles, GPS locators and satellite phones. The biggest new factor of all is China, one of the world's top ivory markets, which is investing heavily in African projects, including roads and other infrastructure that are facilitating the transport of ivory off the continent. More than 100,000 Chinese labourers in Africa are also fuelling demand right at the source.

Susan Hack, *Condé Nast Traveller*, June 2010

Witness

After the 1990 ban on ivory sales CITES gradually softened the ban to allow some countries with healthy elephant numbers the opportunity to auction their government ivory stocks, harvested from elephants that died naturally in their game parks. Proceeds from these sales were to fund conservation and education. Many scientists and law-enforcement officials think that this softening has confused the public about the legality of buying ivory and revived the international black market. However, the African countries that want to sell their ivory argue that a total ban is outdated and that ivory can be a sustainable resource that is traded responsibly.

If the estimate of CITES that 260 tons of ivory was poached in Africa in 2009 is correct, it implies that over 33,000 elephants were killed that year. At that rate, the elephant would be extinct in Africa in 15 years. In countries across Africa, elephant numbers have been decimated. In Chad there were 3,885 elephants in 2006 and fewer than 600 in 2009. There are probably no elephants left in Sierra Leone, Senegal and Liberia. The poachers are brazen in their attacks. In Tanzania, guests at safari lodges in the Selous Game Reserve regularly report hearing gunshots and seeing mutilated elephant carcasses. The tourism industry is worth $2.4 billion a year to the Tanzanian economy and the elephant is an important attraction for many tourists.

Dealing with the problem is not easy for African governments. Kenya has assigned half of its 2,800 park rangers to anti-poaching units and deployed aircraft and a helicopter in an attempt to prevent the killing of elephants

'Ivory from natural mortality is like gold, a resource that we want to reinvest. Elephants give us revenue that enables us to support ourselves and not have to beg from more developed countries.'

Onkokame Kitso Mokaila, Botswana's head of the Ministry of Environment, Wildlife and Tourism, June 2010

and rhinos but it is having little effect. The poachers are often poor Africans who are trying to feed themselves and their families but they are paid and equipped by criminal cartels that have organized across central and southern Africa.

The cost of the widespread action that countries need to take if species like elephants and rhinos are going to be protected is very high and often prohibitive to a developing country. Botswana has developed an alternative approach to try and deal with the poaching problem. It sells hunters licences to kill a certain number of elephants. The number of licences it sells is intended to manage the size of the elephant population and the licences are very expensive. Rich foreign tourists are offered the opportunity to take part in an organized elephant hunt and the money from the licences can be spent on wildlife conservation within Botswana. ∎

An elephant family in Kenya's Amboseli National Park.

The Olympics – a sustainable event?

London was awarded the Olympic Games for 2012 in July 2005, having overcome intense competition from Paris, Moscow, Madrid and Singapore. There was huge jubilation in London after the victory was announced but winning the Olympics bidding war was not greeted with the same enthusiasm by everybody. It undoubtedly offers the chance to gain a massive amount of positive global publicity and attract thousands of tourists to the event but the costs for the host country are very high.

The Olympic bid eventually gained government support because it was seen as a way of enhancing urban regeneration. The East London boroughs of Barking and Dagenham, Hackney, Havering, Newham, Redbridge, Tower Hamlets and Waltham Forest were at the centre of the London bid. Stratford is an economically deprived area in the London Borough of Newham which already had a £4-billion ($6.4-

billion) mixed-use regeneration development planned, and the Olympic Village was to be located on an adjacent site.

Another reason for choosing the area was the availability of brownfield sites for development as a result of deindustrialization that took place in the area, particularly in the 1960s and 1970s. In addition, a new international transport hub in the form of Stratford International Station (opened in November 2009) would provide services to Paris and Brussels via Eurostar.

Sustainability was highlighted by the Olympic Delivery Authority as being central to all planning for the games. It stated: *'London is the first Summer Host City to embed sustainability into our planning from the start. We're aiming to set new standards, creating positive, lasting change for the environment and communities. For London 2012,*

Sustainable stadium?

Key to the sustainability claims of the Olympic project is the future of the Olympic Stadium. This was conceived as a venue designed to cater both for the Olympics – when an 80,000-seat athletics stadium is needed – and for after the Games, when it was thought that London would require a smaller, multi-purpose venue. It therefore included: 55,000 temporary seats and a structure designed to be easily dismantled and reused; a lightweight roof and membrane wrap that could be recycled or reused; temporary hospitality, catering and retail outlets. These measures led to a 50% reduction in the carbon footprint of the stadium compared with a conventional design: but future plans for the stadium have caused controversy.

Feature

An architect's view of the Olympic Village; the Olympic Stadium under construction; David Beckham with Olympic bid leader Sebastian Coe inside the Olympic Stadium.

'sustainability' is far more than being 'green'. It's ingrained into our thinking – from the way we plan, build, work, buy, play, socialize, travel; ultimately everything that we do.'

Will the Games be sustainable?

There were five key themes in the original sustainability plan for the London Olympics.

1. *Climate change*: Minimizing greenhouse-gas emissions and ensuring legacy facilities are able to cope with the impacts of climate change.

2. *Waste*: Minimizing waste at every stage of the project, ensuring no waste is sent to landfill during Games-time, and encouraging the development of new waste-processing infrastructure in East London.

3. *Biodiversity*: Minimizing the impact of the Games on wildlife and their habitats in and around Games venues, leaving a legacy of enhanced habitats where possible, for example in the Olympic Park. The Olympic Park site is mainly former industrial land which was badly degraded and highly polluted.

4. *Inclusion*: Promoting access for all, celebrating the diversity of London and the UK and creating new employment, training and business opportunities.

5. *Healthy living*: Inspiring people across the country to take up sport and develop active, healthy and sustainable lifestyles.

Will the 2012 Olympics be the most sustainable games so far? The question will be debated long after the games have finished.

Indeed, many of the claims for the Games' sustainability are based on its 'legacy' – the benefits that will be felt by local communities in particular after 2012.

The case for

- Only permanent structures that have a long-term use after the Games have been constructed and existing buildings have been used wherever possible
- All new buildings have used technology to reduce their environmental impact
- 800,000 cubic metres of soil contaminated by previous industrial use have been cleaned and reused to create the Olympic Park and land for development
- 90% of demolition materials have been reclaimed for reuse or recycling
- The development of five neighbourhoods around the park will create a total of 11,000 new homes (50% affordable), as well as a network of facilities, including commercial opportunities, sporting venues and visitor attractions
- An estimated 12,000 permanent new jobs will be created by the Olympics development as well as thousands of temporary jobs
- 500 small and medium businesses have won work supplying the Olympics Development Authority, 1 in 10 of them based around the Olympic Park

- There will be a 200-hectare public park after the Games, the biggest new park in Europe for over 100 years
- New transport routes will be available, including rail access to France and improved access to central London
- Wetland habitats in the Park have been restored and native species used in planting; the River Lea and the surrounding area has been cleaned up
- Sport and healthy lifestyles have been encouraged across all ages and communities.

The case against

- There is concern that, as costs have risen beyond the initial estimates, Londoners will have to pay more than was first thought. Taxpayers in Montreal are still paying off debts from the 1976 Games
- Preparing the Olympic precinct involved demolishing every building, business and tree in the existing area. Over 300 businesses had to be relocated and some jobs were lost as a result
- The compulsory purchase of some business properties to make way for Olympic venues and infrastructure improvements caused controversy, with claims that the compensation offered was inadequate
- Claims that London will benefit by £2 billion ($3.2 billion) from tourist revenues are disputed by people who claim that predictions for tourist revenues were exaggerated at the Olympics in Athens and Sydney
- Environmentalists are concerned about potential loss of habitat due to redevelopment. Much of the Lower Lea Valley is an extensive network of waterways, with important wildlife habitats, designated a Site of Metropolitan Importance for Nature Conservation
- Local residents have been adversely affected by the noise, dust and visual pollution of years of construction and associated heavy vehicle movement
- Massive policing will be required because of the potential terrorist threat during the Games and security will have to be tight during construction.

Defining 'sustainable'

A major criticism of the impact of the games is that 'trickle down' economics underlie the approach to regeneration at the heart of the Olympic bid. Research by the New Economics Foundation suggests that it has been consultants, developers and large companies that have been able to exploit the new commercial opportunities offered by the Olympics. Many of the contracts have been so large that small and medium-sized local enterprises have been unable to compete. Strict branding rules and major sponsorship contracts won by major transnational firms are also preventing the local community from maximizing the profits they can make from their geographical proximity to the Games. In addition, local people have been priced out of the housing market because of the gentrification that has happened in the last five years.

Whether the Games are sustainable or not depends on the definition of sustainability you start with. Can an event that results in the temporary migration of many thousands of people and the creation of such huge buildings ever be called a sustainable project when it has such a damaging environmental impact? On the other hand, doesn't the potential regeneration of a very deprived area with all its positive social and economic impacts on the local community deserve sympathetic consideration? ∎

What part does technology play in development?

* Technology can play a key part in the development process.
* Access to technology is uneven.
* Technology is not 'good' in and of itself – it will be used for good or ill depending on the human society that uses it.
* Technology creates both negative externalities and moral dilemmas.

Key points

The term 'technology' has many connotations and different meanings yet, as with many other key terms in development, an exact definition is hard to form. The broadest possible definition might be: 'any human adaptation to the environment'. This would therefore cover the most basic flint tools used by early humans through to microchip implants that help the blind to see. What is clear is that every human on the planet, irrespective of their level of development, is only alive due to their interaction with some form of technology.

Since technology covers such a broad spectrum, it does need some form of classification. A convenient way of doing this is by considering the complexity of the technology and the labour intensity required to use it, as shown in the chart at the top of page 216.

The technological divide

Technology requires both knowledge and capital if it is to be implemented. These twin barriers have created a technological divide between rich and poor, both within and between countries.

Key to understanding this technological divide is the issue of patents. Patents are legal documents that give inventors and researchers legal protection by preventing others from exploiting their ideas and inventions. However, as shown in the bar chart overleaf, patents are almost entirely the exclusive preserve of wealthier countries. The fact

Types of technology and the labour or capital that they require

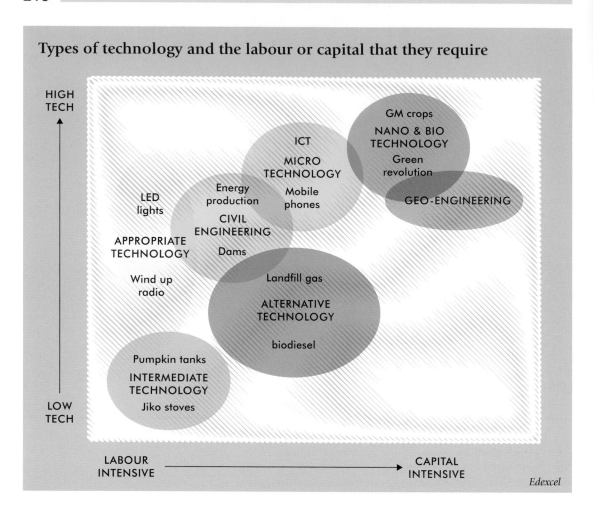

HIGH TECH

GM crops
NANO & BIO TECHNOLOGY
Green revolution

ICT

MICRO TECHNOLOGY

Energy production

Mobile phones

LED lights

CIVIL ENGINEERING

GEO-ENGINEERING

APPROPRIATE TECHNOLOGY

Dams

Wind up radio

Landfill gas

ALTERNATIVE TECHNOLOGY

biodiesel

Pumpkin tanks

INTERMEDIATE TECHNOLOGY

Jiko stoves

LOW TECH

LABOUR INTENSIVE → CAPITAL INTENSIVE

Edexcel

World patent distribution

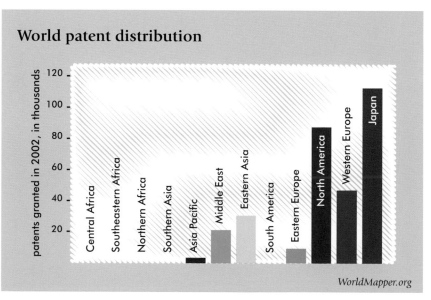

patents granted in 2002, in thousands

120 —
100 —
80 —
60 —
40 —
20 —

Central Africa | Southeastern Africa | Northern Africa | Southern Asia | Asia Pacific | Middle East | Eastern Asia | South America | Eastern Europe | North America | Western Europe | Japan

WorldMapper.org

that developing new technology is often expensive and therefore not affordable to most in developing countries explains a significant part of this inequality. However, obtaining a patent is often expensive and practically impossible in many countries, so even when new technologies are developed in the Global South, researchers often lack the capital or legal knowledge to patent their ideas, allowing others to exploit their research and benefit from the profits.

The fact that the development of technology is so heavily concentrated in the rich world further exacerbates the development gap – countries in the Global South are effectively dependent on technological transfer from the North. This gives the North, and especially the transnational corporations that control many of the patents, significant power both to control the speed of development and to reap the economic benefits.

TRIPS and HIV drugs

In 1995 the members of the WTO approved the Trade-Related Aspects of Intellectual Property Rights (TRIPS) agreement. This introduced minimum standards for enforcing patents and other forms of intellectual property rights. In the case of pharmaceuticals this lasts for 20 years from the filing date of the patent, effectively allowing the pharmaceutical companies to charge high prices, recoup their investments in drug development and make a profit.

The protection offered to the pharmaceutical companies by the agreement caused major problems because of the high cost of drugs used to combat some major diseases. Following the 2001 Doha WTO meeting it was agreed that 'the TRIPS Agreement does not and should not prevent Members from taking measures to protect public health' and that a country can issue a compulsory licence (which prevents companies being prosecuted under the terms of the patent in that country) for a drug that treats a disease causing a severe health emergency without royalties being paid.

Although in theory compulsory licensing offers a legal solution to patent protection for HIV treatment, there are still problems with the agreement:

- Generic manufacturers are limited to producing only the quantities predefined in each compulsory licence. This curbs the large-scale production that is required to produce drugs cheaply
- Some large pharmaceutical companies have demonstrated that countries issuing compulsory licences may face repercussions (see Thailand below)
- It was ruled that licences should be granted 'predominantly' to supply the 'domestic market', making it difficult for poor

countries lacking technological capabilities to access generic drugs manufactured abroad.

Thailand and the use of generic drugs

In 2002 only 3,000 patients were being treated with anti-retrovirals (ARVs) for HIV in Thailand, at a cost of $924 each a year. When Thailand produced its own generic ARVs the cost fell 18-fold and the country was able to treat over 85,000 people.

However, Thailand's decision to stop paying for patented drugs and to produce its own cheaper generic version angered pharmaceutical companies. Abbott (the 10th largest pharmaceutical company in the world) refused to sell seven of its newest products in Thailand and the Pharmaceutical Research and Manufacturers' Association threatened the country with legal action. The US government placed Thailand on its 'priority watchlist' of countries seen to be committing intellectual property piracy.

Despite the massive potential benefit to HIV sufferers around the world, only a few other countries have been prepared to follow Thailand's example and produce their own version of second-generation ARVs for the treatment of HIV.

This issue with patented HIV drugs demonstrates that the decision as to whether to supply or withhold technology is a highly moral one. On other occasions it may be the correct moral decision for high-tech companies not to supply their services. In the recent dispute about censorship, for example, Google redirected its Chinese users to its Hong Kong search engine rather than face censorship imposed by the Chinese government. The battle between Google and the Chinese government appears to have ended in a score-draw.

Google can truthfully say that it has stopped censoring search results in China, fulfilling the promise it made at the end of last year. Its Chinese search business is effectively moribund in the country but it can continue to operate in other areas like music, so that Chinese citizens remain aware of its brand.

The Chinese government has made sure that its citizens cannot receive unfiltered search results because searches have to pass back from Hong Kong through the firewall where sensitive material can be removed.

A source at Google said: 'We've had a lot of messages from China saying don't let Google go dark – we've managed to do that while staying true to our principles.'

BBC news, July 2010

Feature

One Laptop per Child targets Middle East and East Africa

The group behind the '$100 laptop' has formed a partnership which it hopes will deliver computers to every primary schoolchild in East Africa. The partnership between One Laptop per Child (OLPC) and the East African Community (EAC) aims to deliver 30 million laptops in the region by 2015.

OLPC has also announced a partnership with a UN agency which aims to deliver 500,000 machines in the Middle East. Both the UN agency and the EAC first need to raise cash for the laptops. The two groups aim to find donors to help pay for the machines, which currently sell for more than $200, despite intentions to sell them for less.

'At the end of the day, it all comes down to money,' Matt Keller of OLPC told BBC news, talking about the EAC partnership. 'Ideally, we would live in a world where governments can equip every kid to be educated, but that's not the case.'

Jonathan Fildes, BBC news, 29 April 2010

Feature

One way to measure the spread of technology is by tracking global internet use, which has increased by over 400% since 2000. It is estimated that over 28% of the global population had internet access in 2010. Although less than 11% have internet access in Africa, internet use is growing faster there than in any other part of the world. Schemes to provide cheap, solar-powered laptops to rural areas to help the education of young Africans have been taken up by some aid agencies (see box above).

World internet usage statistics

World regions	Population 2010 (millions)	Internet users 31 Dec 2000 (millions)	Internet users 2010 (millions)	Penetration (% population)	Growth 2000-2010
Africa	1,014	4.5	111	10.9%	2,366%
Asia	3,835	114.3	825	21.5%	621%
Europe	813	105.1	475	58.4%	352%
Middle East	212	3.3	63	29.8%	1,810%
North America	344	108.1	266	77.4%	146%
Latin America/ Caribbean	593	18.1	205	34.5%	1,032%
Oceania/ Australia	35	7.6	21	61.3%	179%
WORLD TOTAL	6,845	361	1,966	28.7%	444%

Internet World Statistics 2010

Children in the Rwandan capital, Kigali, relish the chance to try computers supplied by the One Laptop per Child project.

Technological leapfrogging

The internet and other high-tech industries do have a huge potential to accelerate the development process. Critical to this is the process of technological leapfrogging whereby less developed countries can adopt modern technologies without going through the intermediary steps that were followed by industrialized nations. Perhaps the most widespread example of this is the use of mobile-phone technology in developing countries where fixed land lines were often non-existent. This is having a major effect on the development process in isolated rural areas. Afghanistan is one of the countries that has benefited from this technological leapfrogging (see case study on page 222).

Intermediate technology

Although technological leapfrogging can bring huge benefits it is not always practical – especially in the least developed areas, where there is a lack of resources to implement it effectively. In these areas technology can still play a significant role in the development process but it is intermediate technology which is likely to be more effective. Intermediate technology involves using materials, assembly and maintenance methods found in less developed regions. This approach has many advantages. It is:

- Focused on basic needs
- Cheap (using local materials)
- Sustainable (can be repaired by locals)
- Empowers local communities
- Directed at the needs of local groups

One NGO that has specialized in the use of intermediate technology is

> *Spurred on by the experience of societies investing all their physical and mental energies in the propagation of things, development strategists perused the world and, lo and behold, discovered an appalling lack of useful objects wherever they looked.*
>
> *However, what was of primary importance in many villages and communities – the tissue of relationships with neighbours, ancestors and gods – more or less melted into thin air under their gaze. For this reason, the popular image of the Third World was dominated by have-nots desperately battling for mere survival; and whatever constituted their strength, their honour or their hope remained out of sight...*
>
> *Through transfer of technology, generations of development strategists have worked hard to get Southern countries moving. Economically they have had mixed results, yet culturally – entirely unintended – they have had resounding success. The flood of machines which has poured into many regions may or may not have been beneficial, but it has certainly washed away traditional aspirations and ideals. Their place has been taken by aspirations and ideals ordered on the co-ordinates of technological civilization – not only for the limited number who benefit from it, but also for the far larger number who watch its fireworks from the sidelines.*
>
> **Wolfgang Sachs** New Internationalist June 1992

Witness

Practical Action and their work in Darfur, Sudan, illustrates these points well (see case study on page 224).

Is technology a Trojan Horse?

The increasing use of technology in developing countries is not unreservedly acclaimed by everybody. The immediate benefits of technology in promoting development, particularly in medicine, are obvious. The wider impacts of the integration of modern technology in developing countries are not so clear and may pose problems that threaten the traditional way of life and culture of many countries. Indeed, Wolfgang Sachs and others argue that over the last 50 years the desire of development strategists to introduce technology to developing countries has been guided by a flawed interpretation of the development ideal.

Technology is increasingly seen as a key component of the development process. It is certainly clear that the effective transfer of technology has the power both to stimulate economic development and to save millions of people. It is equally clear, however, that this transfer will not take place if it depends solely upon transnational corporations forgoing potential income. Solving this moral dilemma will be a key issue for international development in the 21st century.

Afghanistan CASE STUDY

Mobile phones spread to the least promising areas

Key statistics on Afghanistan	
Total population	28.1 million
GNI per capita	$370
Life expectancy	44 years
Adult literacy rate	28%
Primary enrolment/attendance	61%

Afghanistan is one of the least developed counties in the world, ranked 155th of 169 countries by the UN Human Development Index. Development in Afghanistan faces many challenges:

- Ongoing conflict: Afghanistan has faced conflict almost continuously for 40 years
- Isolation: Afghanistan has a rural population of approximately 75%, many living in some of the most mountainous and isolated locations in the world
- Lack of economic infrastructure: 97% of the population does not have access to a bank and there are only 38 ATMs in the entire country
- Migration: A significant number of Afghans have migrated, either internally or externally, and need to be able to send remittances home
- Lack of education: Over two-thirds of Afghans are illiterate – often making the effective use of technology impossible.

After the fall of the Taliban regime in 2001 and the subsequent formation of a UN-backed government, US advisors have encouraged Afghanistan to replace its state-owned phone company with a number of private companies. In total this has led to over $1 billion in foreign direct investment from four companies, including Emirates Telecommunication Corp, which has alone invested $400 million.

The inward investment has allowed Afghanistan to leapfrog over traditional landline technology and develop its mobile phone infrastructure. This has had a significant impact, with over 25% of the country now having mobile phone coverage and 12% of the population owning a mobile phone. As a result, 75% of the population now enjoys at least limited access to a telephone. In addition to increasing the geographical accessibility, the cost of phone calls has since fallen from $2 a minute to $0.10 per minute, making it more affordable even for Afghans on low incomes. Current rates of subscription in Afghanistan have reached over 150,000 per month.

Horia, 18, learns how to repair a mobile phone at a programme offering vocational training to Afghan women.

This revolution in communication has had some positive impacts:

- Access to banking and microfinance has increased significantly as mobile phone companies have developed applications allowing easy and safe exchange of money, which are used by over 12,000 subscribers. Users can transfer money using text or voice, thus giving many people who are illiterate access to banking for the first time
- Families are able to keep in contact with and receive remittances from family members working away from home
- Farmers can now discover the price of products at market before they set off. This is important as, in the past, farmers often went to the nearest market and were paid low prices, not knowing that they could have sold for higher prices elsewhere
- The mobile-phone industry generated $100 million in taxes for the government in 2009 and Afghanistan's IT and telecommunications industry now employs over 50,000 people.

However, the growth of the mobile-phone industry also has some disadvantages:

- The move to wireless phones is likely to slow down the spread of internet access via broadband
- The Taliban have made extensive use of the mobile-phone network both to communicate with each other and to detonate Improvised Explosive Devices (IEDs)
- The Taliban have targeted mobile-phone masts, which are seen as 'soft targets'. ■

Sudan CASE STUDY
Low-smoke stoves in Kassala and Darfur

Key statistics on Sudan (before independence of the South)	
Total population	42.3 million
GNI per capita	$1,230
Life expectancy	58 years
Infant mortality rate	69 per 1,000 live births
Adult literacy rate	69%

A woman at a clinic in El Fasher, Darfur.

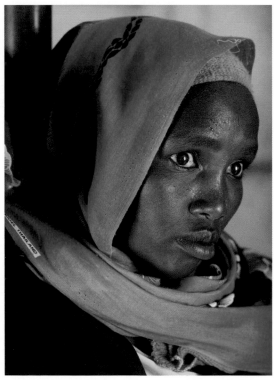

High dependence on biomass fuels for household energy – usually burning wood – not only contributes to environmental degradation, but the smoke from them also causes serious health problems, especially for women and young children.

Practical Action Sudan initiated the first work of its kind in Sudan by monitoring household indoor air pollution (IAP) levels, using participatory research methods with a sample of 30 poor households from a semi-urban residential area, Wau Nour, in Kassala. Traditionally, cooking takes place on inefficient three-stone stoves using firewood. The IAP monitoring revealed high levels of particulate matter and carbon monoxide.

Using a revolving fund, the project enabled a number of households to switch to cooking with liquid petroleum gas (LPG), which reduced levels of IAP by more than

80%. A scaling-up strategy was developed
with the Women's Development Associations
(WDAs) and other partners and stakeholders.
This enabled women to buy ovens and
gas cylinders by establishing a revolving
fund, managed by the women who also
contributed to it financially. The Gas Agent
in Kassala agreed to supply cylinders on an
instalment basis. Based on energy savings
and conservation calculations, households
could repay the cost of LPG appliances over a
maximum period of six months.

Now 2,000 households have switched
from using wood to gas and have acquired
all the necessary appliances. Refilling outlets
were established in Wau Nour and Kadugli
residential areas to give easy access to gas. A
new plate for baking *kisra* (a thin sorghum
pancake which is the main food in central
Sudan) is being manufactured locally.
Training on safety measures is done through
the involvement of the Civil Defence Forces,
and so far no accidents have been reported.

The revolving fund that was established
for provision of clean-energy gas appliances
managed to reach 220 more families in
2007-8.

The situation concerning the availability
of biomass fuel in Darfur is grim. The need
for alternative energy is huge, bearing in
mind the already exhausted environment
and the degradation of the vegetation cover.
Accordingly, a new gas promotion project
has been launched, aiming at serving 5,000
families in El Fasher town directly and
5,000 more as a result of the turnover of the
revolving fund. ∎

Practical Action

Millennium Development Goals

How successful have the MDGs been?

* The MDGs emerged from one of the few agreements reached by virtually all of the global community.
* The success of each MDG is measured by specific targets set in 2000.
* Some MDGs have been harder to meet than others and progress has been uneven.
* Some people are concerned that reaching MDG targets is diverting attention from other urgent development needs.
* There are competing explanations for the expected failure to reach some MDG targets and some criticism of the value of attempting a project structured in this way.

Key points

This final chapter reviews the progress that has been made towards meeting the Millennium Development Goals (MDGs) drawn up at the UN Millennium Summit in New York in 2000. These had specific targets attached to them for the global community to meet by 2015, with the aim of combating extreme poverty. The Millennium Declaration adopted by the world leaders promised to 'free all men, women, and children from the abject and dehumanizing conditions of extreme poverty'.

The Millennium Development Goals were:

1. To eradicate extreme poverty and hunger; by 2015 to halve the proportion of the world's population living in extreme poverty and hunger.
2. To achieve universal primary education.

3. To promote gender equality and empower women.
4. To reduce child mortality.
5. To improve maternal health.
6. To combat HIV/AIDS, malaria and other diseases.
7. To ensure environmental sustainability.
8. To develop a global partnership for development.

All the specific targets were set against a baseline of 1990 rather than 2000.

MDG 1 Eradicate extreme poverty and hunger

Target: Halve, between 1990 and 2015, the proportion of people suffering from extreme poverty and hunger

The World Bank has estimated that the number of people living in extreme poverty in 2009 was between 55 and 90 million higher than had been anticipated before the global economic crisis in 2008. The impact of the crisis varied and in some countries in sub-Saharan Africa and southern Asia both the actual number of poor people and the poverty rate have increased. The World Bank estimates that 920 million people will be living in extreme poverty in 2015 compared to 1.8 billion in 1990. At that rate the first MDG of halving extreme income poverty is likely to be achieved.

Poverty reduction has been particularly successful in Asia, where the rate dropped from nearly 55% of its population in 1990 to 17% in 2005 and is expected to be 5.9% in 2015. A major factor in reducing the number of people living in poverty has been the rapid economic progress of China, which lifted 475 million from extreme poverty between 1990 and 2005 and halved its own poverty rate. India has reduced its poverty rate from 51% in 1990 to an estimated 24% in 2015, reducing its number of extremely poor by 188 million. If the MDG is reached it will be good news but it must be remembered that nearly one billion people will still

'India has become poorer because India has become richer!'

'The World Bank's recent 40% upward revision of the global poverty number was based on an absurd procedure that led to the paradox in the quote.

'To make a long story short, the World Bank decided to boot richer India out of the group of poorest countries used to determine the poverty line, which made the poverty line higher, which made Indian (and global) poverty higher – all because India was richer.'

William Easterly, AIDWATCH, January 2010

Witness

be living in extreme poverty – and there are some people who believe that we should be very sceptical about poverty statistics anyway (see the quotation from William Easterly on page 227).

The second part of MDG1, halving the proportion of the world's population living in hunger, will be more difficult to reach. Food prices fell on the international markets in 2008 but this did not work its way through to better food availability or to the prices that people had to pay in the developing world. There are a number of possible reasons for this, including poor logistics and distribution. An estimated $13 billion worth of food was destroyed by poor storage during the 2009 Indian monsoon season, which caused a huge row in the Indian parliament. Also in 2009, a combination of factors saw wheat and rice prices soar on the global markets. This halted the slow but steady fall in the proportion of the global population suffering from undernourishment, which was reduced from 20% in the early 1990s to 16% in 2008. The number of children suffering from malnutrition has not fallen either and the target of reducing the number of children suffering from malnutrition by half will not be reached by 2015.

MDG2 Universal primary education

Target: Ensure that, by 2015, children everywhere will be able to complete a full course of primary schooling

Other MDGs have also been affected by economic conditions. The global ambition of getting every child into primary education has been hit by a reduction in aid from the developed world as a result of the crisis. In its annual report for 2009, UNESCO warned that the progress made in the last 10 years could be undone as education budgets, particularly in sub-Saharan Africa, get cut back as the flow of aid from rich countries is reduced. However, during 2009, 90% of low- and middle-income countries made progress towards universal primary education and sub-Saharan Africa actually made the greatest progress. The rate of progress is however, still too slow to meet the MDG by 2015.

The number of children out of school worldwide has fallen by 33 million since 2000 but there are still an estimated 72 million children who receive no education at all. At the current rate 56 million will still be not in school in 2015 which means that the target of full primary school enrolment will not be met. Achieving universal primary education would cost an estimated $16 billion per year – less than the amount the US was spending on its military operations in Afghanistan in three months as of 2010.

'Achieving universal primary education would cost less than the US spends on its military operations in Afghanistan in three months.'

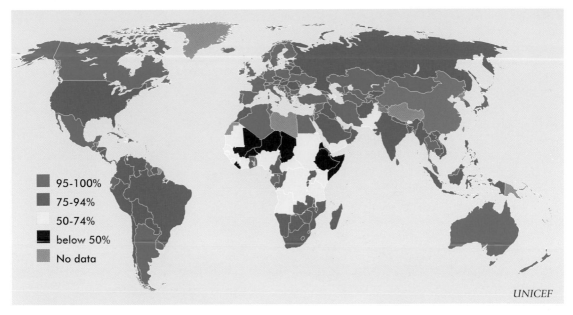

Primary school net enrolment/attendance 2003-09.

Legend:
- 95-100%
- 75-94%
- 50-74%
- below 50%
- No data

Case study in brief: Education progress in Tanzania

Tanzania abolished school fees in 2002 and made school compulsory for all 7-13 year olds. As a result enrolment at primary schools nationwide is reported to have risen from 59% in 2000 to 95.4% in 2010. The total number of primary schools in the country increased from 11,873 in 2001 to 15,624 in 2007. Such rapid progress appears to have put Tanzania well on target to achieving universal education by 2015 but the real situation appears to be more complicated.

There has been significant support for education from donor countries and the government has also increased its funding for education but such a rapid increase in participation has brought problems. Resources and facilities have not increased at the same rate and teachers, books, classrooms and toilets are in short supply. The national pupil-teacher ratio has increased from 1:41 in 2000 to 1:51 in 2010. Many teachers have to manage classes of more than 100 with very few resources. The urgent need to train more teachers to cope with the increase in numbers has given rise to concerns about the length and quality of the training the new teachers receive at government or privately funded colleges. As a result there are concerns about the quality of education the extra students receive.

Some have claimed that the high enrolment figure is not sustained in the more remote rural areas and that the true figure for enrolment is nearer 75%. Drop-out rates after enrolment are also high, particularly for girls, who are vulnerable to cultural expectations, and only half the pupils leaving primary school qualify for secondary school. UNICEF has recognized all these problems but has still praised Tanzania's commitment to universal education, believing that it is safer and better for children to be in school than the alternative. ■

In order to meet the Millennium education goals, governments have to be more inclusive and bring marginalized groups into education instead of simply raising the number of years those already in education remain in school. In 11 sub-Saharan African states over 30% of young adults have less than four years' education and in Burkina Faso and Somalia 50% of school leavers have less than two years' education.

Inequalities between ethnic groups within some countries is a problem. In Turkey, 43% of Kurdish-speaking girls, often from the poorest households, have fewer than two years' education compared to the national average of 6%. In Nigeria, 97% of Hausa-speaking girls have fewer than two years' schooling and a similar figure applies to Somali girls living in the northeast of Kenya. Tanzania, meanwhile, has been praised for its progress towards universal primary education (see case study in brief on page 229).

Girls at a school in the north of Bangladesh, set up by a local NGO to counter child labour in the cigarette industry.

MDG3 Promote gender equality and empower women

Target: Eliminate gender disparity at all levels of education no later than 2015

The third Millennium Goal challenges discrimination against women, and seeks to ensure that girls as well as boys have the chance to go to school. Indicators linked to the goal also try to measure progress towards ensuring that more women become literate and are more widely represented in public policy and decision-making. Without progress towards gender equality and the empowerment of women, none of the other MDGs will be achieved.

The indicators used to measure progress towards MDG3 are:
- Ratios of girls to boys in primary, secondary and tertiary education
- Share of women in wage employment in the non-agricultural sector
- Proportion of seats held by women in national parliament.

The gender gap in education

Access to education has been a long-term problem for women in developing countries. The gender gap is slowly closing in school enrolment in the developing world, with 95 girls of primary school age in school for every 100 boys in 2006 compared with 92 in 1999. Gender parity has been achieved in China and progress has also been made in India. However, significant gender disparities remain. The largest are in West Asia, Oceania and sub-Saharan Africa where 91, 89 and 89 girls are enrolled in primary school for every 100 boys. The gender gap also increases with higher levels of education. The reduced access to education means that women make up around 64% of the estimated 774 million illiterate adults in the world. Globally 77% of adult women are literate, compared to 87% of men.

Women and employment

Worldwide, the income-earning opportunities for women have increased in recent years but these benefits have mostly occurred in the developed world. In developing countries, the majority of women still work in the informal sector or as unpaid family workers and have no income security. In South Asia and sub-Saharan Africa, this type of work accounts for more than 80% of all jobs for women. The same pattern is true for many countries in the Middle East, such as Saudi Arabia and Bahrain. The explanations for low levels of women in employment are mostly found in traditional culture although religion can also be important.

Political representation

True gender equality can only be achieved when women have the opportunity to participate in decision-making processes which affect them and their families. Progress in political representation is slow. Globally, women only occupied 19% of the seats in the different houses of national parliaments in 2010 compared to 11% in 1995. Rwanda is a notable exception, with women making up 56% of its national parliament after the 2008 elections. The explanation for such a significant female representation in Rwanda is that after the 1994 genocide thousands of men fled the country or were jailed for war crimes, leaving a population

Data

that was 70% female. As a result 58% of the workforce in Rwanda is female and 41% of businesses are owned by women. Only the Nordic countries approach these levels of representation for women in governance.

Sex-selective abortion, female infanticide and inferior access to food and medicine have resulted in 60 million fewer women in the world than demographic trends had forecast. For these reasons alone, gender equality and empowerment are urgent global priorities. Slow progress on improving economic participation and empowerment means, however, that MDG3 will not be achieved.

Rank	Country	Rank	Country
1	Iceland	8	Lesotho
2	Norway	9	Philippines
3	Finland	10	Switzerland
4	Sweden	12	South Africa
5	New Zealand	15	UK
6	Ireland	94	Japan
7	Denmark	123	Iran

Global Gender Gap Index 2010, World Economic Forum

Over 93% of the global gender gap on education has been closed. Over 96% of the global gender gap on health has been closed. On the other hand, only about 60% of the economic participation gap has been closed, and only about 18% of the gap on political empowerment.

Saadia Zahidi. Director, World Economic Forum 2010

Data

MDG4 Reduce child mortality

Target: Reduce by two-thirds, between 1990 and 2015, the mortality rate among children under five

Reducing the under-five mortality rate to two-thirds of its 1990 level means bringing it down to 35 per 1,000 live births by 2015. The number of deaths among children under the age of five has dropped from 12.6 million in 1990 to an estimated 8.8 million in 2008, and the mortality rate has declined from 100 deaths per 1,000 live births to 72 in 2008 (a 28% decline) but the rate of progress is too slow to meet the MDG target. Around 40% of the global total of under-five deaths take place in just three countries: Nigeria, India and the Democratic Republic of Congo.

There has been some progress. Measles is capable of killing young children, particularly if they are suffering from malnutrition or a debilitating disease. Some countries, including Botswana, Malawi, South Africa and Namibia, have adopted anti-measles strategies, including vaccination, and have virtually eliminated the disease since 2000. Globally, deaths from measles fell by over 60% between 2000 and 2005. The biggest drop was in Africa, where measles deaths decreased from an

---

Key facts about child deaths

- Of the four million babies that die each year in the first four weeks of life, nearly three-quarters could be saved if women were adequately nourished and received appropriate care during pregnancy, childbirth and the postnatal period.
- Most deaths to children under five years are attributable to acute respiratory infections (mostly pneumonia), diarrhoea, malaria, measles, HIV/AIDS and neonatal conditions – which are all avoidable through existing interventions. .
- Malnutrition increases the risk of dying from these diseases and over half of all child deaths occur in children who are underweight.
- Of the one million malaria deaths each year, more than 90% are among young African children.
- Public health measures have a vital role to play in reducing the number of young children dying. Action will also be required to improve nutrition, gender equality, education and household incomes.
- Discrimination against girls and unequal sharing of food and resources within households have a significant impact on child mortality, especially that of girls.
- Poverty is a considerable barrier to reducing child mortality. Poor families are often unable to obtain even the most basic healthcare for their children. The poor suffer most from food scarcity and lack of access to a safe water source or adequate sanitation.

UNICEF 2009

Data

estimated 506,000 to 126,000.

However, at present rates of progress there is little chance of reaching the 2015 target for child mortality. The means to reduce child mortality further are available – including insecticide-treated bed nets to combat malaria, improved water and sanitation, and enhanced vaccination programmes – but the countries with the highest child mortality rates have generally made the least progress and in some the situation has worsened.

MDG5 Improve maternal health

Target: Between 1990 and 2015, reduce the maternal mortality ratio by three quarters

Most maternal deaths are preventable but every year between 350,000 and 500,000 women die due to complications in pregnancy and childbirth. Around 99% of those deaths occur in the developing world and half of them in sub-Saharan Africa. In developing countries the maternal mortality ratio dropped slightly from 480 per 100,000 births in 1990 to 440 in 2009 but it is nowhere near on target to reach the Millennium Goal of a 75% reduction by 2015. In some countries the

Case study in brief: Free childbirth in Nepal

Free childbirth was introduced in Nepal in January 2009. The measure was made possible with the help of funding from the UK Department for International Development for a five-year Support to Safe Motherhood Programme. Maternal mortality is a major problem in the country and the ratio is currently 281 per 100,000 live births. Until the introduction of free childbirth only 32% of births were attended by a health worker. It meant that one newborn baby died in Nepal every 20 minutes and a woman died of childbirth-related causes every four hours. Making childbirth free will mean that the vast majority of deliveries will be attended by a health worker; 225,000 women are expected to benefit from the measure each year.

The introduction of free childbirth care should help Nepal to achieve its targets for MDG 4 and 5. ■

'The bold initiative is the most beautiful New Year gift to the women of Nepal – a lifeline for them and newborns, particularly in the rural areas where poverty forces women to use unsafe delivery practices, risking their own life and their newborns.'

Bella Bird, head of DFID Nepal

Witness

Case study in brief:
Collapse in Zimbabwe

Maternal mortality has increased dramatically in Zimbabwe. In 1990 the maternal mortality ratio was just over 300 deaths per 100,000 live births but by 2008 it had risen to 790 deaths. During that period Zimbabwe has been through political upheaval that has resulted in civil conflict and the collapse of the national economy. Long-standing president Robert Mugabe has overseen moves to oust white farmers and transfer the land ownership to his political followers amid allegations of corruption and brutal suppression of any opposition.

The collapse of the economy has meant that very little money has been spent on providing healthcare systems within the country and maternal care has been one of the biggest victims of the situation. The shortage of funding has led to a lack of drugs and to chronic shortages of staff. The problem has been exacerbated by the mass emigration of midwives from the country, forced out by the economic difficulties and the threat of violence. More than three million Zimbabweans left the country between 1999 and 2009, many of them professional people the country could little afford to lose.

The improved political stability resulting from the power-sharing agreement signed by the two main political parties in 2009 has enabled some economic improvement and some planning to improve the situation. Primary care nurses are being trained as midwives and funding is being improved but Zimbabwe will certainly not meet its MDG targets. Its dire economic and political malaise led to its being ranked last among the 169 countries ranked in the Human Development Index. Its score of 0.140 compares with 0.239 for the next-lowest country, Democratic Republic of Congo and with the 0.284 that Zimbabwe itself scored in 1990. ■

risks are exceptionally high: in Afghanistan the maternal mortality ratio is 1,400 deaths per 100,000 births.

The attendance of a skilled health worker is vital in improving the care given to women at births and reducing the risk of complications and death. In sub-Saharan Africa and South Asia, less than half of all births are attended by trained personnel. Very young pregnant women are at greater risk of maternal mortality and a child born to a mother who is under the age of 18 in the developing world has a 60% higher risk of dying in its first year of life than a child born to an older mother.

Globally, the average annual decrease in maternal mortality since 2000 has been less than 1% and is well below the 5.5% annual decrease needed to reach the Millennium target. Some countries have done much better than others – the average decrease in the sub-Saharan countries is 0.1% while in East Asia it is 4.2% – but there is little evidence of consistent progress in most low-income developing countries. The disparity in the progress made by some countries compared to others can be illustrated by changes in Zimbabwe and Nepal in recent years (see case studies in brief). A map illustrating levels of maternal mortality worldwide can be found on page 173.

MDG6 Combat HIV/AIDS, malaria and other diseases

Target: To have halted and started to reverse the spread of HIV and AIDS by 2015

MDG indicator: HIV prevalence among young people aged 15-24

About 95% of people living with HIV live in low- and middle-income countries and over two million people died of AIDS-related illnesses in 2008. In the worst-affected countries, average life expectancy has fallen by 20 years since the start of the epidemic. In the 1950s, the large life expectancy gap was between countries in the developed world and developing countries. Now it is between the poorest countries (least developed countries in UN terms) – especially those ravaged by AIDS – and the rest. In Zimbabwe, Zambia and Lesotho the average life expectancy is 46 years.

At last, however, there are signs of some success. The 2009 UNDP report on progress of the MDGs said that for the first time since the epidemic began there had been a decline in the number of deaths in 2008 due to AIDS compared to the previous year. There has been a big increase in the number of people who have been able to access anti-

Region	People given ARV therapy (millions)		People needing ARV therapy (millions)		ARV coverage %	
	Dec 2009	Dec 2008	Dec 2009	Dec 2008	Dec 2009	Dec 2008
Sub-Saharan Africa	3.9	2.95	10.6	10.4	37	28
Eastern & Southern Africa	3.2	2.41	7.8	7.6	41	32
Western & Central Africa	0.71	0.53	2.9	2.8	25	19
Latin America & Caribbean	0.48	0.44	0.95	0.92	50	48
Latin America	0.43	0.4	0.84	0.81	51	49
Caribbean	0.05	0.04	0.11	0.11	48	37
East and Southeast Asia	0.74	0.57	2.4	2.3	31	25
Eastern Europe & Central Asia	0.11	0.08	0.61	0.57	19	15
North Africa & Middle East	0.01	0.009	0.1	0.09	11	10
All low & middle income countries	5.25	4.05	14.6	14.3	36	28

Towards Universal Access, WHO/UNICEF/UNAIDS 2010

An HIV-positive man in Takeo, Cambodia, is examined by a nurse wearing a unifrom with an AIDS ribbon.

retroviral (ARV) drugs that can keep them alive and able to work. The table opposite comes from the 2010 WHO, UNICEF and UNAIDS report *Towards Universal Access*. The data clearly show the big increase in the availability of ARV treatment. By the end of 2009, 36% of people needing the drugs were taking them, a rise of 8% from the previous year.

At the beginning of 2000, the high cost of ARV drugs prohibited their use for millions of HIV sufferers, with only those in the developed world benefiting. The increase in coverage has been possible because the cost has been greatly reduced by the use of cheaper generic drugs, mostly manufactured in developing countries such as India and China.

While ARV expenditures increased from $116.8 million in 2005 to $202.2 million in 2008, procurement increased from 6.2 million to 22.1 million monthly packs. The proportion spent on generic ARVs increased from 9.2% in 2005 to 76.4% in 2008, and the proportion of generic packs procured increased from 14.8% in 2005 to 89.3% in 2008. In 2008, there were eight PEPFAR (US President's Emergency Fund for AIDS Relief) programmes that procured at least 90% of ARV packs in generic form, and deliveries in Ethiopia, Haiti, Namibia, Rwanda, Tanzania and Zimbabwe were more than 99% generic.

Journal of the American Medical Association, July 2010

Data

There have been some disputes between some countries and major drug companies over the use of generic drugs (see Chapter 13) but the fall in price has been so steep that the cost of the ARVs is no longer the biggest barrier to the treatment of HIV. The biggest concern now is having the healthcare systems in place that will enable the ARVs to be distributed effectively. Eight countries are now accredited with having universal access (defined as giving access to at least 80% of those who need them) to ARV treatment. These are: Botswana, Cambodia, Croatia, Cuba, Guyana, Oman, Romania and Rwanda.

The increased use of ARVs has made a massive difference to the lives of people infected with HIV but research has shown that education is the most effective way to halt the spread of the virus. Progress has been disappointing. The target of 90% of young men and women having a comprehensive knowledge of the disease by 2010 has been missed by a long way. Only 31% of young men and 19% of young women aged 15-24 in the developing world are reported to be well informed. Where comprehensive sexual education does take place, there is evidence that it is effective in changing attitudes and practices.

The current evidence suggests that the Millennium target of halting the spread of HIV and AIDS will not be met by 2015. Treatment targets could be met by 2020 but there are potential problems in funding the programmes needed to maintain progress. The WHO has warned of a possible $10 billion shortfall in the $25 billion needed to fund current (2010) programmes and suggests that this may be 'a tipping point' in the fight against HIV and AIDS. The global financial crisis has made countries reluctant to commit money to development projects, although funding for fighting HIV and AIDS has held up better than some other areas of development.

Malaria

The World Health Organization and other agencies with programmes to combat malaria in different countries are hopeful that the target for 2015 will be reached as long as funding is sustained. The impact of malaria in Malawi and the measures being taken to combat the disease there are described in Chapter 9.

'Any decline in malaria funding commitments will run the risk of a resurgence of malaria in countries that have enjoyed the benefits of this funding to provide protection from malaria since 2002. Sustained funding in these countries is crucial or $9·9 billion invested since 2002 will have been in vain.'

Bob Snow, *The Lancet*, October 2010

Case study in brief: Suriname has 'already hit' malaria MDG

The country of Suriname in northern South America has already exceeded its 2015 Millennium Development Goal target for the reduction of malaria. Part of MDG6 is to halt and begin to reverse the incidence of malaria and rates of malaria in Suriname fell by 70% between 2001 and 2006. The intensive campaign against malaria in Suriname began in 2005 and has achieved dramatic results. There were only 700 cases of malaria in 2007. The whole population of the interior of Suriname has access to insecticide-treated bed nets and active case detection is carried out. 'We don't wait for patients to come to us, we look for them – we have mobile teams.'

These measures are complemented by insecticide spraying in high-risk areas, a comprehensive public awareness campaign and good detection systems for possible epidemics. When clusters of malaria cases are found, a team is sent to the area to carry out mass screening for the malaria parasite. ■

Science and Development Network 2007

MDG 7 Ensure environmental sustainability

Target: Integrate the principles of sustainable development into country policies and programmes and reverse the loss of environmental resources.

Key indicators to measure progress are: rates of deforestation, loss of biodiversity and agreement on controlling emissions of gases that contribute to climate change.

Forest loss slowing down

The world's net rate of forest loss has slowed markedly in the last decade, with less logging in the Amazon and China planting trees on a grand scale. Yet forests continue to be lost at 'an alarming rate' in some countries, according to the UN Food and Agriculture Organization (FAO). Its Global Forest Resources Assessment 2010 finds the loss of tree cover is most acute in Africa and South America but Australia also suffered huge losses because of the recent drought.

'It is good news,' said the report's co-ordinator, Mette Loyche Wilkie, a senior forestry officer with FAO.

'This is the first time we've been able to say that the deforestation rate is going down across the world, and when you look at the net rate that is certainly down. But the situation in some countries is still alarming.'

The last decade saw forests being lost or converted at a rate of 13 million hectares per year, compared to 16 million hectares in the 1990s. However, new forests were being planted to the tune of more than seven million hectares per year; so the net rate of loss since the year 2000 has been 5.2 million hectares per year, compared to 8.3 million in the 1990s. Globally, forests now cover about 31% of the Earth's land surface.

Richard Black, BBC news

Feature

Deforestation

Rates of deforestation are an important indicator of environmental sustainability and there is mixed news about the progress that has been made in the last decade. Deforestation is slowing, and important progress is being made in some countries, but overall the rate of loss is still too high.

Biodiversity

Global agreement on limiting the loss of biodiversity has been hard to achieve – as has raising the amount of money needed to protect, conserve and enhance biodiversity. Currently, about $3 billion in official development aid annually goes to help developing countries that are rich in plants and animals but poor in financial and technical resources. Some have estimated, however, that reaching biodiversity targets will require up to $300 billion in assistance from developed nations. There has been a general acknowledgement from all countries of the need to preserve biodiversity but reaching agreement on the measures needed to do that has been much more difficult. The Biodiversity Summit in Nagoya, Japan, in October 2010 was described by many environmentalists as the last chance 'to save the earth'. The outcome was not greeted with universal acclaim but did satisfy some people.

Climate change

The fall in industrial activity caused by the global financial crisis meant that emissions of CO_2 from the rich countries dropped by 7% in 2009. However, this was cancelled out by increased emissions from India and China and total global emissions probably remained the same as the previous year, the first time there has not been an increase since 1992.

The rich countries (except the US, which did not sign the Kyoto Protocol) are legally obliged to reduce their emissions by 5.2% below the 1990 level by 2012. The recession has helped them to reduce emissions by 10% so far – well below the target level. Although China and India have increased emissions they are still well below the average CO_2 emissions per person in industrialized countries. In India the emissions are now 1.4 tonnes per person and in China 6 tonnes, compared with 10 tonnes per person in the Netherlands and 17 tonnes in the United States. In sub-Saharan Africa the average emission is just 0.3 tonnes per person.

The Copenhagen conference on climate change in 2009 failed to produce a significant agreement and the agreement reached at the 2010 follow-up conference in Cancun, Mexico, is only voluntary and in no way binding. For this reason, although global emissions have temporarily stabilized, it is probable that they will increase again if and when normal industrial activity returns to the richer countries.

After nearly two weeks of tense talks on how best to protect the world's threatened ecosystems, delegates from the 193 rich and poor countries attending the UN Biodiversity Summit in the Japanese city of Nagoya, finally reached a 'historic global treaty' last Saturday, pledging to take 'effective and urgent action' to prevent the destruction of nature and halt further loss of the world's genetic wealth. Most were upbeat about the 20-point accord, saying it offered hope that the UN could be forthcoming about helping solve the planet's multiple environmental problems. But the US, being one of the few countries not to have ratified the UN Convention on Biological Diversity (CBD) – initiated at the Rio de Janeiro Earth Summit in 1992 – was not a signatory, as expected. This is likely to 'limit' the pact in many ways.

One of the most significant achievements was the agreement on sharing the knowledge and benefits of genetic resources found in the Amazon basin, for example, and other treasure troves across the globe in developing countries' territories. Brazil, along with other naturally endowed countries, has been arguing over the past 18 years that powerful nations and companies should not be given a blank cheque for exploiting their genetic riches – such as wild plants for making medicines, cosmetics and other products – for sky-high profits that they alone enjoy, unfairly.

The European Union managed to break the stand-off, persuading the rich countries to finally agree to an Access and Benefits Sharing Protocol (ABSP). This has been made legally binding to ensure that countries with the genetic resources in their territories also benefit from at least a modest share of the huge profits generated by the commercial development of those natural assets. So far so good, but the details of the protocol have not yet been worked out. How much this ABSP would cost the conglomerates and countries, so used to the free exploitation of other people's resources, has been left for 'later negotiations', according to reports. It is hoped the merit of this protocol is not lost in unnecessary dilatory tactics – which cynics point out may just be a ploy to prolong the practice of shameless biopiracy as long as possible.

Financial Express, October 2010

Feature

Target: Halve, by 2015, the proportion of people without sustainable access to safe drinking water and basic sanitation

There are an estimated 2.6 billion people who lack access to even a simple latrine and 884 million people who have no access to any type of improved drinking water. As a direct consequence of this:
- 1.6 million people die every year from diarrhoeal diseases (including cholera) attributable to the lack of access to safe drinking water and basic sanitation. Around 90% of these are children under five, nearly all of them in developing countries

Case study in brief: water and sanitation in Afghanistan

There are some countries where it is going to be much harder to achieve environmental sustainability than others. In Afghanistan there has been almost continuous conflict for the last 40 years, and there is no reasonable expectation of the situation improving in the immediate future.

The country has a harsh and difficult environment anyway but the years of conflict have made the situation much worse. Access to clean water and the safe disposal of waste are two of the biggest problems. It is estimated that over 80% of Afghans drink contaminated water. Kabul has a population of over five million and is one of the fastest-growing cities in the world but its authorities say that there are only 35 public toilets in the city and virtually the only access to water is via communal water pumps. The city produces over 2,000 tonnes of solid waste a day but only has the capacity to dispose of 400 tonnes.

Rapid population growth means that in rural areas there is not enough land to grow food and marginal land comes under increasing pressure. Deforestation, soil erosion, conflict over water access and the impacts of climate change are the other ingredients of inevitable environmental degradation. Confronting these problems in the face of intense, prolonged conflict and the threat this poses to the personal security of so many people would appear to be an impossible task. ■

'We can't earn nearly enough. Compared to 20 years ago we are now much poorer. We have new crop diseases we cannot treat, there's conflict between the herders and the settled farmers, and people are cutting down the forests for fuel,' says Mahmoud Saikal, a village elder.

The Guardian, 14 September 2010

Witness

In Kandahar and Herat, dumpsites are sited in dry river valleys above the cities, with the prospect that heavy rains will wash hundreds of tonnes of waste back into the city through the river system. One of Kabul's dumpsites is also upstream of the city and close to wells used to draw drinking water.

Drinking water in urban areas has high concentrations of bacteria from contamination by sewage. It is a threat to public health, particularly for children, who are most susceptible to cholera. Kabul's water-supply system, damaged during the conflict and lacking routine maintenance, is losing as much as 60% of its supply through leaks and illegal use. In Herat, just 10% of the 150 public taps were found to work.

UNEP 2003

Feature

- 160 million people are infected with schistosomiasis, a water-borne disease causing tens of thousands of deaths each year; 500 million people are at risk of trachoma which threatens millions with blindness or visual impairment.

Providing access to safe water has been the target of many national and NGO-sponsored development programmes in the last decade and there has been considerable global progress. Around 87% of the world's population and 84% of people in developing regions now get their water from improved sources. Sub-Saharan Africa accounts for a third of the 884 million who do not have access to safe drinking water. It looks likely that the overall MDG target on safe water will be met, though individual countries will certainly fail to meet it.

Meeting people's basic sanitation requirements is, however, proving much more problematic. The WHO estimates that, in 2008, 2.6 billion people did not use a safe toilet and 1.1 billion people had no option but to defecate in the open. Current estimates suggest that the world is likely to miss the MDG sanitation target by a billion people and that by 2015 there will be 2.7 billion people without access to basic sanitation. The situation is at its worst in South Asia, East Asia and sub-Saharan Africa.

Within developing countries there are disparities in access between urban and rural areas: seven out of ten people without improved sanitation live in rural areas and only 45% of the rural population use latrines of any kind. The number of people in urban areas without safe sanitation is also increasing because of rapid urban population growth.

Fetching water is more fun than it used to be since pumps have been installed in this village near Garango in southeast Burkina Faso.

Inevitably, the poorest are worst affected.

The benefits of improving sanitation are obvious. WHO estimates that meeting the MDG target would avert 470,000 deaths and result in an extra 320 million productive working days every year. The MDG target focuses on sanitation in the home but improving sanitation in schools would also help to ensure that children, and girls in particular, stay in school. UNICEF estimates that only 37% of schools in their priority countries have adequate sanitation facilities.

It is important to provide sanitation facilities that are appropriate. Piped sewerage, for example, is an expensive engineering solution. In the poorest areas, with limited or no access to piped water, the provision of more basic facilities such as pit-latrines is probably a more appropriate measure.

Afghanistan is an example of a country where MDG targets are likely to be missed for both safe water provision and basic sanitation.

MDG 8 Develop a global partnership for development

The goal of addressing the needs of the least developed countries through a global partnership had several objectives:
* Improving the trading and financial systems
* Tackling debt
* Working with pharmaceutical companies to improve access to cheap drugs in developing countries
* Spreading the use of technology.

Trade talks have done little to resolve the problem of the subsidies given by developed countries to agriculture and the distorting effect this has on world trade flows. The value of agricultural subsidies in developed countries was more than 3.5 times larger ($372 billion) than official aid ($104 billion) in 2006. There has also been little progress on measures to ensure that transnational corporations are unable to evade the taxes they owe to developing countries.

The global financial crisis which started in 2008 predictably hit the poorest countries hardest as the wealthier nations failed to meet their aid obligations and the prices of some commodities dropped sharply in world markets. In 2009, aid from the EU countries corresponded to 0.42% of EU GNI, a long way from the target of 0.7% by 2015. The EU is, however, still the largest global donor, providing more than half of global aid. Total official development assistance to developing countries was $20 billion short of its commitments for 2009.

However, some progress was made in tackling debt, and more than 30 countries have received debt relief under the Heavily Indebted Poor Countries Initiative. The money released by this has been successfully

Some perspectives on the MDGs

Sachs

The architect of the MDGs, US economist Jeff Sachs, says the blame for the anti-poverty project being off-track lies in Western capitals. 'Rich countries made promises which they didn't follow through on and now people want to say it was wrong all along,' Professor Sachs says. The UN estimates the gap between funds promised and those delivered is worth $20 billion for this year alone, with $16 billion of that affecting the poorest continent, Africa.

The G8 grouping of wealthier economies committed themselves to spend 0.7% of GDP on Official Development Assistance (ODA) but are lagging behind on 0.34%. Professor Sachs says the targets remain 'realistic and practical' if rich countries would spend less on their military and more on development.

Easterly

Aid sceptic Professor Bill Easterly says the goals were a successful fundraising exercise which then squandered much of the money meant for the poorer world. 'Why waste any more efforts on the MDGs?' Professor Easterly asked recently. '[They] will go down in history as a success in global consciousness-raising, but a failure in using that consciousness for its stated objectives.'

Collier

Paul Collier, author of *The Bottom Billion* and a professor of economics at Oxford University, says both left- and right-wingers have exaggerated the importance of aid. 'Aid is not transformational by itself in either a good or a bad way. It's not that if only we had a lot more aid we'd transform Africa.' The age of slogans such as 'End Poverty Now' is over, he says. 'We have moved beyond that and we have got to recognize complexity.'

Overseas Development Institute

The Overseas Development Institute, the UK's leading thinktank on aid, says that the Millennium Goals should be judged on relative progress, rather than absolute failure. 'The problem with the MDGs was that they were agreed as ends but then confused with means,' says the ODI's Claire Melamed. 'They were a political bargain, not a blueprint for development, but that's how they have been misused.'

Daniel Howden, *The Independent*, 20 September 2010

Feature

channelled into funding essential services such as education and health services. Agreements to allow the production and sale of some cheaper generic drugs manufactured in developing countries have also been helpful. The progress made in developing global partnerships is uneven, however – had there been sufficient will, the 2015 MDG targets could have been met.

Conclusion

The majority of the Millennium Development Goals will not be attained. The reasons for failure are already being debated and even the value of the Millennium exercise itself has been called into question. People will reach their own conclusions about the success of a strategy that sets targets for each part of the development process and how those targets were derived.

Very few people claim that the MDGs have been an unqualified success. Some argue that tying the MDGs to World Bank and IMF prescriptions was a mistake and that the result has been a narrow definition of poverty and little attention to human rights. Another criticism is that trying to meet the MDG targets has prevented a more effective use being made of resources. It does appear that developing countries which can provide evidence that they have made progress towards meeting the key MDG targets appear to be looked at more favourably by the major aid organizations. Aid donors may have their own agenda of promoting economic growth which, in the short term, has little impact on the poor and their standard of living.

Whatever the outcome, the Millennium Development Goals have provided a focus for the development process and highlighted areas where there has been a worrying lack of progress. For that reason at least, they may be judged a partial success by many people – but certainly not by everybody.

References

Bauer P, 'Western Guilt and Third World Poverty', in Karl Brunner (ed), *The First World and the Third World*, University of Rochester Policy Center, 1978

Black M, *No Nonsense Guide to International Development*, New Internationalist 2002

Brautigam D, Knack S, *Foreign Aid, Institutions, and Governance in Sub-Saharan Africa*, Chicago University Press 2004

Codrington Stephen, *Planet Geography* (4th edition), Solid Star Press 2007

Colgan A-L, *Hazardous to Health: The World Bank and IMF in Africa*, Africa Action 2002

Collier P, *The Bottom Billion: Why the Poorest Countries are Failing and What Can be Done About It*, Grove Art 2007

Desai V, Potter R, *A Companion to Development Studies*, Arnold 2002

Easterly W, *The Elusive Quest for Growth*, MIT 2002

Easterly W, *The White Man's Burden: Why the West's Efforts to Aid the Rest Have Done So Much Ill and So Little Good*, Penguin 2006

Eberstadt N, *Too Many People?* International Policy Press 2007

Gill P, *Famine and Foreigners: Ethiopia Since Live Aid*, OUP 2010

Escobar A, *Encountering Development: The Making and Unmaking of the Third World*, Princetown University Press 1995

Hanlon J, Smart T, *Do Bicycles Equal Development in Mozambique?* James Currey 2009

Hay C, Marsh D (eds), *Demystifying Globalization*, Palgrave 2000

Kaplan R, *The Ends of the Earth*, Random House 1994

Klein N, *No Logo*, Harper Collins 2000

Mehta L and Nicol A, *Water*, Oxfam 2006

Nagle, Garrett, *Advanced Geography*, OUP 2000

Naughton B, *The Chinese Economy, Transitions and Growth*, Cambridge 2007

Potter R, Binns T, Elliott J, Smith D, *Geographies of Development*, Pearson 2004

Polman L, *The Crisis Caravan: What's Wrong With Humanitarian Aid?* Metropolitan Books 2010

Ransom D, *No Nonsense Guide to Fair Trade*, New Internationalist 2002

Regan C (ed), *80:20 Development In An Unequal World*, Tide 2002

Sachs J, *The End of Poverty: How can we make it happen in our lifetime?* Allen Lane 2005

Sachs J, *Common Wealth: Economics for a Crowded Planet*, Penguin 2008

Sachs W, *The Development Dictionary: A Guide to Knowledge as Power*, Zed Books 1992

Saquet A-M, *World Atlas of Sustainable Development* Anthem Press 2005

Seabrook J, *No Nonsense Guide to World Poverty*, New Internationalist 2003

Seager J, *The Atlas of Women in the World*, Earthscan 2003

Sen A, *Development As Freedom*, OUP 1999

Southall R, Melber H, *A New Scramble for Africa? Imperialism, Investment and Development*, University of KwaZulu-Natal Press 2009

Spencer N, *Health Consequences of Poverty for Children*, End Child Poverty Report 2010

Stiglitz J, *Globalization and its discontents*, Norton 2003

Terry G, *Women's Rights, Poverty and Development*, Oxfam 2006

Williams G, Meth P, Willis K, *Geographies of Developing Areas: The Global South in a Changing World*, Routledge 2009

Willis K, *Theories and Practices of Development*, Routledge 2005

Usdin S, *No Nonsense Guide to World Health*, New Internationalist 2007

Online Information

Useful journals, newspapers and other online sources

Aid Watch – information on aid, trade and debt
www.aidwatchers.com

All Africa – African news and information provider
http://allafrica.com

BBC online www.bbc.co.uk

Development Education Association www.dea.org.uk

Global Health Watch www.ghwatch.org

Global Link online resources www.globalink.org

The Guardian and The Observer – newspapers www.guardian.co.uk

The Independent – newspaper www.independent.co.uk

International Development Research Centre www.idrc

New Internationalist www.newint.org

Panos – global development information provider www.panos.org.uk

People and Planet www.peopleandplanet.net

NGOs and charities

Action Aid www.ActionAid.org.uk

Bill and Melinda Gates Foundation www.gatesfoundation.org

Christian Aid www.christianaid.org.uk

End Child Poverty http://endchildpoverty.org.uk

Excellent Development – NGO supporting farmers in Africa www.excellentdevelopment.com

Fairtrade Foundation www.fairtrade.org.uk

Jubilee Debt Campaign www.jubileedebtcampaign.org.uk

Oxfam www.oxfam.org.uk

Plan International http://planinternational.org

Practical Action, charity that promotes appropriate technology www.PracticalAction.org

Wateraid www.wateraid.org

National and international organizations involved in development

Food and Agricultural Organization of the United Nations www.fao.org

International Monetary Fund www.imf.org

Organization for Economic Cooperation and Development www.oecd.org

UK Department for International Development www.dfid.gov.uk

United Nations Children's Fund www.unicef.org

United Nations Conference on Trade and Development www.unctad.org

United Nations Education, Scientific and Cultural Organization www.unesco.org

UNAIDS www.unaids.org

UK Government statistics www.statistics.gov.uk

World Bank www.worldbank.org

World Economic Forum www.weforum.org

World Food Programme www.wfp.org

World Trade Organization www.wto.org

About the New Internationalist

The New Internationalist is an independent not-for-profit
publishing co-operative. Our mission is to report on
issues of world poverty and inequality; to focus attention
on the unjust relationship between the powerful and the
powerless worldwide; to debate and campaign for the
radical changes necessary if the needs of all are to be met.

Books, diaries & calendars
We publish informative current affairs books, such as the
No-Nonsense Guides and the World Changing titles,
complemented by world food, fiction, photography and
alternative gift books, as well as calendars and diaries,
maps and posters.

Magazine
The New Internationalist magazine tackles subjects of
global significance, exploring each issue in a concise way
which is easy to understand. Feature articles are packed
full of photos, charts and graphs and each issue also
contains reviews, country profiles, interviews and news.

Mail order
We operate mail order businesses in the UK, North America,
Australia and New Zealand/Aotearoa, for our supporters
and other clients. Besides our branded publications and
products, we specialize in sourcing and marketing useful,
fair trade, eco-friendly, organic and educational gift items.

www.newint.org